Student Companion

Boston, Massachusetts • Chandler, Arizona • Glenview, Illinois • Upper Saddle River, New Jersey

Acknowledgements **Illustration:** Stephen Durke: 29, 124; Jeff Grunwald represented by Wilkinson Studios, Inc.: 156, 164, 189, 192, 200; Phil Guzy: 225, 272; XNR Productions: 228 **Photo:** All photographs not listed are the property of Pearson Education; **Back Cover,** © Bon Appetit/Almay; **Page 16,** Pete Saloutos/zefa/Corbis; **108,** John Wells/Photo Researchers, Inc.; **151,** Eric Hood/iStockphoto; **232,** Ron Kimball/kimballstock; **236,** iStockphoto; Andy Crawford/Dorling Kindersley; **247,** M.C. Escher's "Symmetry E56" © 2009 The M.C. Escher Company-Holland. All rights reserved. www.mcescher.com; **275,** Matthias Tunger/Photonica/Getty Images; **281,** amana images inc./Alamy.

ISBN-13: 978-0-13368884-9
ISBN-10: 0-13-368884-4

5 6 7 8 9 10   V039   13 12 11 10

Contents

Chapter 1 **Tools of Geometry** 2
1-1 Nets and Drawings for Visualizing Geometry 2
1-2 Points, Lines, and Planes 6
1-3 Measuring Segments 10
1-4 Measuring Angles 14
1-5 Exploring Angle Pairs 18
1-6 Basic Constructions 22
1-7 Midpoint and Distance in the Coordinate Plane 26
1-8 Perimeter, Circumference, and Area 30

Chapter 2 **Reasoning and Proof** 34
2-1 Patterns and Inductive Reasoning 34
2-2 Conditional Statements 38
2-3 Biconditionals and Definitions 42
2-4 Deductive Reasoning 46
2-5 Reasoning in Algebra and Geometry 50
2-6 Proving Angles Congruent 54

Chapter 3 **Parallel and Perpendicular Lines** 58
3-1 Lines and Angles 58
3-2 Properties of Parallel Lines 62
3-3 Proving Lines Parallel 66
3-4 Parallel and Perpendicular Lines 70
3-5 Parallel Lines and Triangles 74
3-6 Constructing Parallel and Perpendicular Lines 78
3-7 Equations of Lines in the Coordinate Plane 82
3-8 Slopes of Parallel and Perpendicular Lines 86

Chapter 4 **Congruent Triangles** 90
4-1 Congruent Figures 90
4-2 Triangle Congruence by SSS and SAS 94
4-3 Triangle Congruence by ASA and AAS 98
4-4 Using Corresponding Parts of Congruent Triangles 102
4-5 Isosceles and Equilateral Triangles 106
4-6 Congruence in Right Triangles 110
4-7 Congruence in Overlapping Triangles 114

Chapter 5 **Relationships Within Triangles** 118
5-1 Midsegments of Triangles 118
5-2 Perpendicular and Angle Bisectors. 122
5-3 Bisectors in Triangles 126
5-4 Medians and Altitudes 130
5-5 Indirect Proof 134
5-6 Inequalities in One Triangle. 138
5-7 Inequalities in Two Triangles 142

Chapter 6 **Polygons and Quadrilaterals** 146
6-1 The Polygon-Angle Sum Theorems 146
6-2 Properties of Parallelograms 150
6-3 Proving That a Quadrilateral Is a Parallelogram 154
6-4 Properties of Rhombuses, Rectangles, and Squares 158
6-5 Conditions for Rhombuses, Rectangles, and Squares 162
6-6 Trapezoids and Kites 166
6-7 Polygons in the Coordinate Plane. 170
6-8 Applying Coordinate Geometry 174
6-9 Proofs Using Coordinate Geometry 178

Chapter 7 **Similarity** 182
7-1 Ratios and Proportions 182
7-2 Similar Polygons. 186
7-3 Proving Triangles Similar 190
7-4 Similarity in Right Triangles 194
7-5 Proportions in Triangles. 198

Chapter 8 **Right Triangles and Trigonometry**. 202
8-1 The Pythagorean Theorem and Its Converse 202
8-2 Special Right Triangles 206
8-3 Trigonometry. 210
8-4 Angles of Elevation and Depression 214
8-5 Vectors 218

Chapter 9 **Transformations** 222
9-1 Translations 222
9-2 Reflections 226
9-3 Rotations 230
9-4 Symmetry 234
9-5 Dilations 238
9-6 Compositions of Reflections 242
9-7 Tessellations 246

Contents

Chapter 10   **Area**. 250
                   10-1 Areas of Parallelograms and Triangles 250
                   10-2 Areas of Trapezoids, Rhombuses, and Kites 254
                   10-3 Areas of Regular Polygons 258
                   10-4 Perimeters and Areas of Similar Figures 262
                   10-5 Trigonometry and Area 266
                   10-6 Circles and Arcs. 270
                   10-7 Areas of Circles and Sectors 274
                   10-8 Geometric Probability. 278

Chapter 11   **Surface Area and Volume** 282
                   11-1 Space Figures and Cross Sections. 282
                   11-2 Surface Areas of Prisms and Cylinders 286
                   11-3 Surface Areas of Pyramids and Cones 290
                   11-4 Volumes of Prisms and Cylinders 294
                   11-5 Volumes of Pyramids and Cones 298
                   11-6 Surface Areas and Volumes of Spheres 302
                   11-7 Areas and Volumes of Similar Solids. 306

Chapter 12   **Circles**. 310
                   12-1 Tangent Lines 310
                   12-2 Chords and Arcs. 314
                   12-3 Inscribed Angles. 318
                   12-4 Angle Measures and Segment Lengths 322
                   12-5 Circles in the Coordinate Plane 326
                   12-6 Locus: A Set of Points 330

Welcome to **Geometry!**

Your Prentice Hall Geometry program is designed to help you achieve mastery of Geometry topics. Your *Prentice Hall Geometry Student Companion* is written to support you as you study. Your Student Companion is designed to work with your Student Edition textbook and PowerGeometry.com by providing a place to practice the concepts, skills, and vocabulary you'll learn in each lesson.

Using the Geometry Student Companion

Your Student Companion provides daily support for each lesson by targeting the following areas:

- **Vocabulary** Building your math vocabulary is an important part of success this year. You'll use your Student Companion to learn and understand the vocabulary words you need for Geometry.

- **Got It?** You'll use your Student Companion to check your understanding of example problems from your Student Edition.

- **Lesson Check** You'll use your Student Companion to make sure you're ready to tackle your homework.

Together, these sections will help you prepare to master the topics covered in your Student Edition — and lead to a successful year in Geometry.

Using PowerGeometry.com

All your Student Companion pages are available for downloading and printing from PowerGeometry.com.

🔊 Vocabulary

● Review

Identify each figure as *two-dimensional* or *three-dimensional*.

1.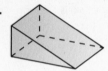

2.

3.

● Vocabulary Builder

polygon

polygon (noun) PAHL **ih gahn**

Definition A **polygon** is a two-dimensional figure with three or more sides, where each side meets exactly two other sides at their endpoints.

Main Idea: A **polygon** is a closed figure, so all sides meet. No sides cross each other.

Examples: Triangles, rectangles, pentagons, hexagons, and octagons are **polygons**.

● Use Your Vocabulary

Underline the correct word(s) to complete each sentence.

4. A *polygon* is formed by two / three or more straight sides.

5. A circle is / is not a *polygon*.

6. A triangle / rectangle is a *polygon* with three sides.

7. The sides of a *polygon* are curved / straight .

8. Two / Three sides of *polygon* meet at the same point.

Cross out the figure(s) that are NOT *polygons*.

9.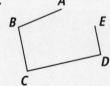

10.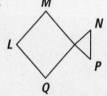

11.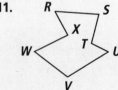

Underline the correct word(s) to complete the sentence.

12. A *net* is a two-dimensional / three-dimensional diagram that you can fold to form

a two-dimensional / three-dimensional figure.

13. Circle the *net* that you can NOT fold into a cube.

Use the net of a cube at the right for Exercises 14 and 15.

14. Suppose you fold the net into a cube. What color will be opposite each face?

red   blue   green

_____   _____   _____

15. Suppose you fold the net into a cube. What color is missing from each view?

_____   _____   _____

✓ **Problem 1** **Identifying a Solid From a Net**

Got It? The net at the right folds into the cube shown.
Which letters will be on the top and right side of the cube?

16. Four of the five other letters will touch some side of Face B when
the net is folded into a cube. Cross out the letter of the side that
will NOT touch some side of Face B.

A   C   D   E   F

17. Which side of the cube will that letter be on? Circle your answer.

Top   Bottom   Right   Left   Back

18. Use the net. Which face is to the right of Face B? How do you know?

_____

_____

19. Use the net. Which face is on the top of the cube? How do you know?

_____

_____

Lesson 1-1

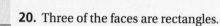

Problem 2 Drawing a Net From a Solid

Got It? What is a net for the figure at the right? Label the net with its dimensions.

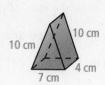

Write T for *true* or F for *false*.

_____ **20.** Three of the faces are rectangles.

_____ **21.** Four of the faces are triangles.

_____ **22.** The figure has five faces in all.

23. Now write a description of the net.

_____

_____

24. Circle the net that represents the figure above.

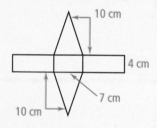

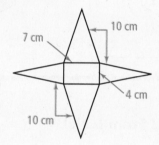

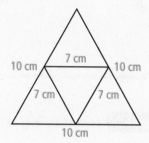

Problem 3 Isometric Drawing

Got It? What is an isometric drawing of this cube structure?

25. The cube structure has

[ ] edges that you can see and

[ ] vertices that you can see.

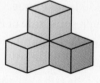

26. The isometric dot paper shows 2 vertices and 1 edge of the cube structure. Complete the isometric drawing.

Problem 4 Orthographic Drawing

Got It? What is the orthographic drawing for this isometric drawing?

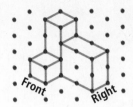

27. Underline the correct word to complete the sentence.

If you built the figure out of cubes, you would use seven / eight cubes

28. Cross out the drawing below that is NOT part of the orthographic drawing. Then label each remaining drawing. Write *Front*, *Right*, or *Top*.

   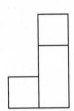      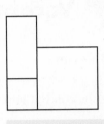

_____   _____   _____   _____

Lesson Check • Do you UNDERSTAND?

Vocabulary Tell whether each drawing is *isometric*, *orthographic*, a *net*, or *none*.

29. Write *dot paper, one view, three views* or *none*. Then label each figure.

Top

Front   Right

_____   _____   _____   _____

Math Success

Check off the vocabulary words that you understand.

☐ net   ☐ isometric drawing   ☐ orthographic drawing

Rate how well you can *use nets, isometric drawings, and orthographic drawings.*

Need to review 0   2   4   6   8   10   Now I get it!

Vocabulary

● Review

Draw a line from each *net* in Column A to the three-dimensional figure it represents in Column B.

Column A   Column B

1.

2.

3.

● Vocabulary Builder

conjecture (noun, verb) kun JEK chur

Main Idea: A **conjecture** is a guess or a prediction.

Definition: A **conjecture** is a conclusion reached by using inductive reasoning.

● Use Your Vocabulary

Write *noun* or *verb* to identify how the word *conjecture* is used in each sentence.

4. You make a *conjecture* that your volleyball team will win.

5. Assuming that your sister ate the last cookie is a *conjecture*.

6. You *conjecture* that your town will build a swimming pool.

Key Concept   Undefined and Defined Terms

Write the correct word from the list on the right. Use each word only once.

	Undefined or Defined Term	Diagram	Name
7.	_____	A•	A
8.	_____	ℓ, B, A (line $\overrightarrow{AB}$)	$\overleftrightarrow{AB}$
9.	_____	P, A, B, C (plane P)	P
10.	_____	A•——•B	$\overline{AB}$
11.	_____	A•——•B→	$\overrightarrow{AB}$
12.	_____	←A•—C•—B•→	$\overrightarrow{CA}, \overrightarrow{CB}$

Word list:
line
opposite rays
plane
point
ray
segment

Draw a line from each item in Column A to its description in Column B.

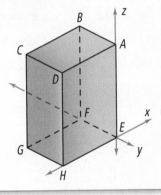

Column A

13. plane *HGE*

14. $\overline{BF}$

15. plane *DAE*

16. line *y*

17. point *A*

Column B

intersection of $\overline{AB}$ and line *z*

plane *AEH*

line through points *F* and *E*

intersection of planes *ABF* and *CGF*

plane containing points *E*, *F*, and *G*

Postulates 1–1, 1–2, 1–3, and 1–4

18. Complete each postulate with *line, plane,* or *point.*

Postulate 1-1 Through any two points there is exactly one __?__ .   _____

Postulate 1-2 If two distinct lines intersect, then they intersect in exactly one __?__ .   _____

Postulate 1-3 If two distinct planes intersect, then they intersect in exactly one __?__ .   _____

Postulate 1-4 Through any three noncollinear points there is exactly one __?__ .   _____

Lesson 1-2

Write P if the statement describes a *postulate* or U if it describes an *undefined term*.

_____ **19.** A point indicates a location and has no size.

_____ **20.** Through any two points there is exactly one line.

_____ **21.** A line is represented by a straight path that has no thickness and extends in two opposite directions without end.

_____ **22.** If two distinct planes intersect, then they intersect in exactly one line.

_____ **23.** If two distinct lines intersect, then they intersect in exactly one point.

_____ **24.** Through any three noncollinear points there is exactly one plane.

Problem 2 Naming Segments and Rays

Got It? Reasoning $\overrightarrow{EF}$ and $\overrightarrow{FE}$ form a line. Are they opposite rays? Explain.

For Exercises 25–29, use the line below.

25. Draw and label points E and F. Then draw $\overrightarrow{EF}$ in one color and $\overrightarrow{FE}$ in another color.

26. Do $\overrightarrow{EF}$ and $\overrightarrow{FE}$ share an endpoint?   Yes / No

27. Do $\overrightarrow{EF}$ and $\overrightarrow{FE}$ form a line?   Yes / No

28. Are $\overrightarrow{EF}$ and $\overrightarrow{FE}$ opposite rays?   Yes / No

29. Explain your answer to Exercise 28.

_____

_____

Problem 3 Finding the Intersection of Two Planes

Got It? Each surface of the box at the right represents part of a plane. What are the names of two planes that intersect in $\overleftrightarrow{BF}$?

30. Circle the points that are on $\overleftrightarrow{BF}$ or in one of the two planes.

A	B	C	D	E	F	G	H

31. Circle another name for plane *BFG*. Underline another name for plane *BFE*.

ABF	*BCD*	*BCG*	*CDH*	*FGH*

32. Now name two planes that intersect in $\overleftrightarrow{BF}$.

_____   _____

Got It? What plane contains points *L*, *M*, and *N*? Shade the plane.

33. Use the figure below. Draw $\overline{LM}$, $\overline{LN}$, and $\overline{MN}$ as dashed segments. Then shade plane *LMN*.

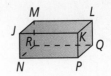

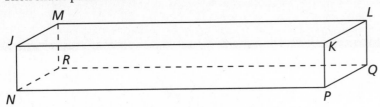

Underline the correct word to complete the sentence.

34. $\overline{LM}$, $\overline{LN}$, and $\overline{MN}$ form a triangle / rectangle .

35. Name the plane.

_____

Lesson Check • Do you UNDERSTAND?

Are $\overrightarrow{AB}$ and $\overrightarrow{BA}$ the same ray? Explain.

Underline the correct symbol to complete each sentence.

36. The endpoint of $\overrightarrow{AB}$ is *A* / *B* .

37. The endpoint of $\overrightarrow{BA}$ is *A* / *B* .

38. Use the line. Draw and label points *A* and *B*. Then draw $\overrightarrow{AB}$ and $\overrightarrow{BA}$.

⟵————————————————————⟶

39. Are $\overrightarrow{AB}$ and $\overrightarrow{BA}$ the same ray? Explain.

_____

Math Success

Check off the vocabulary words that you understand.

☐ point   ☐ line   ☐ plane   ☐ segment   ☐ ray   ☐ postulate   ☐ axiom

Rate how well you *understand points, lines, and planes.*

| Need to review | 0 | 2 | 4 | 6 | 8 | 10 | Now I get it! |

Vocabulary

● **Review**

Draw an example of each.

1. *point*

2. $\overleftrightarrow{AB}$

3. $\overrightarrow{DF}$

● **Vocabulary Builder**

segment HJ

H ●————————● J

segment (noun) SEG **munt**

Definition: A **segment** is part of a line that consists of two endpoints and all points between them.

Main Idea: You name a **segment** by its endpoints.

● **Use Your Vocabulary**

Complete each sentence with *endpoint, endpoints, line,* or *points*.

4. A *ray* has one ? .

5. A *line* contains infinitely many ? .

6. A *segment* has two ? .

7. A *segment* is part of a ? .

Place a check ✓ if the phrase describes a *segment*. Place an ✗ if it does not.

____ **8.** Earth's equator   ____ **9.** the right edge of a book's cover   ____ **10.** one side of a triangle

---

take note

Postulate 1–5 Ruler Postulate

Every point on a line can be paired with a real number, called the *coordinate* of the point.

Problem 1 Measuring Segment Lengths

Got It? What are *UV* and *SV* on the number line?

11. Label each point on the number line with its coordinate.

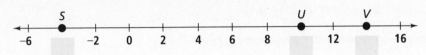

12. Find *UV* and *SV*. Write a justification for each statement.

$UV = \left| \boxed{} - \boxed{} \right|$ _____

$UV = \left| \boxed{} \right|$ _____

$UV = \boxed{}$ _____

$SV = \left| \boxed{} - \boxed{} \right|$

$SV = \left| \boxed{} \right|$

$SV = \boxed{}$

---

take note

Postulate 1–6   Segment Addition Postulate

If three points *A*, *B*, and *C* are collinear and *B* is between *A* and *C*, then $AB + BC = AC$.

Given points *A*, *B*, and *C* are collinear and *B* is between *A* and *C*, complete each equation.

13. $AB = 5$ and $BC = 4$, so $AB + BC = \boxed{} + \boxed{}$ and $AC = \boxed{}$.

14. $AC = 12$ and $BC = 7$, so $AC - BC = \boxed{} - \boxed{}$ and $AB = \boxed{}$.

Problem 2 Using the Segment Addition Postulate

Got It? In the diagram, $JL = 120$. What are *JK* and *KL*?

15. Write a justification for each statement.

$JK + KL = JL$ _____

$(4x + 6) + (7x + 15) = 120$ _____

$11x + 21 = 120$ _____

$11x = 99$ _____

$x = 9$ _____

16. You know that $JK = 4x + 6$ and $KL = 7x + 15$. Use the value of *x* from Exercise 15 to to find *JK* and KL. Find *JK* and *KL*.

17. $JK = \boxed{}$ and $KL = \boxed{}$.

11

Lesson 1-3

Problem 3 Comparing Segment Lengths

Got It? Use the diagram below. Is $\overline{AB}$ congruent to $\overline{DE}$?

```
        A       B  C       D       E
◄──┼──┼──●──┼──┼●─●┼──┼──●──┼──●──┼──►
  -6  -4  -2   0  2   4   6   8  10  12  14  16
```

In Exercises 18 and 19, circle the expression that completes the equation.

18. $AB = $ ■

| $-2 - 2$ | $\lvert -2 - 2 \rvert$ | $\lvert -2 - 3 \rvert$ | $\lvert -2 - 4 \rvert$ |

19. $DE = $ ■

| $3 - 14$ | $10 + 14$ | $\lvert 5 - 14 \rvert$ | $\lvert 10 - 14 \rvert$ |

20. After simplifying, $AB = $ ▭ and $DE = $ ▭.

21. Is $\overline{AB}$ congruent to $\overline{DE}$? Explain.

_____

The *midpoint* of a segment is the point that divides the segment into two congruent segments.

Use the number line below for Exercises 22–25.

```
  A   B   C   D   E   F   G   H   I   J   K
◄─●───●───●───●───●───●───●───●───●───●───●─►
 -5  -4  -3  -2  -1   0   1   2   3   4   5
```

22. Point ▭ is halfway between points B and J.   **23.** The midpoint of $\overline{AE}$ is point ▭ .

24. Point ▭ divides $\overline{EK}$ into two congruent segments.

25. Find the midpoint of each segment. Then write the coordinate of the midpoint.

	$\overline{AG}$	$\overline{DH}$	$\overline{AK}$
Midpoint	▭	▭	▭
Coordinate	▭	▭	▭

26. Find the coordinate of the midpoint of each segment.

	segment with endpoints at −4 and 2	segment with endpoints at −2 and 4
Coordinate of midpoint	▭	▭

27. Circle the expression that relates the coordinate of the midpoint to the coordinates of the endpoints.

| $x_1 + x_2$ | $\dfrac{(x_1 + x_2)}{2}$ | $\dfrac{(x_1 - x_2)}{2}$ |

Problem 4 Using the Midpoint

Got It? U is the midpoint of $\overline{TV}$. What are TU, UV, and TV?

$$\underset{T}{\overset{8x + 11}{\bullet}} \quad \underset{U}{\overset{12x - 1}{\bullet}} \quad \underset{V}{\bullet}$$

28. Use the justifications at the right to complete the steps below.

Step 1 Find x.

$$TU = UV \qquad\qquad\qquad \text{Definition of midpoint}$$

$$8x + 11 = \boxed{} \qquad\qquad \text{Substitute.}$$

$$8x + 11 + \boxed{} = \boxed{} + \boxed{} \qquad \text{Add 1 to each side.}$$

$$\boxed{} = \boxed{} \qquad\qquad \text{Subtract } 8x \text{ from each side.}$$

$$\boxed{} = x \qquad\qquad\qquad \text{Divide each side by 4.}$$

Step 2 Find TU and UV.

$$TU = 8 \cdot \boxed{} + 11 = \boxed{} \qquad \text{Substitute } \boxed{} \text{ for } x.$$

$$UV = 12 \cdot \boxed{} - 1 = \boxed{} \qquad \text{Substitute.}$$

Step 3 Find TV.

$$TV = TU + UV \qquad\qquad \text{Definition of midpoint}$$

$$= \boxed{} + \boxed{} \qquad\qquad \text{Substitute.}$$

$$= \boxed{} \qquad\qquad\qquad \text{Simplify.}$$

Lesson Check • Do you UNDERSTAND?

Vocabulary Name two segment bisectors of $\overline{PR}$.

Underline the correct word or symbol to complete each sentence.

29. A bisector / midpoint may be a point, line, ray, or segment.

30. The midpoint of $\overline{PR}$ is point $P / Q / R$.

31. Line ℓ passes through point $P / Q / R$.

32. Two bisectors of $\overline{PR}$ are $\boxed{}$ and $\boxed{}$.

Math Success

Check off the vocabulary words that you understand.

☐ congruent segments ☐ coordinate ☐ midpoint ☐ segment bisector

Rate how well you can *find lengths of segments*.

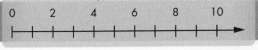

Lesson 1-3

Measuring Angles

Vocabulary

● Review

Write T for *true* or F for *false*.

_____ **1.** $\overrightarrow{AB}$ names a *ray* with endpoints A and B.

_____ **2.** You name a *ray* by its endpoint and another point on the *ray*.

● Vocabulary Builder

> **angle** (noun, verb) **ANG gul**
>
> **Other Word Forms:** angular (adjective), angle (verb), angled (adjective)
>
> **Definition:** An **angle** is formed by two rays with the same endpoint.

● Use Your Vocabulary

Name the rays that form each *angle*.

3.

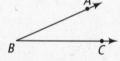 and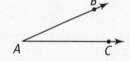

4.

and

---

take note

Key Concept   Angle

Definition	How to Name It	Diagram
An **angle** is formed by two rays with the same endpoint. The rays are the **sides** of the angle. The endpoint is the **vertex** of the angle.	You can name an angle by • its vertex • a point on each ray and the vertex • a number	

For Exercises 5–8, use the diagram in the Take Note on page 14. Name each part of the angle.

5. the *vertex*

6. two points that are NOT the vertex

[ ] and [ ]

7. the *sides*

$\overrightarrow{}$ and $\overrightarrow{}$

8. Name the angle three ways.

by its *vertex*

by a point on each side and the vertex

by a number

Problem 1 Naming Angles

Got It? What are two other names for $\angle KML$?

9. Cross out the ray that is NOT a ray of $\angle KML$.

$\overrightarrow{MK}$ $\overrightarrow{MJ}$ $\overrightarrow{ML}$

10. Circle all the possible names of $\angle KML$.

$\angle 1$ $\angle 2$ $\angle JKL$ $\angle JMK$ $\angle JML$ $\angle KMJ$ $\angle LMK$

take note

Key Concept   Types of Angles

11. Draw your own example of each type of angle.

acute   right   obtuse   straight

$0 < x <$ [ ] $x =$ [ ]   [ ] $< x <$ [ ] $x =$ [ ]

In the diagram, $m\angle ABC = 70$ and $m\angle BFE = 90$. Describe each angle as *acute, right, obtuse* or *straight*. Give an angle measure to support your description.

12. $\angle ABC$

13. $\angle CBD$

14. $\angle CFG$

15. $\angle CFH$

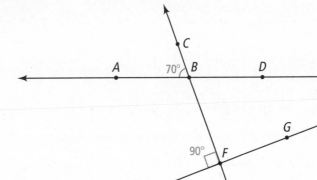

15

Problem 2 Measuring and Classifying Angles

Got It? What are the measures of ∠LKH, ∠HKN, and ∠MKH in the art below?
Classify each angle as *acute, right, obtuse,* or *straight.*

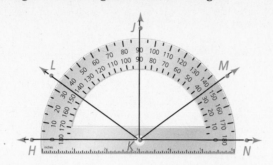

16. Write the measure of each angle. Then classify each angle.

∠LKH

∠HKN

∠MKH

Problem 3 Using Congruent Angles

Got It? Use the photo at the right. If m∠ABC = 49, what is m∠DEF?

17. ∠ABC has ___ angle mark(s).

18. The other angle with the same number of

marks is ∠ ___ .

19. Underline the correct word to complete the sentence.

The measure of ∠ABC and the measure of the angle

in Exercise 18 are equal / unequal .

20. m∠DEF = ___

take note

Postulate 1–8 Angle Addition Postulate

If point B is in the interior of ∠AOC, then m∠AOB + m∠BOC = m∠AOC.

21. Draw ∠ABT with point L in the interior and ∠ABL and ∠LBT.

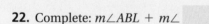

22. Complete: m∠ABL + m∠ ___ = m∠ ___

Problem 4 — Using the Angle Addition Postulate

Got It? ∠*DEF* is a straight angle. What are *m*∠*DEC* and *m*∠*CEF*?

$(11x - 12)°$ $(2x + 10)°$

D   E   F   C

23. Write a justification for each statement.

$$m\angle DEF = 180$$ _____

$$m\angle DEC + m\angle CEF = 180$$ _____

$$(11x - 12) + (2x + 10) = 180$$ _____

$$13x - 2 = 180$$ _____

$$13x = 182$$ _____

$$x = 14$$ _____

24. Use the value of *x* to find *m*∠*DEC* and *m*∠*CEF*.

$$m\angle DEC = 11x - 12 = 11(\quad) - 12 = \boxed{\quad}$$

$$m\angle CEF = \boxed{\qquad\qquad\qquad}$$

Lesson Check • Do you know How?

Algebra If *m*∠*ABD* = 85, what is an expression to represent *m*∠*ABC*?

25. Use the justifications at the right to complete the statements below.

$$m\angle ABC + m\angle CBD = m\angle ABD \qquad \text{Angle Addition Postulate}$$

$$m\angle ABC + \boxed{\quad} = \boxed{\quad} \qquad \text{Substitute.}$$

$$m\angle ABC + \boxed{\quad} - \boxed{\quad} = \boxed{\quad} - \boxed{\quad} \qquad \text{Subtract } \boxed{\quad} \text{ from each side.}$$

$$m\angle ABC = \boxed{\quad} \qquad \text{Simplify.}$$

A   C
   1 x° D
   B

Math Success

Check off the vocabulary words that you understand.

☐ acute angle   ☐ obtuse angle   ☐ right angle   ☐ straight angle

Rate how well you can *classify angles.*

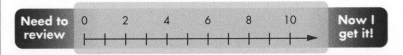

Need to review   0   2   4   6   8   10   Now I get it!

Vocabulary

● Review

Use a word from the list below to complete each sentence. Use each word just once.

> interior   rays   vertex

1. The _?_ of an *angle* is the region containing all of the points between the two sides of the angle.

2. When you use three points to name an *angle*, the _?_ must go in the middle.

3. The sides of ∠*QRS* are _?_ *RS* and *RQ*.

Use the figure below for Exercises 4–7. Identify each angle as *acute*, *right*, *obtuse*, or *straight*.

4. ∠*SRV*

5. ∠*TRS*

6. ∠*TRQ*

7. ∠*VRQ*

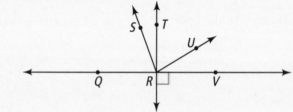

● Vocabulary Builder

conclusion (noun) **kun KLOO zhun**

Other Word Forms: conclude (verb)

Definition: A **conclusion** is the end of an event or the last step in a reasoning process.

● Use Your Vocabulary

Complete each sentence with *conclude* or *conclusion*.

8. If it rains, you can _?_ that soccer practice will be canceled.

9. The last step of the proof is the _?_ .

Key Concept Types of Angle Pairs

Angle Pair	Definition
Adjacent angles	Two coplanar angles with a common side, a common vertex, and no common interior points
Vertical angles	Two angles whose sides are opposite rays
Complementary angles	Two angles whose measures have a sum of 90
Supplementary angles	Two angles whose measures have a sum of 180

Draw a line from each word in Column A to the angles it describes in Column B.

Column A   Column B

10. supplementary   ∠1 and ∠2

11. adjacent   ∠2 and ∠3

12. vertical   ∠2 and ∠5

13. complementary   ∠3 and ∠6

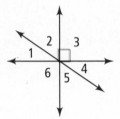

Problem 1 Identifying Angle Pairs

Got It? Use the diagram at the right. Are ∠AFE and ∠CFD vertical angles? Explain.

14. The rays of ∠AFE are $\overrightarrow{FE}$ and $\overrightarrow{FC}$ / $\overrightarrow{FA}$.

15. The rays of ∠CFD are $\overrightarrow{FC}$ and $\overrightarrow{FD}$ / $\overrightarrow{FA}$.

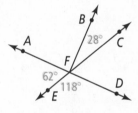

Complete each statement.

16. $\overrightarrow{FE}$ and ⬜ are opposite rays.

17. $\overrightarrow{FA}$ and ⬜ are opposite rays.

18. Are ∠AFE and ∠CFD vertical angles?   Yes / No

Problem 2 Making Conclusions From a Diagram

Got It? Can you conclude that $\overline{TW} \cong \overline{WV}$ from the diagram? Explain.

19. Circle the items marked as congruent in the diagram.

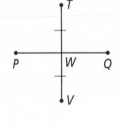

$\overline{PW}$ and $\overline{WQ}$ $\overline{TW}$ and $\overline{WV}$

       ∠TWQ and ∠PWT   ∠TWQ and ∠VWQ

20. Can you conclude that $\overline{TW} \cong \overline{WV}$? Why or why not?

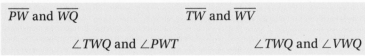

Lesson 1-5

Postulate 1-9 Linear Pair Postulate

If two angles form a linear pair, then they are supplementary.

21. If $\angle A$ and $\angle B$ form a linear pair, then $m\angle A + m\angle B = $ [ ] .

Problem 3 **Finding Missing Angle Measures**

Got It? Reasoning $\angle KPL$ and $\angle JPL$ are a linear pair, $m\angle KPL = 2x + 24$, and $m\angle JPL = 4x + 36$. How can you check that $m\angle KPL = 64$ and $m\angle JPL = 116$?

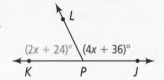

22. What is one way to check solutions? Place a ✓ in the box if the response is correct. Place an ✗ in the box if it is incorrect.

[ ]   Draw a diagram. If it looks good, the solutions are correct.

[ ]   Substitute the solutions in the original problem statement.

23. Use your answer(s) to Exercise 22 to check the solutions.

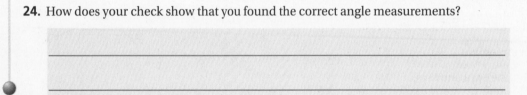

24. How does your check show that you found the correct angle measurements?

_____

_____

Problem 4 **Using an Angle Bisector to Find Angle Measures**

Got It? $\overrightarrow{KM}$ bisects $\angle JKL$. If $m\angle JKL = 72$, what is $m\angle JKM$?

25. Write a justification for each step.

$m\angle JKM = m\angle MKL$ _____

$m\angle JKM + m\angle MKL = m\angle JKL$ _____

$2m\angle JKM = m\angle JKL$ _____

$m\angle JKM = \frac{1}{2}m\angle JKL$ _____

26. Complete.

$m\angle JKL =$ [ ] , so $m\angle JKM =$ [ ] .

27. Now complete the diagram below.

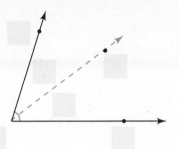

✓ **Lesson Check** • **Do you UNDERSTAND?**

Error Analysis Your friend calculated the value of x below. What is her error?

$4x + 2x = 180$
$6x = 180$
$x = 30$

28. Circle the best description of the largest angle in the figure.

acute	obtuse	right	straight

29. Complete: $4x + 2x =$ [ ]

30. What is your friend's error? Explain.

_____

_____

_____

✓ **Math Success**

Check off the vocabulary words that you understand.

☐ angle   ☐ complementary   ☐ supplementary   ☐ angle bisector   ☐ vertical

Rate how well you can *find missing angle measures*.

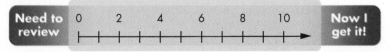

Lesson 1-5

Basic Constructions

Vocabulary

● Review

Draw a line from each word in Column A to its symbol or picture in Column B.

Column A	Column B
1. congruent	
2. point	
3. ray	
4. vertex	
5. intersection of segments	

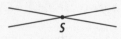

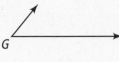

● Vocabulary Builder

perpendicular (adjective) **pur pun** DIK **yoo lur**

Definition: **Perpendicular** means at right angles to a given line or plane.

Example: Each corner of this paper is formed by **perpendicular** edges of the page.

Non-Examples: Acute, obtuse, and straight angles do not have **perpendicular** rays.

● Use Your Vocabulary

6. Circle the figure that shows *perpendicular* segments.

Problem 1 **Constructing Congruent Segments**

Got It? Use a straightedge to draw $\overline{XY}$. Then construct $\overline{RS}$ so that $RS = 2XY$.

7. A student did the construction at the right. Describe each
   step of the construction.

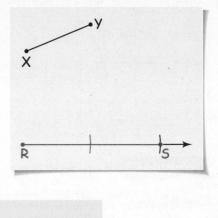

Step 1 _____

Step 2 _____

Step 3 _____
   _____

Step 4 _____

Step 5 _____

 Problem 2 **Constructing Congruent Angles**

Got It? Construct $\angle F$ so that $m\angle F = 2m\angle B$ at the right.

8. Use *arc* or *compass* to complete the sentence(s) in each step.
   In the large box, construct $\angle F$.

Step 1 Use a straightedge to construct a ray with endpoint *F*.

Step 2 With your ___?___ point on vertex *B*, draw a(n) ___?___ that intersects both sides of $\angle B$. Label the points of intersection *A* and *C*.
   _____

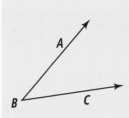

Step 3 Use the same compass setting. Put the ___?___ point on point *F*. Draw a long ___?___ and label its intersection with the ray as *S*.
   _____

Step 6 Draw $\overrightarrow{FR}$.

Step 5 Use the same compass setting. Put the ___?___ point on point *T*. Draw an ___?___ and label its intersection with the first ___?___ as point *R*.
   _____

Step 4 Open the ___?___ to the length of $\overline{AC}$. With the compass point on point *S*, draw an ___?___. Label where this arc intersects the other arc as point *T*.
   _____

Lesson 1-6

A *perpendicular bisector* of a segment is a line, segment, or ray that is perpendicular to the segment at its midpoint.

9. Circle the drawing that shows the perpendicular bisector of a segment.

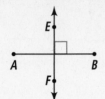   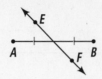   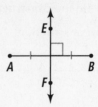

Problem 3 **Constructing the Perpendicular Bisector**

Got It? Draw $\overline{ST}$. Construct its perpendicular bisector.

10. Error Analysis A student's construction of the perpendicular bisector of $\overline{ST}$ is shown below. Describe the student's error.

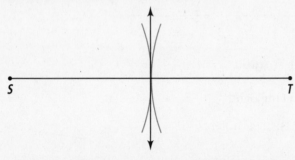

_____

_____

11. Do the construction correctly in the box below.

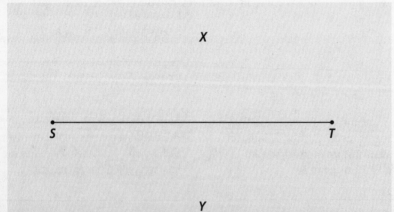

Problem 4 **Constructing the Angle Bisector**

Got It? Draw obtuse ∠XYZ. Then construct its bisector $\overrightarrow{YP}$.

12. Obtuse ∠XYZ is drawn in the box at the right. Complete the flowchart and do each step of the construction.

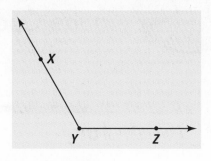

Step 1 Put the compass point on vertex ▢ . Draw an arc that intersects the sides of ▢ . Label the points of intersection A and B.

↓

Step 2 Put the compass point on point A and draw an arc. With the same / a different compass setting, draw an arc using point B. Be sure the arcs intersect. Label the point where the two arcs intersect P.

↓

Step 3 Draw ▢ .

 Lesson Check • **Do you UNDERSTAND?**

Vocabulary What two tools do you use to make constructions?

Draw a line from each task in Column A to the tool used in Column B.

Column A	Column B
13. measure lines	compass
14. measure angles	protractor
15. construct arcs	ruler
16. construct lines	straightedge

 Math Success

Check off the vocabulary words that you understand.

☐ straightedge   ☐ compass   ☐ construction   ☐ perpendicular bisector

Rate how well you can *construct angles and bisectors*.

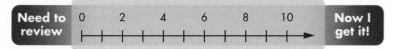

1-7 Midpoint and Distance in the Coordinate Plane

Vocabulary

● Review

Use the figure at the right for Exercises 1–6. Write T for *true* or F for *false*.

_____ **1.** Points *A* and *B* are both at the *origin*.

_____ **2.** If *AB* = *BC*, then *B* is the midpoint of $\overline{AC}$.

_____ **3.** The *midpoint* of $\overline{AE}$ is *F*.

_____ **4.** The *Pythagorean Theorem* can be used for any triangle.

_____ **5.** Point *C* is at (6, 0).

_____ **6.** Point *E* has a *y-coordinate* of −8.

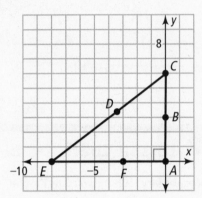

● Vocabulary Builder

> **midpoint** (noun) MID **poynt**
>
> **Definition:** A *midpoint* of a segment is a point that divides the segment into two congruent segments.

● Use Your Vocabulary

Use the figure at the right for Exercises 7–9.

7. The *midpoint* of $\overline{EF}$ is *G*(____ , ____).

8. The *midpoint* of $\overline{AB}$ is (____ , ____), or the origin.

9. The *midpoint* of $\overline{CD}$ is (____ , ____).

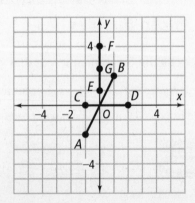

Key Concept Midpoint Formulas

On a Number Line	In the Coordinate Plane
The coordinate of the midpoint M of $\overline{AB}$ with endpoints at a and b is $\dfrac{a+b}{2}$.	Given $A(x_1, y_1)$ and $B(x_2, y_2)$, the coordinates of the midpoint of $\overline{AB}$ are $M\left(\dfrac{x_1 + x_2}{2}, \dfrac{y_1 + y_2}{2}\right)$

Find the coordinate of the midpoint M of each segment with the given endpoints on a number line.

10. endpoints 5 and 9

11. endpoints -3 and 5

12. endpoints -10 and -3

13. endpoints -8 and -1

14. Complete the diagram below.

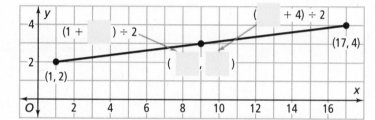

✓ **Problem 2** **Finding an Endpoint**

Got It? The midpoint of $\overline{AB}$ has coordinates $(4, -9)$. Endpoint A has coordinates $(-3, -5)$. What are the coordinates of B?

15. Complete the equations below.

Endpoint A Coordinates	Midpoint Formula	Midpoint Coordinates
(□ , □)	$\left(\dfrac{x_1 + \;\square\;}{2}, \dfrac{y_1 + \;\square\;}{2}\right)$	(□ , □)

$$\frac{x_1 + \square}{2} = \square$$

$$x_1 + \square = \square$$

$$x_1 = \square$$

← Solve two equations. →

$$\frac{y_1 + \square}{2} = \square$$

$$y_1 + \square = \square$$

$$y_1 = \square$$

16. The coordinates of endpoint B are (□).

27

Lesson 1-7

Formula   The Distance Formula

The distance between two points $A(x_1, y_1)$ and $B(x_2, y_2)$ is $d = \sqrt{(x_2 - x_1)^2 + (y_2 - y_1)^2}$.

The Distance Formula is based on the Pythagorean Theorem.

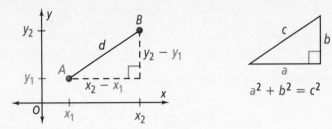

Use the diagrams above. Draw a line from each triangle side in Column A to the corresponding triangle side in Column B.

Column A	Column B
17. $y_2 - y_1$	a
18. $x_2 - x_1$	b
19. distance, d	c

 Problem 3   **Finding Distance**

Got It? $\overline{SR}$ has endpoints $S(-2, 14)$ and $R(3, -1)$. What is SR to the nearest tenth?

20. Complete the diagram at the right.

21. Let $S(-2, 14)$ be (x_1, y_1) and let $R(3, -1)$ be (x_2, y_2). Use the justifications and complete the steps below to find SR.

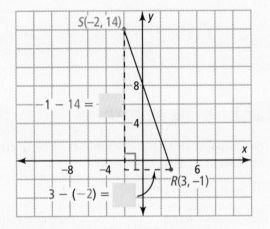

$d = \sqrt{\left(\boxed{} - x_1\right)^2 + \left(\boxed{} - y_1\right)^2}$ Use the Distance Formula.

$SR = \sqrt{\left(\boxed{} - (-2)\right)^2 + \left(\boxed{} - 14\right)^2}$ Substitute.

$= \sqrt{\left(\boxed{}\right)^2 + \left(\boxed{}\right)^2}$ Subtract.

$= \sqrt{\boxed{} + \boxed{}}$ Simplify powers.

$= \sqrt{\boxed{}}$ Add.

$\approx \boxed{}$ Use a calculator.

Got It? On a zip-line course, you are harnessed to a cable that travels through the treetops. You start at Platform *A* and zip to each of the other platforms. How far do you travel from Platform *D* to Platform *E*? Each grid unit represents 5 m.

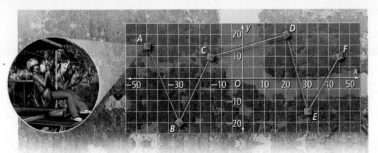

22. The equation is solved below. Write a justification for each step.

$$d = \sqrt{(x_2 - x_1)^2 + (y_2 - y_1)^2}$$

_____

$$DE = \sqrt{(30 - 20)^2 + (-15 - 20)^2}$$

_____

$$= \sqrt{10^2 + (-35)^2} = \sqrt{100 + 1225} = \sqrt{1325}$$

_____

23. To the nearest tenth, you travel about _____ m.

Reasoning How does the Distance Formula ensure that the distance between two different points is positive?

24. A radical symbol with no sign in front of it indicates a positive / negative square root.

25. Now answer the question.

_____

Check off the vocabulary words that you understand.

☐ midpoint   ☐ distance   ☐ coordinate plane

Rate how well you can *use the Midpoint and Distance Formulas.*

Need to review | 0   2   4   6   8   10 | Now I get it!

Lesson 1-7

Perimeter, Circumference, and Area

Vocabulary

● Review

1. Cross out the shapes that are NOT *polygons*.

2. Write the name of each figure. Use each word once.

triangle   square   rectangle   circle

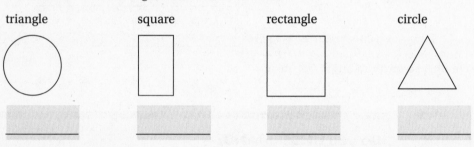

_____   _____   _____   _____

● Vocabulary Builder

consecutive (adjective) **kun SEK yoo tiv**

Definition: **Consecutive** means following in order without interruption.

Related Word: sequence

Example: The numbers 2, 4, 6, 8, . . . are **consecutive** even numbers.

Non-Example: The numbers 1, 3, 2, 5, 4, . . . are NOT **consecutive** numbers.

● Use Your Vocabulary

Draw a line from each sequence of letters in Column A to the next *consecutive* letter in Column B.

Column A	Column B
3. L, M, N, O, . . .	R
4. V, U, T, S, . . .	I
5. A, C, E, G. . . .	P

Key Concept Perimeter, Circumference, and Area

6. Label the parts of each of the figures below.

Square   Triangle   Rectangle    Circle

$P = 4s$

$A = s^2$

$P = a + b + c$

$A = \frac{1}{2}bh$

$P = 2b + 2h$

$A = bh$

$C = \pi d$ or $C = 2\pi r$

$A = \pi r^2$

Problem 1 Finding the Perimeter of a Rectangle

Got It? You want to frame a picture that is 5 in. by 7 in. with a 1-in.-wide frame. What is the perimeter of the picture?

7. The picture is ____ in. by ____ in.

8. Circle the formula that gives the perimeter of the picture.

$P = 4s$ $P = 2b + 2h$ $P = a + b + c$ $C = \pi d$

9. Solve using substitution.

10. The perimeter of the picture is ____ in.

Problem 2 Finding Circumference

Got It? What is the circumference of a circle with radius 24 m in terms of π?

11. Error Analysis At the right is one student's solution. What error did the student make?

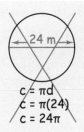

$c = \pi d$
$c = \pi(24)$
$c = 24\pi$

12. Find the correct circumference.

Problem 3 **Finding Perimeter in the Coordinate Plane**

Got It? Graph quadrilateral *JKLM* with vertices *J*(−3, −3), *K*(1, −3), *L*(1, 4), and *M*(−3, 1). What is the perimeter of *JLKM*?

13. Graph the quadrilateral on the coordinate plane at the right.

14. Use the justifications at the right to find the length of each side.

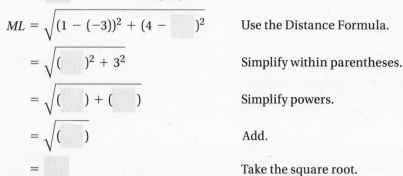

$JK = \left| -3 - 1 \right|$ Use the Ruler Postulate.

$= \boxed{}$ Simplify.

$KL = \left| 4 - \boxed{} \right|$ Use the Ruler Postulate.

$= \boxed{}$ Simplify.

$JM = \left| -3 - \boxed{} \right|$ Use the Ruler Postulate.

$= \boxed{}$ Simplify.

$ML = \sqrt{(1 - (-3))^2 + (4 - \boxed{})^2}$ Use the Distance Formula.

$= \sqrt{(\boxed{})^2 + 3^2}$ Simplify within parentheses.

$= \sqrt{(\boxed{}) + (\boxed{})}$ Simplify powers.

$= \sqrt{(\boxed{})}$ Add.

$= \boxed{}$ Take the square root.

15. Add the side lengths to find the perimeter.

$JK + KL + JM + ML = \boxed{} + \boxed{} + \boxed{} + \boxed{} = \boxed{}$

16. The perimeter of *JKLM* is $\boxed{}$ units.

Problem 5 **Finding Area of a Circle**

Got It? The diameter of a circle is 14 ft. What is its area in terms of π?

17. Label the diameter and radius of the circle at the right.

18. Use the formula $A = \pi r^2$ to find the area of the circle in terms of π.

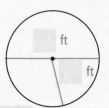

19. The area of the circle is $\boxed{}$ π ft^2.

take note

Key Concept Postulate 1-10 Area Addition Postulate

20. The area of a region is the **sum / difference** of the areas of its nonoverlapping parts.

 ft

ft

Got It? Reasoning The figure below shows one way to separate the figure at the left. What is another way to separate the figure?

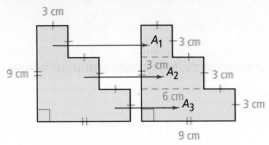

21. Draw segments to show two different ways to separate the figure. Separate the left-hand figure into three squares.

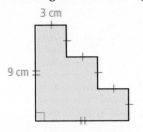 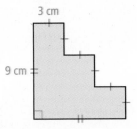

 Lesson Check • **Do you UNDERSTAND?**

Compare and Contrast Your friend can't remember whether $2\pi r$ computes the circumference or the area of a circle. How would you help your friend? Explain.

22. Underline the correct word(s) to complete each sentence.

Area involves units / square units .

Circumference involves units / square units .

The formula $2\pi r$ relates to area / circumference because it involves units / square units .

 Math Success

Check off the vocabulary words that you understand.

☐ perimeter   ☐ area

Rate how well you can *find the area of irregular shapes.*

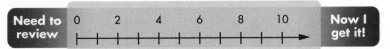

Vocabulary

● Review

Tell whether the statement is a *conjecture*. Explain your reasoning.

1. All apples are sweet.

_____

2. The sun sets in the west.

_____

● Vocabulary Builder

reason (noun, verb) **REE zun**

Related Words: reasonable (adjective), reasonably (adverb)

Definition: A **reason** is an explanation.

Main Idea: A logical argument uses **reasons** to arrive at a conclusion.

● Use Your Vocabulary

3. Complete each statement with the appropriate form of the word *reason*.

NOUN	In a logical argument, you state each ? .	_____
ADJECTIVE	The student did a ? job on the last math test.	_____
ADVERB	The workers cleaned up ? well after the party.	_____
VERB	To make a good decision, we ? together.	_____

Write R if the estimate is *reasonable* or U if it is *unreasonable*.

_____ **4.** $32 + 11 + 6 \approx 60$

_____ **5.** A 15% tip on $36 is $6.

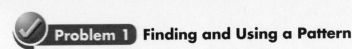

Problem 1 Finding and Using a Pattern

Got It? What are the next two terms in the sequence?

45, 40, 35, 30, . . .

For Exercises 6–9, circle the correct answer.

6. Do the numbers increase or decrease?

7. Does the amount of change *vary* or remain *constant*?

8. Which operation helps you form the next term?

9. Which number helps you form the next term?

Increase / Decrease
Vary / Constant
Addition / Subtraction
5 / 15

10. Now find the next two terms in the sequence.

Problem 2 Using Inductive Reasoning

Got It? What conjecture can you make about the twenty-first term in R, W, B, R, W, B, ...?

11. Complete the table.

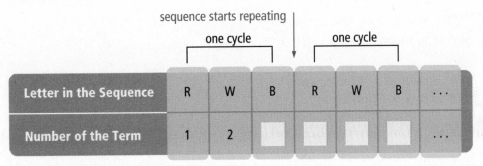

sequence starts repeating

one cycle   one cycle

Letter in the Sequence	R	W	B	R	W	B	...
Number of the Term	1	2					...

12. There are ____ letters in the pattern before it starts repeating.

13. R is the 1st term, 4th term, ____ term, ...

W is the 2nd term, ____ term, ____ term, ...

B is the 3rd term, ____ term, ____ term, ...

Underline the correct words to complete the sentence.

14. The twenty-first term is

one more than a multiple of 3 / two more than a multiple of 3 / a multiple of 3 .

15. Now make a conjecture.

The twenty-first term of the sequence is ____ .

Lesson 2-1

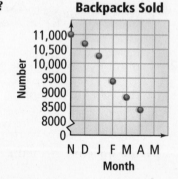

Problem 3 Collecting Information to Make a Conjecture

Got It? What conjecture can you make about the sum of the first 30 odd numbers?

16. Complete the table.

Number of Terms	Sum
1	1 = 1 = 1 • 1
2	1 + 3 = 4 = 2 • ☐
3	1 + ☐ + ☐ = 9 = ☐ • ☐
4	☐ + ☐ + ☐ + ☐ = ☐ = ☐ • ☐
5	☐ + ☐ + ☐ + ☐ + ☐ = ☐ = ☐ • ☐
⋮	⋮

17. Now make a conjecture.

The sum of the first 30 odd numbers is ☐ • ☐ , or ☐ .

Problem 4 Making a Prediction

Got It? What conjecture can you make about backpack sales in June?

For Exercises 18–22, write T for *true* or F for *false*.

_____ **18.** The graph shows a pattern of points.

_____ **19.** Each month, the number of backpacks sold increases.

_____ **20.** The change in sales varies from month to month, so you need to estimate this change.

_____ **21.** If sales change by about 500 each month, you can subtract 500 from April's sales to estimate May's sales.

_____ **22.** If sales change by about 500 each month, you can add 500 to May's sales to estimate June's sales.

23. Now make a conjecture about backpack sales in June.

About ☐ backpacks will be sold in June.

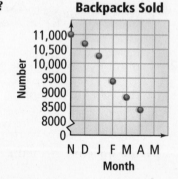

Backpacks Sold

Number

11,000
10,500
10,000
9500
9000
8500
8000
0

N D J F M A M
Month

Problem 5 Finding a Counterexample

Got It? What is a counterexample for the conjecture?

If a flower is red, it is a rose.

24. Circle the flowers below that are or can be red.

| rose | bluebell | carnation | geranium | tulip |

25. Is every flower you named a rose?   Yes / No

26. Write a word to complete the counterexample.

A ___?___ is a red flower but it is not a rose.

_____

 Lesson Check • **Do you UNDERSTAND?**

Compare and Contrast Clay thinks the next term in the sequence 2, 4, . . . is 6. Given the same pattern, Ott thinks the next term is 8, and Stacie thinks the next term is 7. What conjecture is each person making? Is there enough information to decide who is correct?

Choose the letter that describes the rule for each sequence.

A Multiply by 2   **B** Add 2, add 3, add 4, ...   **C** Add 2

____ 27. 2, 4, 6, 8, ...   ____ 28. 2, 4, 8, 16, ...   ____ 29. 2, 4, 7, 1, ...

____ 30. Clay's conjecture   ____ 31. Ott's conjecture   ____ 32. Stacie's conjecture

33. Circle the correct answer.

Are two numbers enough to show a pattern?   Yes / No

 Math Success

Check off the vocabulary words that you understand.

☐ inductive reasoning   ☐ conjecture   ☐ counterexample

Rate how well you can *use inductive reasoning*.

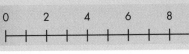

Lesson 2-1

Conditional Statements

Vocabulary

● Review

Underline the *conclusion* of each statement.

1. If the weather is nice, we will go swimming.

2. If I ride my bike to softball practice, then I will get there on time.

● Vocabulary Builder

converse (noun) **KAHN vurs**

Related Words: convert, conversion

Definition: The **converse** of something is its opposite.

Word Source: The prefix *con-,* which means "together," and *vertere,* which means "to turn," come from Latin. So, a **converse** involves changing the order of more than one thing.

● Use Your Vocabulary

Finish writing the *converse* of each statement.

3. **Statement:** If I study, then I pass the Geometry test.

   Converse: If __?__ , then I study.

   _____

4. **Statement:** If I am happy, then I laugh.

   Converse: If __?__ , then __?__ .

   _____   _____

5. **Statement:** If I have a summer job, then I can buy a new bicycle.

   Converse: __?__ .

   _____

take note

Key Concept Conditional Statements

Definition	Symbols	Diagram

Definition

A **conditional** is an if-then statement.

The **hypothesis** is the part *p* following *if*.

The **conclusion** is the part *q* following *then*.

Symbols

$p \rightarrow q$

Read as "If *p* then *q*"

or "*p* implies *q*."

Diagram

6. If *p* = tears and *q* = sadness, what are two ways to read $p \rightarrow q$?

_____   _____

Problem 1 **Identifying the Hypothesis and the Conclusion**

Got It? What are the hypothesis and the conclusion of the conditional?

If an angle measures 130, then the angle is obtuse.

Complete each sentence with *if* or *then*.

7. The hypothesis is the part following __?__.

_____

8. The conclusion is the part following __?__.

_____

9. Circle the hypothesis. Underline the conclusion.

If an angle measures 130, then the angle is obtuse.

Problem 2 **Writing a Conditional**

Got It? How can you write "Dolphins are mammals" as a conditional?

10. Circle the correct statement.

All dolphins are mammals.   All mammals are dolphins.

Underline the correct words to complete each statement.

11. The set of dolphins / mammals is inside the set of dolphins / mammals .

12. The smaller/larger set is the hypothesis and the smaller / larger set is the conclusion.

13. Use your answers to Exercises 11 and 12 to write the conditional.

If __?__ , then __?__ .

If an animal is _____ ,

then it is _____ .

Lesson 2-2

Problem 3 **Finding the Truth Value of a Conditional**

Got It? Is the conditional *true* or *false*? If it is false, find a counterexample.

If a month has 28 days, then it is February.

14. Cross out the month(s) that have at least 28 days.

January	February	March	April	May	June
July	August	September	October	November	December

15. Is the conditional *true* or *false*? Explain.

_____

_____

Key Concept **Related Conditional Statements**

Statement	How to Write It	Symbols	How to Read It
Conditional	Use the given hypothesis and conclusion.	$p \rightarrow q$	If p, then q.
Converse	Exchange the hypothesis and the conclusion.	$q \rightarrow p$	If q, then p.
Inverse	Negate both the hypothesis and the conclusion of the conditional.	$\sim p \rightarrow \sim q$	If not p, then not q.
Contrapositive	Negate both the hypothesis and the conclusion of the converse.	$\sim q \rightarrow \sim p$	If not q, then not p.

Use the statement below to write each conditional.

∠A measures 98, so ∠A is obtuse.

16. **Conditional** If _?_, then _?_.

If ∠A measures 98, then _____.

17. **Converse** If _?_, then _?_.

If _____, then _____.

18. **Inverse** If *not* _?_, then *not* _?_.

If _____,

then _____.

19. **Contrapositive** If *not* _?_, then *not* _?_.

If _____,

then _____.

Problem 4 Writing and Finding Truth Values of Statements

Got It? What are the converse, inverse, and contrapositive of the conditional statement below? What are the truth values of each? If a statement is false, give a counterexample.

If a vegetable is a carrot, then it contains beta carotene.

20. Converse: If a vegetable contains beta carotene, then _?_ .

_____

21. Inverse: If a vegetable is not a carrot, then _?_ .

_____

22. Contrapositive: If a vegetable does not contain beta carotene, then _?_ .

_____

23. The converse is true / false . The inverse is true / false . The contrapositive is true / false .

24. Give counterexamples for the statements that are false.

_____

_____

 Lesson Check • Do you UNDERSTAND?

Error Analysis Your classmate rewrote the statement "You jog every Sunday" as "If you jog, then it is Sunday." What is your classmate's error? Correct it.

25. Circle the hypothesis and underline the conclusion of your classmate's conditional.

If you jog, then it is Sunday.

26. Circle the counterexample for your classmate's conditional.

You don't jog, and it is not Sunday.   You also jog on Saturday.

27. Write the conditional that best represents "You jog every Sunday."

_____

Math Success

Check off the vocabulary words that you understand.

☐ conditional   ☐ hypothesis   ☐ conclusion

Rate how well you can *write conditional statements*.

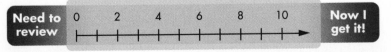

Lesson 2-2

Vocabulary

● Review

Underline the *hypothesis* in each statement.

1. If it rains on Friday, I won't have to cut the grass on Saturday.

2. If I go to sleep early tonight, then I won't be late for school tomorrow.

3. A triangle is equilateral if it has three congruent sides.

4. I'll know how to write biconditionals if I can identify a hypothesis and a conclusion.

● Vocabulary Builder

> **bi-** (prefix) **by**
>
> **Definition:** *bi-* is a prefix that means having two.
>
> **Examples:** A *bicycle* has two wheels. Someone who is *bilingual* speaks two languages fluently.

● Use Your Vocabulary

Draw a line from each word in Column A to its meaning in Column B.

Column A	Column B
5. biannually (adverb)	occurring every two hundred years
6. biathlon (noun)	a two-footed animal
7. bicentennial (adjective)	having two coasts
8. bicoastal (adjective)	supported by two parties
9. biped (noun)	occurring every two weeks
10. bipartisan (adjective)	occurring every two years
11. biplane (noun)	a plane with two sets of wings
12. biweekly (adjective)	a two-event athletic contest

Key Concept Biconditional Statements

A *biconditional* combines $p \rightarrow q$ and $q \rightarrow p$ as $p \leftrightarrow q$.

You read $p \leftrightarrow q$ as "p if and only if q."

13. Complete the biconditional.

A ray is an angle bisector ___?___ it divides an angle into two congruent angles.

 **Problem 1** **Writing a Biconditional**

Got It? What is the converse of the following true conditional? If the converse is also true, rewrite the statements as a biconditional.

If two angles have equal measure, then the angles are congruent.

14. Identify the hypothesis (p) and the conclusion (q).

p: _____ q: _____

15. Circle the converse ($q \rightarrow p$) of the conditional.

| If two angles do *not* have equal measure, then the angles are *not* congruent. | If two angles are congruent, then the angles have equal measure. | If two angles are *not* congruent, then the angles do *not* have equal measure. |

16. Now write the statements as a biconditional ($p \leftrightarrow q$).

_____ if and only if _____.

Problem 2 **Identifying the Conditionals in a Biconditional**

Got It? What are the two conditionals that form this biconditional?

Two numbers are reciprocals if and only if their product is 1.

17. Identify p and q.

p: _____ q: _____

18. Write the conditional $p \rightarrow q$.

If _____,

then _____.

19. Write the conditional $q \rightarrow p$.

If _____,

then _____.

Lesson 2-3

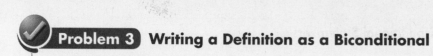

Problem 3 Writing a Definition as a Biconditional

Got It? Is this definition of *straight angle* reversible? If yes, write it as a true biconditional.

A straight angle is an angle that measures 180.

20. *Reversible* means you can reverse *p* and ⬜ in the conditional.

21. Write the conditional.

If _____ ,

then _____ .

22. Write the converse.

If _____ ,

then _____ .

23. Write the biconditional.

_____ ,

if and only if _____ .

Problem 4 Identifying Good Definitions

Got It? Is the following statement a good definition? Explain.

A square is a figure with four right angles.

24. Write the *conditional*.

_____

_____

25. Write the *converse*.

_____

_____

26. Which statement is true, the *conditional*, the *converse*, or *both*?

_____

27. Is the definition of a square a good definition? Explain.

_____

_____

Lesson Check • Do you UNDERSTAND?

Compare and Contrast Which of the following statements is a better definition of a linear pair?

A linear pair is a pair of supplementary angles.

A linear pair is a pair of adjacent angles with noncommon sides that are opposite rays.

Use the figures below for Exercises 28–31.

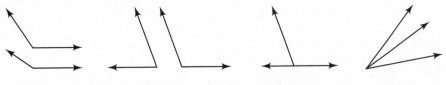

Figure 1   Figure 2   Figure 3   Figure 4

Underline the correct number or numbers to complete each sentence.

28. Figure(s) 1 / 2 / 3 / 4 show(s) linear pairs.

29. Figure(s) 1 / 2 / 3 / 4 show(s) supplementary angles.

30. Figure(s) 1 / 2 / 3 / 4 show(s) adjacent angles.

31. Figure(s) 1 / 2 / 3 / 4 show(s) adjacent angles whose noncommon sides are opposite rays.

32. Underline the correct word to complete the sentence.

Supplementary angles are always / sometimes / never linear pairs.

33. Write the better definition of a linear pair.

Math Success

Check off the vocabulary words that you understand.

☐ biconditional   ☐ conditional   ☐ hypothesis   ☐ conclusion

Rate how well you can *use biconditionals*.

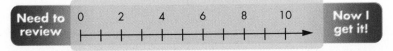

Lesson 2-3

Deductive Reasoning

Vocabulary

● Review

Write the *converse* of each conditional.

1. If I am thirsty, then I drink water.

_____

2. If the car outside is wet, then it rained.

_____

● Vocabulary Builder

deduce (verb) **dee DOOS**

Related Words: deductive (adjective), deduction (noun)

Definition: To **deduce** is to use known facts to reach a conclusion.

Main Idea: When you use general principles and facts to come to a conclusion, you **deduce** the conclusion.

Example: Your friend is wearing red today. He wears red only when there is a home game. You use these facts to **deduce** that there is a home game today.

● Use Your Vocabulary

Complete each statement with a word from the list. Use each word only once.

deduce   deduction   deductive

3. You use __?__ reasoning to draw a conclusion based on facts.

_____

4. The conclusion of your reasoning is a __?__ .

_____

5. The teacher will not __?__ that a dog ate your homework.

_____

Property   Law of Detachment

Law

If the hypothesis of a true conditional is true, then the conclusion is true.

Symbols

If $p \rightarrow q$ is true and p is true, then q is true.

 Problem 1 **Using the Law of Detachment**

Got It? What can you conclude from the given information?

> If there is lightning, then it is not safe to be out in the open.
> Marla sees lightning from the soccer field.

6. Underline the hypothesis of the conditional. Circle the conclusion.

> If there is lightning, then it is not safe to be out in the open.

Underline the correct word or phrase to complete each sentence.

7. "Marla sees lightning from the soccer field" fits / does not fit the hypothesis of the conditional.

8. It is safe / not safe to be on the soccer field.

Property   Law of Syllogism

You can state a conclusion from two true conditional statements when the conclusion of one statement is the hypothesis of the other statement.

If $p \rightarrow q$ is true and $q \rightarrow r$ is true, then $p \rightarrow r$ is true.

Complete each conclusion.

9. If it is July, then you are on summer vacation.

If you are on summer vacation, then you work in a smoothie shop.

Conclusion: If it is July, then _____ .

10. If a figure is a rhombus, then it has four sides.

If a figure has four sides, then it is a quadrilateral.

Conclusion: If a figure is a rhombus, then _____ .

 Problem 2 **Using the Law of Syllogism**

Got It? What can you conclude from the given information? What is your reasoning?

> If a number ends in 0, then it is divisible by 10.
> If a number is divisible by 10, then it is divisible by 5.

11. Identify p, q, and r.

p: a number ends in ☐ q: a number is divisible by ☐ r: a number is divisible by ☐

Lesson 2-4

12. Decide whether each part of the given information is *true* or *false*. Write T for *true* or F for *false*.

_____ $p \rightarrow q$ _____ $q \rightarrow r$ _____ $p \rightarrow r$

13. Circle the part of the Law of Syllogism that you will write.

$p \rightarrow q$ $q \rightarrow r$ $p \rightarrow r$

14. Now write your conclusion.

If _____ , then _____ .

Problem 3 **Using the Laws of Syllogism and Detachment**

Got It? What can you conclude from the given information? What is your reasoning?

If a river is more than 4000 mi long, then it is longer than the Amazon.
If a river is longer than the Amazon, then it is the longest river in the world.
The Nile is 4132 mi long.

15. Identify p, q, and r in the given information.

p: _____

q: _____

r: _____

16. Use the Law of Syllogism to complete the conditional.

If a river is more than _____ .

then it _____ .

17. Use the Law of Detachment and the conditional in Exercise 16 to write a conclusion.

The Nile is _____ .

Lesson Check • **Do you know HOW?**

If possible, make a conclusion from the given true statements. What reasoning did you use?

If a figure is a three-sided polygon, then it is a triangle.
Figure *ABC* is a three-sided polygon.

18. Identify p and q in the first statement.

p: _____

q: _____

19. Underline the correct words to complete each sentence.

The second statement matches the hypothesis / conclusion of the first statement.

I can use the Law of Detachment / Syllogism to state a conclusion.

20. Write your conclusion.

_____

Lesson Check • Do you UNDERSTAND?

Error Analysis What is the error in the reasoning below?

Birds that weigh more than 50 pounds
cannot fly. A kiwi cannot fly. So, a kiwi
weighs more than 50 pounds.

21. Write "Birds that weigh more than 50 pounds cannot fly" as a conditional.

_____

_____

22. Write the hypothesis of the conditional in Exercise 21.

_____

Underline the correct word to complete each sentence.

23. "A kiwi cannot fly" matches the hypothesis / conclusion of the conditional.

24. The student incorrectly applied the Law of Detachment / Syllogism .

Math Success

Check off the vocabulary words that you understand.

☐ Law of Detachment   ☐ Law of Syllogism   ☐ deductive reasoning   ☐ conditional

Rate how well you can use *deductive reasoning*.

| Need to review | 0 | 2 | 4 | 6 | 8 | 10 | Now I get it! |

Lesson 2-4

2-5 Reasoning in Algebra and Geometry

Vocabulary

● Review

1. Circle each *equation*.

$$2(a - 5)^2 \qquad 3x + 2 = 4 \qquad 5 + 3^4 \qquad 9 < x - 2$$

Write an *equation* to represent each problem.

2. Sara has five more than twice the number of apples that Gregg has. If Sara has 21 apples, how many apples does Gregg have?

3. Your brother does one less than twice the number of chores that you do. If he does seven chores, how many chores do you do?

● Vocabulary Builder

justify (verb) JUS **tuh fy**

Related Words: justice (noun), justification (noun), justifiable (adjective), justly (adverb)

Definition: To **justify** a step in a solution means to provide a mathematical reason why the step is correct.

Main Idea: When you **justify** an action, you explain why it is reasonable.

● Use Your Vocabulary

4. Draw a line from each equation in Column A to the property you would use to *justify* it in Column B.

Column A	Column B
$3 + 7 = 7 + 3$	Associative Property of Addition
$12(4) = 4(12)$	Associative Property of Multiplication
$2 \cdot (5 \cdot x) = (2 \cdot 5) \cdot x$	Commutative Property of Addition
$1 + (9 + 53) = (1 + 9) + 53$	Commutative Property of Multiplication

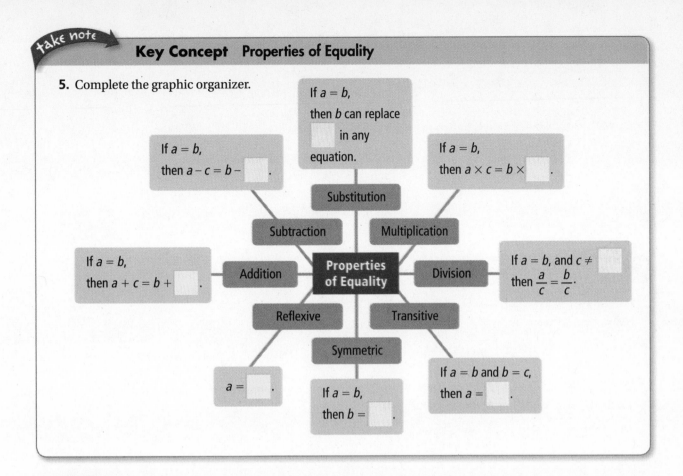

take note

Key Concept   Properties of Equality

5. Complete the graphic organizer.

If $a = b$,
then b can replace ☐ in any equation.

If $a = b$,
then $a - c = b -$ ☐.

If $a = b$,
then $a \times c = b \times$ ☐.

Substitution

Subtraction

Multiplication

If $a = b$,
then $a + c = b +$ ☐.

Addition

Properties of Equality

Division

If $a = b$, and $c \neq$ ☐
then $\dfrac{a}{c} = \dfrac{b}{c}$.

Reflexive

Transitive

Symmetric

$a =$ ☐.

If $a = b$,
then $b =$ ☐.

If $a = b$ and $b = c$,
then $a =$ ☐.

take note

Key Concept   The Distributive Property

Use multiplication to distribute a to each term of the sum or difference within the parentheses.

Sum

$a(b + c) = ab + ac$

Difference

$a(b - c) = ab - ac$

Use the Distributive Property to simplify each expression.

6. $5(24) = 5(20 + $ ☐ $)$

$= 5($ ☐ $) + 5($ ☐ $)$

$=$ ☐ $+$ ☐

$=$ ☐

7. $17(3) = (20 - 3)($ ☐ $)$

$= 20($ ☐ $) - 3($ ☐ $)$

$=$ ☐ $-$ ☐

$=$ ☐

✓ Problem 1   Justifying Steps When Solving an Equation

Got It? What is the value of x? Justify each step.

Given: $\overrightarrow{AB}$ bisects $\angle RAN$.

8. Circle the statement you can write from the given information.

$\angle RAB$ is obtuse. $\angle RAB \cong \angle NAB$ $\angle NAB \cong \angle RAN$

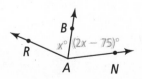

Lesson 2-5

9. Use the justifications below to find the value of *x*.

$\overrightarrow{AB}$ bisects $\angle RAN$.   Given

$\angle RAB \cong \angle$ [____]   Definition of angle bisector

$m\angle RAB = m\angle$ [____]   Congruent angles have equal measures.

$x =$ [____]   Substitute.

$0 =$ [____]   Subtraction Property of Equality

$75 =$ [____]   Addition Property of Equality

Key Concept   Properties of Congruence

Reflexive	**Symmetric**	**Transitive**
$\overline{AB} \cong \overline{AB}$	If $\overline{AB} \cong \overline{CD}$, then $\overline{CD} \cong \overline{AB}$.	If $\overline{AB} \cong \overline{CD}$ and $\overline{CD} \cong \overline{EF}$, then $\overline{AB} \cong \overline{EF}$.
$\angle A \cong \angle A$	If $\angle A \cong \angle B$, then $\angle B \cong \angle A$.	If $\angle A \cong \angle B$ and $\angle B \cong \angle C$, then $\angle A \cong \angle C$.

Complete each statement.

10. If $\angle P \cong \angle R$ and $\angle R \cong \angle A$, then $\angle P \cong \angle$ [____].

11. If $\angle X \cong \angle N$ and $\angle$ [____] $\cong \angle Y$, then $\angle X \cong \angle Y$.

12. If $\angle L \cong \angle T$ and $\angle T \cong \angle$ [____], then $\angle L \cong \angle Q$.

Problem 3   Writing a Two-Column Proof

Got It? Write a two-column proof.

Given: $\overline{AB} \cong \overline{CD}$ **Prove:** $\overline{AC} \cong \overline{BD}$

13. The statements are given below. Write a reason for each statement.

Statements	Reasons
1) $\overline{AB} \cong \overline{CD}$	1) _____
2) $AB = CD$	2) _____
3) $BC = BC$	3) _____
4) $AB + BC = BC + CD$	4) _____
5) $AC = BD$	5) _____
6) $\overline{AC} \cong \overline{BD}$	6) _____

Lesson Check • Do you UNDERSTAND?

Developing Proof Fill in the reasons for this algebraic proof.

Given: $5x + 1 = 21$

Prove: $x = 4$

Statements	Reasons
1) $5x + 1 = 21$	1) ?
2) $5x = 20$	2) ?
3) $x = 4$	3) ?

14. The first step in a proof is what you are given / to prove .

Underline the correct word(s) to complete each sentence. Then circle the property of equality that justifies the step.

15. First, the number 1 was added to / subtracted from each side of the equation.

    Addition Property of Equality   Subtraction Property of Equality   Reflexive Property

16. Then, each side of the equation was multiplied / divided by 5.

    Division Property of Equality   Multiplication Property of Equality   Transitive Property

17. Now write a reason for each step.

1) _____

2) _____

3) _____

Math Success

Check off the vocabulary words that you understand.

☐ Reflexive Property   ☐ Symmetric Property   ☐ Transitive Property

☐ proof   ☐ two-column proof

Rate how well you can *use properties of equality and congruence in proofs.*

Need to review   0   2   4   6   8   10   Now I get it!

Lesson 2-5

Vocabulary

● **Review**

Complete each sentence with *proof* or *prove*.

1. Galileo wanted to __?__ that the planets revolve around the sun.

_____

2. His observations and discoveries supported his theory but were not a __?__ of it.

_____

● **Vocabulary Builder**

theorem (noun) THEE **uh rum**

Definition: A **theorem** is a conjecture or statement that you prove true.

Main Idea: You use definitions, postulates, properties, and previously proven theorems to prove **theorems.**

● **Use Your Vocabulary**

Write T for *true* or F for *false*.

_____ **3.** A postulate is a *theorem*.

_____ **4.** A *theorem* may contain definitions.

_____ **5.** An axiom is a *theorem*.

Complete each statement with *lines, planes,* or *points*.

6. Postulate 1-1 Through any two __?__ there is exactly one line.

_____

7. Postulate 1-2 If two distinct __?__ intersect, then they intersect in exactly one point.

_____

8. Postulate 1-3 If two distinct __?__ intersect, then they intersect in exactly one line.

_____

9. Postulate 1-4 Through any three noncollinear __?__ there is exactly one plane.

_____

Theorem 2-1 Vertical Angles Theorem

Vertical angles are congruent.

10. If $\angle A$ and $\angle B$ are vertical angles and $m\angle A = 15$, then $m\angle B =$ [ ] .

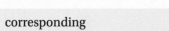

Problem 1 Using the Vertical Angles Theorem

Got It? What is the value of x?

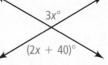

11. Circle the word that best describes the labeled angle pair in the diagram.

| corresponding | perpendicular | vertical |

12. Circle the word that best describes the relationship between the labeled angles in the diagram.

| congruent | perpendicular | supplementary |

13. Use the labels in the diagram to write an equation.

$3x =$ [ ]

14. Now solve the equation.

15. The value of x is [ ] .

Problem 2 Proof Using the Vertical Angles Theorem

Got It? Use the Vertical Angles Theorem to prove the following.

Given: $\angle 1 \cong \angle 2$

Prove: $\angle 1 \cong \angle 2 \cong \angle 3 \cong \angle 4$

16. Write a reason for each statement below.

Statements	Reasons
1) $\angle 1 \cong \angle 2$	1) _____
2) $\angle 1 \cong \angle 3$	2) _____
3) $\angle 2 \cong \angle 4$	3) _____
4) $\angle 1 \cong \angle 2 \cong \angle 3 \cong \angle 4$	4) _____

Lesson 2-6

Theorem 2-2 Congruent Supplements Theorem

If two angles are supplements of the same angle (or of congruent angles), then the two angles are congruent.

If ∠1 and ∠3 are supplements and ∠2 and ∠3 are supplements, then ∠1 ≅ ∠2.

17. Complete the diagram below to illustrate Theorem 2-2.

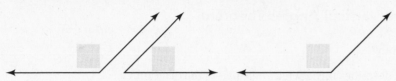

18. If $m\angle D = 135$ and $m\angle G = 45$ and ∠F and ∠G are supplements, then $m\angle F = $ _____ .

If ∠A and ∠B are supplements and $m\angle C = 85$ and $m\angle B = 95$, then $m\angle A = $ _____ .

Problem 3 Writing a Paragraph Proof

Got It? Write a paragraph proof for the Vertical Angles Theorem.

> **Given:** ∠1 and ∠3 are vertical angles.
>
> **Prove:** ∠1 ≅ ∠3

Circle the correct word to complete each sentence.

19. ∠1 and ∠3 are __?__ angles because it is given. → supplementary / vertical

20. ∠1 and ∠2 are __?__ angles because they form a linear pair. → supplementary / vertical

21. ∠2 and ∠3 are __?__ angles because they form a linear pair. → supplementary / vertical

22. $m\angle 1 + m\angle 2 = 180$ because the sum of the measures of __?__ angles is 180. → complementary / supplementary

23. $m\angle 2 + m\angle 3 = 180$ because the sum of the measures of __?__ angles is 180. → complementary / supplementary

24. By the __?__ Property of Equality, $m\angle 1 + m\angle 2 = m\angle 2 + m\angle 3$. → Reflexive / Transitive

25. By the __?__ Property of Equality, $m\angle 1 = m\angle 3$. → Subtraction / Symmetric

26. Angles with the same __?__ are congruent, so ∠1 ≅ ∠3. → properties / measure

---

Theorem 2-3 Congruent Complements Theorem

If two angles are complements of the same angle (or of congruent angles), then the two angles are congruent.

27. ∠A is a supplement of a 165° angle. ∠B is a complement of a 75° angle. Circle the relationship between ∠A and ∠B.

complementary   congruent   supplementary

Theorems 2-4 and 2-5

Theorem 2-4 All right angles are congruent.

Theorem 2-5 If two angles are congruent and supplementary, then each is a right angle.

28. If ∠R and ∠S are right angles, then ☐ ≅ ☐ .

29. If ∠H ≅ ∠J and ∠H and ∠J are supplements, then m∠H = m☐ = ☐ .

Lesson Check • Do you know HOW?

What are the measures of ∠1, ∠2, and ∠3?

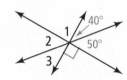

30. Cross out the theorem you CANNOT use to find an angle measure.

Congruent Complements Theorem   Congruent Supplements Theorem   Vertical Angles Theorem

31. m∠1 = ☐   **32.** m∠2 = ☐   **33.** m∠3 = ☐

Lesson Check • Do you UNDERSTAND?

Reasoning If ∠A and ∠B are supplements, and ∠A and ∠C are supplements, what can you conclude about ∠B and ∠C? Explain.

34. Since ∠A and ∠B are supplements, m∠A + m∠B = ☐ .

35. Since ∠A and ∠C are supplements, m∠A + m∠C = ☐ .

36. By the Transitive Property of Equality, ☐ + m∠B = ☐ + m∠C.

37. By the Subtraction Property of Equality, m∠B = ☐ , so ∠B ≅ ☐ .

Math Success

Check off the vocabulary words that you understand.

☐ theorem   ☐ paragraph proof   ☐ complementary   ☐ supplementary   ☐ right angle

Rate how well you can *write proofs*.

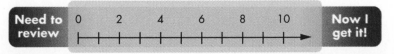

57

Lesson 2-6

Copyright © by Pearson Education, Inc. or its affiliates. All Rights Reserved.

Vocabulary

● **Review**

Write T for *true* or F for *false*.

_____ **1.** You can name a *plane* by a capital letter, such as *A*.

_____ **2.** A *plane* contains a finite number of lines.

_____ **3.** Two points lying on the same *plane* are coplanar.

_____ **4.** If two distinct *planes* intersect, then they intersect in exactly one line.

● **Vocabulary Builder**

> The symbol for
> **parallel** is ‖.

parallel (noun) PA **ruh lel**

Definition: *Parallel* lines lie in the same plane but never intersect, no matter how far they extend.

● **Use Your Vocabulary**

5. Circle the segment(s) that are *parallel* to the *x*-axis.

$\overline{AB}$ $\overline{BC}$ $\overline{CD}$ $\overline{AD}$

6. Circle the segment(s) that are *parallel* to the *y*-axis.

$\overline{AB}$ $\overline{BC}$ $\overline{CD}$ $\overline{AD}$

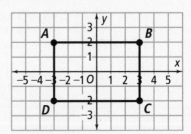

7. Circle the polygon(s) that have two pairs of *parallel* sides.

rectangle   parallelogram   square   trapezoid

Complete each statement below with *line* or *segment*.

8. A __?__ consist of two endpoints and all the points between them.

_____

9. A __?__ is made up of an infinite number of points.

_____

Key Concept Parallel and Skew

Parallel lines are coplanar lines that do not intersect.

Skew lines are noncoplanar; they are not parallel and do not intersect.

Parallel planes are planes that do not intersect.

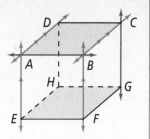

Use arrows to show $\overleftrightarrow{AE} \parallel \overleftrightarrow{BF}$ and $\overleftrightarrow{AD} \parallel \overleftrightarrow{BC}$.

10. Write each word, phrase, or symbol in the correct oval.

noncoplanar   coplanar   do not intersect

intersect $\overleftrightarrow{AE}$ and $\overleftrightarrow{CG}$ $\overleftrightarrow{CB}$ and $\overleftrightarrow{AE}$

Parallel

Skew

Problem 1 Identifying Nonintersecting Lines and Planes

Got It? Use the figure at the right. Which segments are parallel to $\overline{AD}$?

11. In plane *ADHE*, ____ is parallel to $\overline{AD}$.

12. In plane *ADBC*, ____ is parallel to $\overline{AD}$.

13. In plane *ADGF*, ____ is parallel to $\overline{AD}$.

Got It? Reasoning Explain why $\overline{FE}$ and $\overline{CD}$ are *not* skew.

14. Cross out the words or phrases below that do NOT describe skew lines.

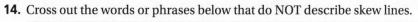

coplanar	do not intersect	intersect
parallel	noncoplanar	not parallel

15. Circle the correct statement below.

Segments and rays can be skew if they lie in skew lines.

Segments and rays are never skew.

16. Underline the correct words to complete the sentence.

$\overline{FE}$ and $\overline{CD}$ are in a plane that slopes from the bottom / top left edge to the

bottom / top right edge of the figure.

17. Why are $\overline{FE}$ and $\overline{CD}$ NOT skew?

_____

_____

Lesson 3-1

Key Concept Angle Pairs Formed by Transversals

Alternate interior angles are nonadjacent interior angles that lie on opposite sides of the transversal.

Same-side interior angles are interior angles that lie on the same side of the transversal.

Corresponding angles lie on the same side of a transversal *t* and in corresponding positions.

Alternate exterior angles are nonadjacent exterior angles that lie on opposite sides of the transversal.

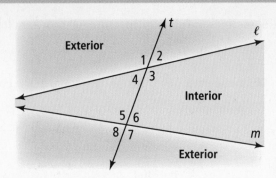

Use the diagram above. Draw a line from each angle pair in Column A to its description in Column B.

Column A	Column B
18. ∠4 and ∠6	alternate exterior angles
19. ∠3 and ∠6	same-side interior angles
20. ∠2 and ∠6	alternate interior angles
21. ∠2 and ∠8	corresponding angles

Problem 2 Identifying an Angle Pair

Got It? What are three pairs of corresponding angles in the diagram at the right?

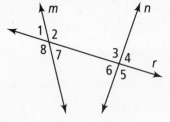

Underline the correct word(s) or letter(s) to complete each sentence.

22. The transversal is line *m / n / r*.

23. Corresponding angles are on the same side / different sides of the transversal.

24. Name three pairs of corresponding angles.

∠ ___ and ∠ ___   ∠ ___ and ∠ ___   ∠ ___ and ∠ ___   ∠ ___ and ∠ ___

Problem 3 Classifying an Angle Pair

Got It? Are angles 1 and 3 *alternate interior angles, same-side interior angles, corresponding angles,* or *alternate exterior angles*?

25. Are ∠1 and ∠3 on the same side of the transversal?   Yes / No

26. Cross out the angle types that do NOT describe ∠1 and ∠3.

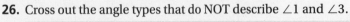

alternate exterior   alternate interior   corresponding   same-side interior

27. ∠1 and ∠3 are __?__ angles.

Lesson Check • Do you know HOW?

Name one pair each of the segments or planes.

28. parallel segments

$\overline{AB} \parallel$ ___

29. skew segments

$\overline{HD}$ and ___

30. parallel planes

$ABCD \parallel$ ___

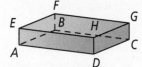

Name one pair each of the angles.

31. alternate interior

$\angle 8$ and $\angle$ ___

32. same-side interior

$\angle 8$ and $\angle$ ___

33. corresponding

$\angle 1$ and $\angle$ ___

34. alternate exterior

$\angle 7$ and $\angle$ ___

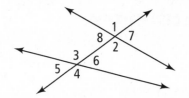

Lesson Check • Do you UNDERSTAND?

Error Analysis Carly and Juan examine the figure at the right. Carly says $\overline{AB} \parallel \overline{HG}$. Juan says $\overline{AB}$ and $\overline{HG}$ are skew. Who is correct? Explain.

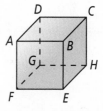

Write T for *true* or F for *false*.

_____ **35.** Parallel segments are coplanar.

_____ **36.** There are only six planes in a cube.

_____ **37.** No plane contains $\overline{AB}$ and $\overline{HG}$.

38. Who is correct? Explain.

_____

_____

Math Success

Check off the vocabulary words that you understand.

☐ angle   ☐ parallel   ☐ skew   ☐ transversal

Rate how well you can *classify angle pairs*.

Lesson 3-1

3-2 Properties of Parallel Lines

Copyright © by Pearson Education, Inc. or its affiliates. All Rights Reserved.

Vocabulary

● Review

1. Circle the symbol for *congruent*.   ≅   =   ∥

Identify each angle below as *acute*, *obtuse*, or *right*.

2.
125°

3.

4.
72°

_____   _____   _____

● Vocabulary Builder

interior (noun) **in TEER ee ur**

Main Idea: The **interior** is the inside of a figure.

Related Words: inside (noun), exterior (noun, antonym)

Definition: The **interior** of a pair of lines is the region between the two lines.

Example: A painter uses **interior** paint for the inside of a house.

interior ℓ
m ← interior

● Use Your Vocabulary

Use the diagram at the right for Exercises 5 and 6. Underline the correct point to complete each sentence.

5. The *interior* of the circle contains point *A / B / C*.

6. The *interior* of the angle contains point *A / B / C*.

7. Underline the correct word to complete the sentence.

The endpoint of an *angle* is called its ray / vertex .

8. Write two other names for ∠ABC in the diagram at the right.

_____   _____

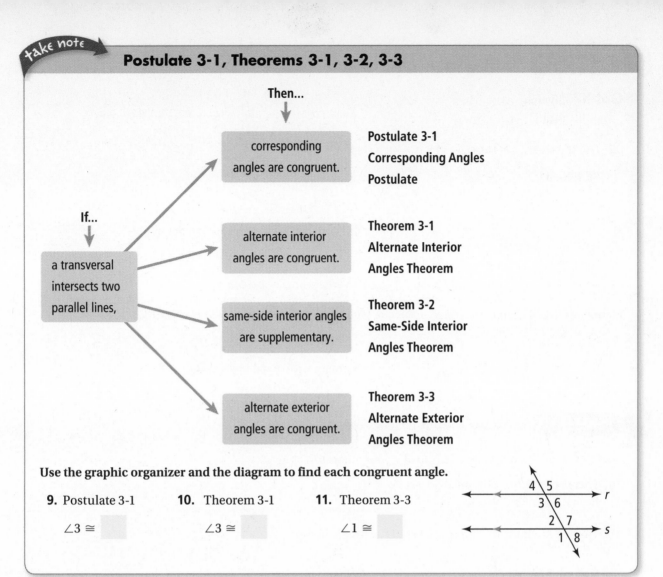

Then...

corresponding angles are congruent.

Postulate 3-1
Corresponding Angles
Postulate

If...

a transversal intersects two parallel lines,

alternate interior angles are congruent.

Theorem 3-1
Alternate Interior
Angles Theorem

same-side interior angles are supplementary.

Theorem 3-2
Same-Side Interior
Angles Theorem

alternate exterior angles are congruent.

Theorem 3-3
Alternate Exterior
Angles Theorem

Use the graphic organizer and the diagram to find each congruent angle.

9. Postulate 3-1

$\angle 3 \cong$ ▢

10. Theorem 3-1

$\angle 3 \cong$ ▢

11. Theorem 3-3

$\angle 1 \cong$ ▢

Problem 1 Identifying Congruent Angles

Got It? **Reasoning** One way to justify $m\angle 5 = 55$ is shown below. Can you find another way to justify $m\angle 5 = 55$? Explain.

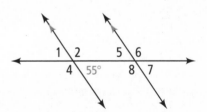

$m\angle 1 = 55$ by the Vertical Angles Theorem.

$m\angle 5 = 55$ by the Corresponding Angles Postulate because $\angle 1$ and $\angle 5$ are corresponding angles.

12. Write a reason for each statement.

$m\angle 7 = 55$

_____

$m\angle 5 = m\angle 7$

_____

$m\angle 5 = 55$

_____

Problem 2 Proving an Angle Relationship

Got It? Given: $a \parallel b$

Prove: $\angle 1 \cong \angle 7$

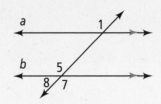

13. Use the reasons at the right to write each step of the proof.

Statements	Reasons
1)	1) Given
2)	2) If lines are $\parallel$, then corresp. angles are $\cong$.
3)	3) Congruent angles have equal measure.
4)	4) Vertical angles are congruent.
5)	5) Congruent angles have equal measure.
6)	6) Transitive Property of $\cong$
7)	7) Angles with equal measure are $\cong$.

Problem 3 Finding Measures of Angles

Got It? Find the measure of $\angle 1$. Justify your answer.

14. There are two sets of parallel lines.
Each parallel line also acts as a ___?___ .

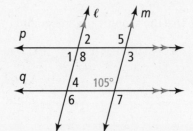

15. The steps to find $m\angle 1$ are given below. Justify each step.

Statements	Reasons
1) $\angle 1 \cong \angle 4$	1)
2) $m\angle 1 = m\angle 4$	2)
3) $\angle 4$ and $\angle 6$ are supplementary.	3)
4) $m\angle 4 + m\angle 6 = 180$	4)
5) $m\angle 1 + m\angle 6 = 180$	5)
6) $m\angle 5 = 105$	6)
7) $m\angle 6 = 105$	7)
8) $m\angle 1 + 105 = 180$	8)
9) $m\angle 1 = 75$	9)

Chapter 3

64

Problem 4 **Using Algebra to Find an Angle Measure**

Got It? In the figure at the right, what are the values of *x* and *y*?

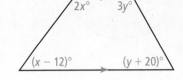

16. The bases of a trapezoid are parallel / perpendicular .

17. Use the Same-Side Interior Angles Theorem to complete each statement.

$2x +$ [ ] $= 180$ $3y +$ [ ] $= 180$

18. Solve each equation.

 Lesson Check • **Do you UNDERSTAND?**

In the diagram at the right, $\angle 1$ and $\angle 8$ are supplementary. What is a good name for this pair of angles? Explain.

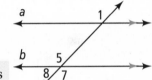

19. Circle the best name for lines *a* and *b*.

parallel perpendicular skew transversals

20. Circle the best name from the list below for $\angle 1$ and $\angle 8$.

alternate congruent corresponding same-side

21. Circle the best name from the list below for $\angle 1$ and $\angle 8$.

exterior interior

22. Use your answers to Exercises 20 and 21 to write a name for $\angle 1$ and $\angle 8$.

_____

 **Math Success**

Check off the vocabulary words that you understand.

☐ alternate interior angles ☐ alternate exterior angles

Rate how well you can *prove angle relationships*.

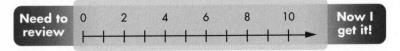

3-3 Proving Lines Parallel

Vocabulary

● Review

Write the *converse* of each statement.

1. Statement: If you are cold, then you wear a sweater.

Converse: If __?__, then __?__.

If _____, then _____.

2. Statement: If an angle is a right angle, then it measures 90°.

Converse: _____

3. The *converse* of a true statement is always / sometimes / never true .

● Vocabulary Builder

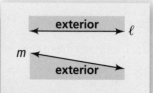

exterior (adjective) **ek STEER ee ur**

Related Words: **exterior** (noun), external, interior (antonym)

Definition: **Exterior** means on the outside or in an outer region.

Example: Two lines crossed by a transversal form four **exterior** angles.

● Use Your Vocabulary

Underline the correct word to complete each sentence.

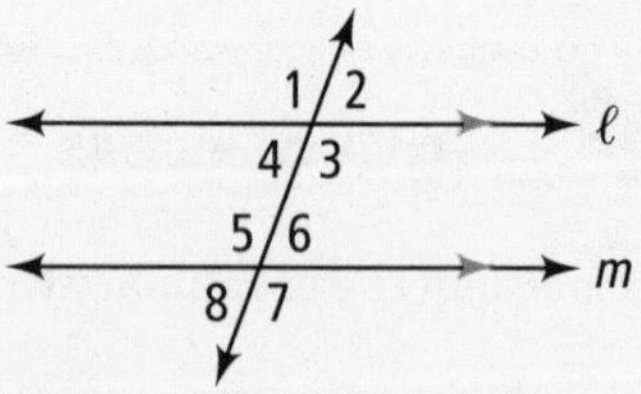

4. To paint the outside of your house, buy interior / exterior paint.

5. The protective cover prevents the interior / exterior of the book from being damaged.

6. In the diagram at the right, angles 1 and 7 are alternate interior / exterior angles.

7. In the diagram at the right, angles 4 and 5 are same-side interior / exterior angles.

Underline the *hypothesis* and circle the *conclusion* in the following statements.

8. If the lines do not intersect, then they are parallel lines.

9. If the angle measures 180°, then it is a straight angle.

Postulate 3-1 Corresponding Angles Postulate

If a transversal intersects two parallel lines, then corresponding angles are congruent.

10. Complete the statement of Postulate 3-2.

Postulate 3-2 Converse of the Corresponding Angles Postulate

If two lines on a transversal form corresponding angles that are congruent, then the lines are ___?___ .

11. Use the diagram below. Place appropriate marking(s) to show that ∠1 and ∠2 are congruent.

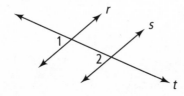

12. Circle the diagram that models Postulate 3-2.

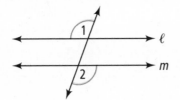 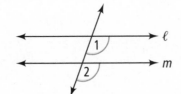

Theorem 3-4 Converse of the Alternate Interior Angle Theorem

If two lines and a transversal form alternate interior angles that are congruent, then the two lines are parallel.

Theorem 3-5 Converse of the Same-Side Interior Angles Theorem

If two lines and a transversal form same-side interior angles that are supplementary, then the two lines are parallel.

Theorem 3-6 Converse of the Alternate Exterior Angles Theorem

If two lines and a transversal form alternate exterior angles that are congruent, then the two lines are parallel.

13. Use the diagram at the right to complete each example.

Theorem 3-4	**Theorem 3-5**	**Theorem 3-6**
If ∠4 ≅ ▢ , then $b \parallel c$.	If ∠3 and ▢ are supplementary, then $b \parallel c$.	If ∠1 ≅ ▢ , then $b \parallel c$.

Lesson 3-3

Problem 1 Identifying Parallel Lines

Got It? Which lines are parallel if ∠6 ≅ ∠7? Justify your answer.

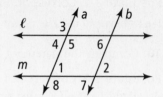

14. Underline the correct word(s) to complete each sentence.

∠6 ≅ ∠7 is given / to prove .

∠6 and ∠7 are alternate / same-side angles.

∠6 and ∠7 are corresponding / exterior / interior angles.

I can use Postulate 3-1 / Postulate 3-2 to prove the lines parallel.

Using ∠6 ≅ ∠7, lines *a* and *b* / *ℓ* and *m* are parallel and the transversal is *a* / *b* / *ℓ* / *m* .

Problem 2 Writing a Flow Proof of Theorem 3-6

Got It? Given that ∠1 ≅ ∠7. Prove that ∠3 ≅ ∠5 using a flow proof.

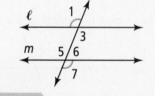

15. Use the diagram at the right to complete the flow proof below.

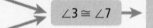

	Given

∠1 ≅ ∠3

∠3 ≅ ∠7 → ∠7 ≅ ☐ → ∠3 ≅ ∠5

Vertical angles
are ≅.

Problem 3 Determining Whether Lines Are Parallel

Got It? Given that ∠1 ≅ ∠2, you can use the Converse of the Alternate Exterior Angles Theorem to prove that lines *r* and *s* are parallel. What is another way to explain why *r*∥*s*? Justify your answer.

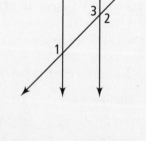

16. Justify each step.

∠1 ≅ ∠2 _____

∠2 ≅ ∠3 _____

∠1 ≅ ∠3 _____

17. Angles 1 and 3 are alternate / corresponding .

18. What postulate or theorem can you now use to explain why *r*∥*s*?

_____

Got It? What is the value of *w* for which *c* ∥ *d*?

Underline the correct word to complete each sentence.

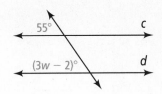

19. The marked angles are on opposite sides / the same side of the transversal.

20. By the Corresponding Angles Postulate, if *c* ∥ *d* then corresponding angles are
complementary / congruent / supplementary .

21. Use the theorem to solve for *w*.

Lesson Check • Do you UNDERSTAND?

Error Analysis A classmate says that $\overleftrightarrow{AB} \parallel \overleftrightarrow{DC}$ based on the diagram at right. Explain your classmate's error.

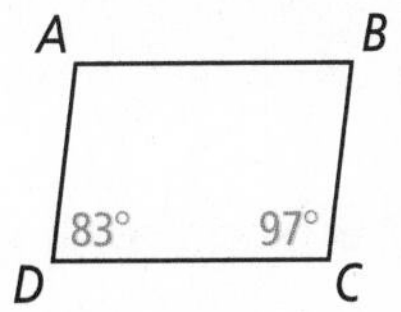

22. Circle the segments that are sides of ∠*D* and ∠*C*. Underline the transversal.

$\overline{AB}$ $\qquad\qquad$ $\overline{BC}$ $\qquad\qquad$ $\overline{DC}$ $\qquad\qquad$ $\overline{DA}$

23. Explain your classmate's error.

_____

_____

_____

Math Success

Check off the vocabulary words that you understand.

☐ flow proof $\qquad$ ☐ two-step proof $\qquad$ ☐ parallel lines

Rate how well you can *prove that lines are parallel.*

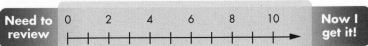

Lesson 3-3

Parallel and Perpendicular Lines

Vocabulary

● Review

Complete each statement with *always*, *sometimes* or *never*.

1. A *transversal* __?__ intersects at least two lines.

_____

2. A *transversal* __?__ intersects two lines at more than two points.

_____

3. A *transversal* __?__ intersects two parallel lines.

_____

4. A *transversal* __?__ forms angles with two other lines.

_____

● Vocabulary Builder

transitive (adjective) TRAN **si tiv**

Related Words: transition, transit, transitivity

Main Idea: You use the **Transitive** Property in proofs when what you know implies a statement that, in turn, implies what you want to prove.

Definition: **Transitive** describes the property where one element in relation to a second element and the second in relation to the third implies the first element is in relation to the third element.

> **Transitive**
> If $A \to B$
> and $B \to C$
> then $A \to C$.

● Use Your Vocabulary

Complete each example of the *Transitive* Property.

5. If $a > b$
and $b > c$,
then _____.

6. If Joe is younger than Ann
and Ann is younger than
Sam, then

_____
_____.

7. If you travel from
Station 2 to Station 3
and you travel from

_____
_____,

then you travel from
Station 2 to Station 4.

Theorem 3-7 Transitive Property of Parallel Lines and **Theorem 3-8**

8. Complete the table below.

	Theorem 3-7 Transitive Property of Parallel Lines	Theorem 3-8
	If two lines are parallel to the same line, then they are parallel to each other.	In a plane, if two line are perpendicular to the same line, then they are parallel to each other.
If	$a \parallel b$	$m \perp t$
and	☐ $\parallel$ ☐	$n \perp t$
then	$a \parallel c$	m ☐ n

Problem 1 Solving a Problem With Parallel Lines

Got It? Can you assemble the pieces at the right to form a picture frame with opposite sides parallel? Explain.

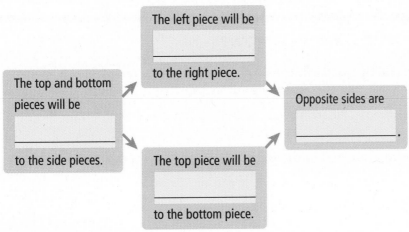

9. Circle the correct phrase to complete the sentence.

To make the picture frame, you will glue __?__ .

the same angle to the same angle   two different angles together

10. The angles at each connecting end measure ☐° and ☐°.

11. When the pieces are glued together, each angle of the frame will measure ☐°.

12. Complete the flow chart below with *parallel* or *perpendicular*.

The top and bottom pieces will be _____ to the side pieces.

The left piece will be _____ to the right piece.

The top piece will be _____ to the bottom piece.

Opposite sides are _____.

13. Underline the correct words to complete the sentence.

Yes / No , I can / cannot assemble the pieces to form a picture frame with opposite sides parallel.

Theorem 3-9   Perpendicular Transversal Theorem

In a plane, if a line is perpendicular to one of two parallel lines, then it is also perpendicular to the other.

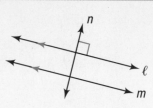

14. Place a right angle symbol in the diagram at the right to illustrate Theorem 3-9.

Use the information in each diagram to complete each statement.

15.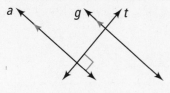

16.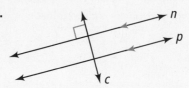

$a \parallel$ ▢ and $a \perp$ ▢ , so ▢ $\perp$ ▢ .

$c \perp$ ▢ and $n \parallel$ ▢ , so ▢ $\perp$ ▢ .

 Problem 2 **Proving a Relationship Between Two lines**

Got It? Use the diagram at the right. In a plane, $c \perp b$, $b \perp d$, and $d \perp a$. Can you conclude that $a \parallel b$? Explain.

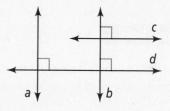

17. Circle the line(s) perpendicular to a. Underline the line(s) perpendicular to b.

| a | b | c | d |

18. Lines that are perpendicular to the same line are parallel / perpendicular .

19. Can you conclude that $a \parallel b$? Explain.

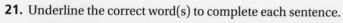

Lesson Check • **Do you know HOW?**

In one town, Avenue A is parallel to Avenue B. Avenue A is also perpendicular to Main Street. How are Avenue B and Main Street related? Explain.

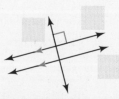

20. Label the streets in the diagram A for *Avenue A*, B for *Avenue B*, and M for *Main Street*.

21. Underline the correct word(s) to complete each sentence.

The Perpendicular Transversal Theorem states that, in a plane, if a line is

parallel / perpendicular to one of two parallel / perpendicular lines, then it is

also parallel / perpendicular to the other.

Avenue B and Main Street are parallel / perpendicular streets.

Lesson Check • Do you UNDERSTAND?

Which theorem or postulate from earlier in the chapter supports the conclusion in Theorem 3-8? In the Perpendicular Transversal Theorem? Explain.

Use the diagram at the right for Exercises 22 and 23.

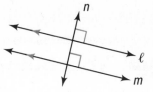

22. Complete the conclusion to Theorem 3-8.

In a plane, if two lines are perpendicular to the same line, then __?__ .

_____

23. Complete the statement of Postulate 3-2.

If two lines and a transversal form __?__ angles that are congruent, then the lines are parallel.

Use the diagram at the right for Exercises 24 and 25.

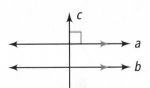

24. Complete the conclusion to the Perpendicular Transversal Theorem.

In a plane, if a line is perpendicular to one of two parallel lines, then it is also __?__ .

_____

25. Explain how any congruent angle pairs formed by parallel lines support the conclusion to the Perpendicular Transversal Theorem.

_____

_____

_____

_____

_____

Math Success

Check off the vocabulary words that you understand.

☐ parallel   ☐ perpendicular

Rate how well you can *understand parallel and perpendicular lines.*

| Need to review | 0 | 2 | 4 | 6 | 8 | 10 | Now I get it! |

Parallel Lines and Triangles

Vocabulary

● Review

Identify the part of speech for the word *alternate* in each sentence below.

1. You vote for one winner and one *alternate*. _____

2. Your two friends *alternate* serves during tennis. _____

3. You and your sister babysit on *alternate* nights. _____

4. Write the *converse* of the statement.

Statement: If it is raining, then I need an umbrella.

Converse: _____

● Vocabulary Builder

tri- (prefix) **try**

Related Word: triple

Main Idea: **Tri-** is a prefix meaning three that is used to form compound words.

Examples: triangle, tricycle, tripod

● Use Your Vocabulary

Write T for *true* or F for *false*.

_____ **5.** A *tri*pod is a stand that has three legs.

_____ **6.** A *tri*angle is a polygon with three or more sides.

_____ **7.** A *tri*atholon is a race with two events — swimming and bicycling.

_____ **8.** In order to *tri*ple an amount, multiply it by three.

Postulate 3-3 Parallel Postulate

Through a point not on a line, there is one and only one line parallel to the given line.

9. You can draw [ ] line(s) through P parallel to line ℓ.

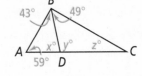

Theorem 3-10 Triangle Angle-Sum Theorem

The sum of the measures of the angles of a triangle is 180.

Find each angle measure.

10.

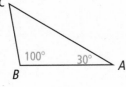

$m\angle C = $ [ ]

11.

$m\angle L = $ [ ]

Problem 1 Using the Triangle Angle-Sum Theorem

Got It? Use the diagram at the right. What is the value of z?

Complete each statement.

12. $m\angle A = $ [ ]

13. $m\angle ABC = $ [ ] $+$ [ ] $= $ [ ]

14. $m\angle A + m\angle ABC + m\angle C = $ [ ]

  [ ] $+$ [ ] $+ z = $ [ ]

  $z = $ [ ] $-$ [ ] $-$ [ ] $= $ [ ]

Check your result by solving for z another way.

15. Find $m\angle BDA$.

16. Then find $m\angle BDC$.

17. Use your answers to Exercises 15 and 16 to find the value of z.

Lesson 3-5

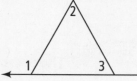

Theorem 3-11 Triangle Exterior Angle Theorem

An **exterior angle of a polygon** is an angle formed by a side and an extension of an adjacent side. For each exterior angle of a triangle, the two nonadjacent interior angles are its **remote interior angles.**

The measure of each exterior angle of a triangle equals the sum of the measures of its two remote interior angles.

18. ⬜ $= m\angle 2 + m\angle 3$

Circle the number of each exterior angle and draw a box around the number of each remote interior angle.

19.    20.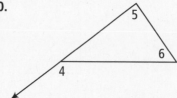

✓ **Problem 2** Using the Triangle Exterior Angle Theorem

Got It? Two angles of a triangle measure 53. What is the measure of an exterior angle at each vertex of the triangle?

21. Use the diagram at the right.

Label the interior angles 53°, 53°, and a.

Label the exterior angles adjacent to the 53° angles as x and y. Label the third exterior angle z.

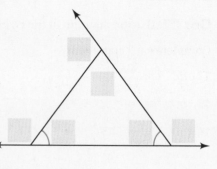

22. Complete the flow chart.

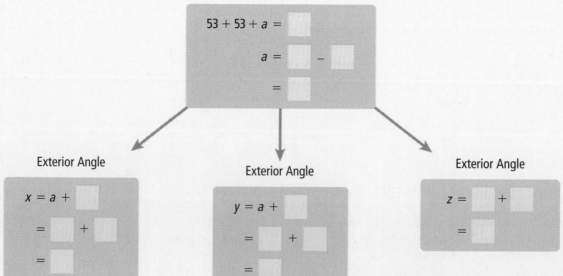

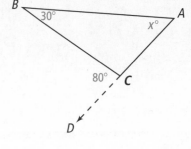

 Problem 3 **Applying the Triangle Theorems**

Got It? **Reasoning** Can you find $m\angle A$ without using the Triangle Exterior Angle Theorem? Explain.

23. $\angle ACB$ and $\angle DCB$ are complementary / supplementary angles.

24. Find $m\angle ACB$.

25. Can you find $m\angle A$ if you know two of the angle measures? Explain.

_____

 Lesson Check • **Do you UNDERSTAND?**

Explain how the Triangle Exterior Angle Theorem makes sense based on the Triangle Angle-Sum Theorem.

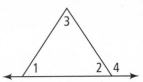

26. Use the triangle at the right to complete the diagram below.

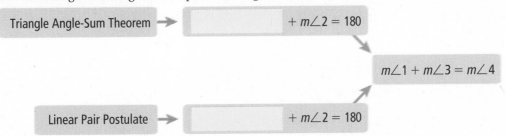

27. Explain how the Triangle Exterior Angle Theorem makes sense based on the Triangle Angle-Sum Theorem.

_____

_____

_____

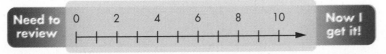 **Math Success**

Check off the vocabulary words that you understand.

☐ exterior angle   ☐ remote interior angles

Rate how well you can *use the triangle theorems.*

Need to review   0   2   4   6   8   10   Now I get it!

Lesson 3-5

3-6 Constructing Parallel and Perpendicular Lines

Vocabulary

● **Review**

Write T for *true* or F for *false*.

_____ **1.** A rectangle has two pairs of *parallel* segments.

_____ **2.** A rectangle has two pairs of *perpendicular* segments.

Write *alternate exterior, alternate interior,* or *corresponding* to describe each angle pair.

3.

4.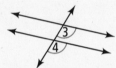

5.

_____ _____ _____

● **Vocabulary Builder**

construction (noun) **kun struck shun**

Other Word Forms: construct (verb), constructive (adjective)

Main Idea: **Construction** means how something is built or *constructed*.

Math Usage: A **construction** is a geometric figure drawn using a straightedge and a compass.

● **Use Your Vocabulary**

6. Complete each statement with the correct form of the word *construction*.

VERB   You __?__ sand castles at the beach.   _____

NOUN   The __?__ on the highway caused quite a traffic jam.   _____

ADJECTIVE   The time you spent working on your homework was __?__ .   _____

 **Problem 1** **Constructing Parallel Lines**

Got It? Reasoning The diagram at the right shows the construction of line *m* through point *N* with line *m* parallel to line ℓ. Why must lines ℓ and *m* be parallel?

7. The diagram shows the construction of congruent

   angles [   ] and [   ].

8. Circle the description(s) of the angle pairs that were constructed.

alternate interior	congruent	corresponding	same-side interior

9. Now explain why lines ℓ and *m* must be parallel.

   _____

   _____

   _____

 Problem 2 **Constructing a Special Quadrilateral**

Got It? Draw a segment. Label its length *m*. Construct quadrilateral *ABCD* with $\overleftrightarrow{AB} \parallel \overleftrightarrow{CD}$, so that $AB = m$ and $CD = 2m$.

Underline the correct word or symbol to complete each sentence.

10. Construct parallel / perpendicular lines.

11. Draw $\overleftrightarrow{AB}$. Draw point *D* not on $\overleftrightarrow{AB}$. Draw $\overleftrightarrow{AD}$. The length of
    $\overline{AB}$ / $\overline{AD}$ is *m*.

12. At *D*, construct $\angle TDZ$ perpendicular / congruent to $\angle DAB$ so that $\angle TDZ$ and
    $\angle DAB$ are corresponding angles. Then $\overleftrightarrow{DZ} \parallel \overleftrightarrow{AB}$.

13. Now, you need a side of length 2*m*. Construct *C* on $\overleftrightarrow{DZ}$ so that $DC = 2m$.
    Draw $\overline{BC}$ / $\overline{BA}$.

14. Do the construction below.

Lesson 3-6

Got It? Use a straightedge to draw $\overleftrightarrow{EF}$. Construct $\overleftrightarrow{FG}$ so that $\overleftrightarrow{FG} \perp \overleftrightarrow{EF}$ at point F.

15. Use the diagram at the right. Write each construction step.

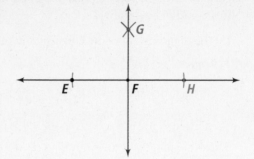

Step 1 _____

_____

Step 2 _____

_____

_____

Step 3 _____

_____

_____

Step 4 _____

_____

_____

_____

Step 5 _____

take note

Postulate 3-4 **Perpendicular Postulate**

Complete the statement of Postulate 3-4 below.

16. Through a point not on a line, there is one and only one line parallel / perpendicular
to the given line.

17. Circle the diagram that models Postulate 3-4.

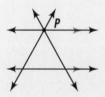 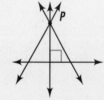 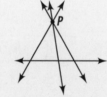

Problem 4 Perpendicular From a Point to a Line

Got It? Draw a line $\overleftrightarrow{CX}$ and a point Z not on $\overleftrightarrow{CX}$. Construct $\overleftrightarrow{ZB}$ so that $\overleftrightarrow{ZB} \perp \overleftrightarrow{CX}$.

Underline the correct word(s) to complete each sentence.

18. Open your compass to a size equal to / greater than the distance from Z to line ℓ.

19. With the compass tip on point Z, draw an arc that intersects line ℓ at one / two point(s).

20. Label the point(s) C and X / Z .

21. Place the compass point on C / Z and make an arc below line ℓ.

22. With the same opening and the compass tip on C / X, draw an arc that intersects the arc you made in Exercise 21. Label the point of intersection B.

23. Draw $\overleftrightarrow{ZB} / \overleftrightarrow{CX}$.

24. Use line ℓ and point Z at the right. Construct a line through point Z perpendicular to line ℓ.

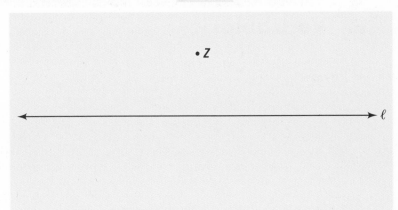

Lesson Check • Do you UNDERSTAND?

Suppose you use a wider compass setting in Exercise 18. Will you construct a different perpendicular line? Explain.

25. Explain why you will NOT construct a different perpendicular line.

_____

_____

Math Success

Check off the vocabulary words that you understand.

☐ construction   ☐ parallel   ☐ perpendicular

Rate how well you can *construct parallel and perpendicular lines.*

Need to review 0 2 4 6 8 10 Now I get it!

Lesson 3-6

Equations of Lines in the Coordinate Plane

Vocabulary

● Review

Write T for *true* or F for *false*.

_____ **1.** An *ordered pair* describes the location of a point in a coordinate grid.

_____ **2.** An *ordered pair* can be written as (*x*-coordinate, *y*-coordinate) or (*y*-coordinate, *x*-coordinate).

_____ **3.** The *ordered pair* for the origin is (0, 0).

● Vocabulary Builder

slope (noun, verb) **slohp**

$$\text{Slope} = \frac{\text{rise}}{\text{run}}$$

Definition: The **slope** of a line m between two points (x_1, y_1) and (x_2, y_2) on a coordinate plane is the ratio of the vertical change (rise) to the horizontal change (run). $\quad m = \dfrac{\text{rise}}{\text{run}} = \dfrac{y_2 - y_1}{x_2 - x_1}$

● Use Your Vocabulary

Complete each statement with the appropriate word from the list. Use each word only once.

slope   sloping   sloped

4. The __?__ of the hill made it difficult for bike riding.

_____

5. The driveway __?__ down to the garage.

_____

6. The __?__ lawn led to the river.

_____

Draw a line from each word in Column A to its corresponding part of speech in Column B.

Column A	Column B
7. linear	ADJECTIVE
8. line	NOUN

Problem 1 Finding Slopes of Lines

Got It? Use the graph at the right. What is the slope of line *a*?

9. Complete the table below to find the slope of line *a*.

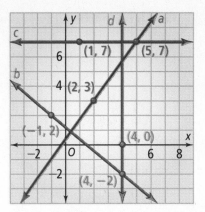

Think	Write
I know the slope is the ratio $\dfrac{\text{change in } y\text{-coordinates}}{\text{change in } x\text{-coordinates}}$.	$m = \dfrac{y_2 - y_1}{x_2 - x_1}$
Two points on line *a* are (2, 3) and (5, 7).	$= \dfrac{\boxed{} - \boxed{}}{\boxed{} - \boxed{}}$
Now I can simplify.	$= \boxed{}$

---

take note

Key Concept   Forms of Linear Equations

Definition

The **slope-intercept form** of an equation of a nonvertical line is $y = mx + b$, where *m* is the slope and *b* is the *y*-intercept.

The **point-slope form** of an equation of a nonvertical line is $y - y_1 = m(x - x_1)$, where *m* is the slope and (x_1, y_1) is a point on the line.

Symbols

$y = mx + b$

   ↑   ↑

 slope   *y*-intercept

$y - y_1 = m(x - x_1)$

  ↑   ↑   ↑

y-coordinate   slope   *x*-coordinate

Problem 2 Graphing Lines

Got It? Graph $y = 3x - 4$.

10. In what form is the given equation written?

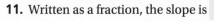

_____

11. Written as a fraction, the slope is $\boxed{}$.

12. One point on the graph is ($\boxed{}$, −4).

13. From that point, move $\boxed{}$ unit(s) *up* and $\boxed{}$ unit (s) *to the right*.

14. Graph $y = 3x - 4$ on the coordinate plane.

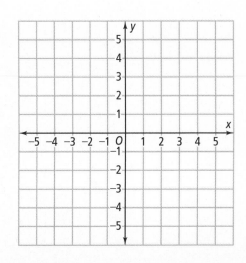

Problem 3 Writing Equations of Lines

Got It? What is an equation of the line with slope $-\frac{1}{2}$ and y-intercept 2?

15. Complete the problem-solving model below.

Know	Need	Plan
slope $m = \boxed{}$ y-intercept $= \boxed{}$	Write an equation of a line.	Use $\boxed{}$, the slope-intercept form of a linear equation.

16. Now write the equation.

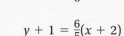

Problem 4 Using Two Points to Write an Equation

Got It? You can use the two points given on the line at the right to show that the slope of the line is $\frac{6}{5}$. So one equation of the line is $y - 5 = \frac{6}{5}(x - 3)$. What is an equation of the line if you use $(-2, -1)$ instead of $(3, 5)$ in the point-slope form of the equation?

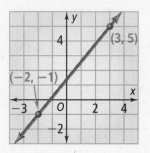

17. The equation is found below. Write a justification for each step.

$$y - y_1 = m(x - x_1) \qquad \text{Write in } \underline{\hspace{4cm}}$$

$$y - (-1) = \tfrac{6}{5}(x - (-2)) \qquad \underline{\hspace{5cm}}$$

$$y + 1 = \tfrac{6}{5}(x + 2) \qquad \underline{\hspace{5cm}}$$

Got It? Use the two equations for the line shown above. Rewrite the equations in slope-intercept form and compare them. What can you conclude?

18. Write each equation in slope-intercept form.

$$y - 5 = \tfrac{6}{5}(x - 3) \qquad\qquad\qquad y + 1 = \tfrac{6}{5}(x + 2)$$

19. Underline the correct word(s) to complete each sentence.

The equations are different / the same .

Choosing $(-2, -1)$ gives a different / the same equation as choosing $(3, 5)$.

The equations $y - 5 = \frac{6}{5}(x - 3)$ and $y + 1 = \frac{6}{5}(x + 2)$ are / are not equivalent.

Writing Equations of Horizontal and Vertical Lines

Got It? **What are the equations for the horizontal and vertical
lines through $(4, -3)$?**

Write T for *true* or F for *false*.

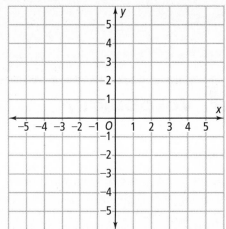

_____ **20.** Every point on a horizontal line through $(4, -3)$
has y-coordinate of -3.

_____ **21.** The equation of a vertical line through $(4, -3)$
is $y = -3$.

_____ **22.** The equation of a vertical line through $(4, -3)$
is $x = 4$.

23. Graph the horizontal and vertical lines through $(4, -3)$
on the coordinate plane at the right.

Lesson Check • Do you UNDERSTAND?

Error Analysis A classmate found the slope of the line passing through $(8, -2)$
and $(8, 10)$ as shown at the right. Describe your classmate's error. Then find
the correct slope of the line passing through the given points.

$$m = \frac{8 - 8}{10 - (-2)}$$

$$m = \frac{0}{12}$$

$$m = 0$$

24. What is your classmate's error?

_____

25. Find the slope, m.

26. The run is $8 - 8 = $ _____ , so the slope is _____ .

Math Success

Check off the vocabulary words that you understand.

☐ slope   ☐ slope-intercept form   ☐ point-slope form

Rate how well you can write and graph *linear equations*.

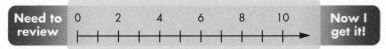

Lesson 3-7

Slopes of Parallel and Perpendicular Lines

Vocabulary

● **Review**

Use the graph at the right for Exercises 1–4. Write *parallel* or *perpendicular* to complete each sentence.

1. Line *b* is __?__ to line *a*.

2. Line *b* is __?__ to the *x*-axis.

3. Line *a* is __?__ to the *y*-axis.

4. The *x*-axis is __?__ to the *y*-axis.

Write the *converse, inverse,* and *contrapositive* of the statement below.

If a polygon is a triangle, then the sum of the measures of its angles is 180.

5. **CONVERSE** If the sum of the measures of the angles of a polygon is 180, then __?__ .

6. **INVERSE** If a polygon is *not* a triangle, then __?__ .

7. **CONTRAPOSITIVE** If the sum of the measures of the angles of a polygon is *not* 180, then __?__ .

● **Vocabulary Builder**

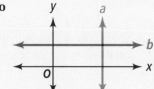

The **reciprocal** of x is $\frac{1}{x}$.

reciprocal (noun) rih sɪp ruh kul

Other Word Forms: reciprocate (verb)

Definition: The **reciprocal** of a number is a number such that the product of the two numbers is 1. The **reciprocal** of $\frac{numerator}{denominator}$ is $\frac{denominator}{numerator}$.

● Use Your Vocabulary

Complete each statement with *reciprocal* or *reciprocate*. Use each word only once.

8. VERB   After your friend helps you with your homework, you _?_ by helping your friend with his chores.

_____

9. NOUN   The _?_ of $\frac{2}{3}$ is $\frac{3}{2}$.

_____

Key Concept   Slopes of Parallel Lines

- If two nonvertical lines are parallel, then their slopes are equal.
- If the slopes of two distinct nonvertical lines are equal, then the lines are parallel.
- Any two vertical lines or horizontal lines are parallel.

Circle the correct statement in each exercise.

10. A vertical line is parallel to any other vertical line.

A vertical line is parallel to any horizontal line.

11. Any two nonvertical lines have the same slope.

Any two nonvertical lines that are parallel have the same slope.

Problem 1   Checking for Parallel Lines

Got It? Line ℓ_3 contains $A(-13, 6)$ and $B(-1, 2)$. Line ℓ_4 contains $C(3, 6)$ and $D(6, 7)$. Are ℓ_3 and ℓ_4 parallel? Explain.

12. To determine whether lines ℓ_3 and ℓ_4 are are parallel check whether the lines have the same _?_ .

_____

13. Find the slope of each line.

slope of ℓ_3

$$\frac{2 - 6}{-1 - (-13)} = \frac{\quad}{\quad} = \boxed{}$$

slope of ℓ_4

14. Are the slopes equal?   Yes / No

15. Are lines ℓ_3 and ℓ_4 parallel? Explain.

_____

_____

Lesson 3-8

Got It? What is an equation of the line parallel to $y = -x - 7$ that contains $(-5, 3)$?

16. The slope of the line $y = -x - 7$ is [ ] .

17. The equation of the line parallel to $y = -x - 7$ will have slope $m =$ [ ] .

18. Find the equation of the line using point-slope form. Complete the steps below.

$y - y_1 =$	[ ]	Write in point-slope form.
$y - 3 =$	[ ]	Substitute point and slope into equation.
$y - 3 =$	[ ]	Simplify.
$y =$	[ ]	Add 3 to both sides.

take note

Key Concept   Slopes of Perpendicular Lines

- If two nonvertical lines are perpendicular, then the product of their slopes is -1.

- If the slopes of two lines have a product of -1, then the lines are perpendicular.

- Any horizontal line and vertical line are perpendicular.

Write T for *true* or F for *false*.

_____ **19.** The second bullet in the Take Note is the contrapositive of the first bullet.

_____ **20.** The product of the slopes of any horizontal line and any vertical line is -1.

 Problem 3 **Checking for Perpendicular Lines**

Got It? Line ℓ_3 contains $A(2, 7)$ and $B(3, -1)$. Line ℓ_4 contains $C(-2, 6)$ and $D(8, 7)$. Are ℓ_3 and ℓ_4 perpendicular? Explain.

21. Find the slopes and multiply them.

$m_3 =$ [ ] $m_4 =$ [ ]

$m_3 \times m_4 =$ [ ]

22. Underline the correct words to complete the sentence.

Lines ℓ_3 and ℓ_4 are / are not   perpendicular because the product of their slopes

does / does not   equal -1.

Problem 4 **Writing Equations of Perpendicular Lines**

Got It? What is an equation of the line perpendicular to $y = -3x - 5$ that contains $(-3, 7)$?

23. Complete the reasoning model below.

Think	Write
I can identify the slope, m_1, of the given line.	$y = -3x - 5$ is in point-slope form, so $m_1 = \boxed{}$.
I know that the slope, m_2, of the perpendicular line is the negative reciprocal of m_1.	m_2 is $\dfrac{\boxed{}}{\boxed{}}$ because $\boxed{} \times \dfrac{\boxed{}}{\boxed{}} = -1$.
I can use m_2 and $(-3, 7)$ to write the equation of the perpendicular line in point-slope form.	$y - y_1 = m(x - x_1)$

 Lesson Check • **Do you UNDERSTAND?**

Error Analysis Your classmate tries to find an equation for a line parallel to $y = 3x - 5$ that contains $(-4, 2)$. What is your classmate's error?

24. Parallel lines have the same / different slopes.

25. Show a correct solution in the box below.

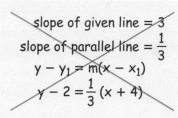

slope of given line = 3
slope of parallel line = $\frac{1}{3}$
$y - y_1 = m(x - x_1)$
$y - 2 = \frac{1}{3}(x + 4)$

 Math Success

Check off the vocabulary words that you understand.

☐ slope ☐ reciprocal ☐ parallel ☐ perpendicular

Rate how well you *understand perpendicular lines*.

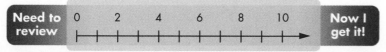

Need to review 0 2 4 6 8 10 Now I get it!

Lesson 3-8

Congruent Figures

Vocabulary

● Review

1. Underline the correct word to complete the sentence.

A *polygon* is a two-dimensional figure with two / three or more segments that meet exactly at their endpoints.

2. Cross out the figure(s) that are NOT *polygons*.

● Vocabulary Builder

congruent (adjective) **kahng GROO unt**

Main Idea: **Congruent** figures have the same size and shape.

Related Word: congruence (noun)

● Use Your Vocabulary

3. Circle the triangles that appear to be *congruent*.

Write T for *true* or F for *false*.

_____ **4.** *Congruent* angles have different measures.

_____ **5.** A prism and its net are *congruent* figures.

_____ **6.** The corresponding sides of *congruent* figures have the same measure.

Key Concept Congruent Figures

Congruent polygons have congruent corresponding parts—their matching sides and angles. When you name congruent polygons, you must list corresponding vertices in the same order.

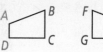

$ABCD \cong EFGH$

7. Use the figures at the right to complete each congruence statement.

$\overline{AB} \cong$ ☐ $\overline{BC} \cong$ ☐ $\overline{CD} \cong$ ☐ $\overline{DA} \cong$ ☐

$\angle A \cong$ ☐ $\angle B \cong$ ☐ $\angle C \cong$ ☐ $\angle D \cong$ ☐

Problem 1 Using Congruent Parts

Got It? If $\triangle WYS \cong \triangle MKV$, what are the congruent corresponding parts?

8. Use the diagram at the right. Draw an arrow from each vertex of the first triangle to the corresponding vertex of the second triangle.

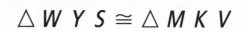

$\triangle\, W\ Y\ S \cong \triangle\, M\ K\ V$

9. Use the diagram from Exercise 8 to complete each congruence statement.

Sides	$\overline{WY} \cong$ ☐	$\overline{YS} \cong$ ☐	$\overline{WS} \cong$ ☐
Angles	$\angle W \cong$ ☐	$\angle Y \cong$ ☐	$\angle S \cong$ ☐

Problem 2 Finding Congruent Parts

Got It? Suppose that $\triangle WYS \cong \triangle MKV$. If $m\angle W = 62$ and $m\angle Y = 35$, what is $m\angle V$? Explain.

Use the congruent triangles at the right.

10. Use the given information to label the triangles. Remember to write corresponding vertices in order.

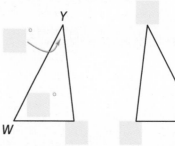

11. Complete each congruence statement.

$\angle W \cong$ ☐

$\angle Y \cong$ ☐

$\angle S \cong$ ☐

12. Use the Triangle Angle-Sum theorem.

$m\angle S + m$ ☐ $+ m$ ☐ $= 180$, so $m\angle S = 180 - ($ ☐ $+$ ☐ $)$, or ☐ .

13. Complete.

Since $\angle S \cong$ ☐ and $m\angle S =$ ☐ , $m\angle V =$ ☐ .

Problem 3 Finding Congruent Triangles

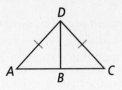

Got It? Is △ABD ≅ △CBD? Justify your answer.

14. Underline the correct word to complete the sentence.

To prove two triangles congruent, show that all adjacent / corresponding parts are congruent.

15. Circle the name(s) for △ACD.

acute	isosceles	right	scalene

16. Cross out the congruence statements that are NOT supported by the information in the figure.

$\overline{AD} \cong \overline{CD}$	$\overline{BD} \cong \overline{BD}$	$\overline{AB} \cong \overline{CB}$
$\angle A \cong \angle C$	$\angle ABD \cong \angle CBD$	$\angle ADB \cong \angle CDB$

17. You need _____ congruence statements to prove two triangles congruent, so you

can / cannot prove that △ABD ≅ △CBD.

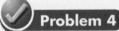

Theorem 4-1 Third Angles Theorem

Theorem	**If . . .**	**Then . . .**
If two angles of one triangle are congruent to two angles of another triangle, then the third angles are congruent.	$\angle A \cong \angle D$ and $\angle B \cong \angle E$ 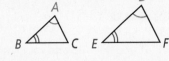	$\angle C \cong \angle F$

Use △ABC and △DEF above.

18. If $m\angle A = 74$, then $m\angle D =$ _____ .

19. If $m\angle B = 44$, then $m\angle E =$ _____ .

20. If $m\angle C = 62$, then $m\angle F =$ _____ .

Problem 4 Proving Triangles Congruent

Got It? Given: $\angle A \cong \angle D$, $\overline{AE} \cong \overline{DC}$,

$\overline{EB} \cong \overline{CB}$, $\overline{BA} \cong \overline{BD}$

Prove: △AEB ≅ △DCB

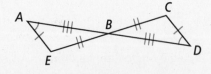

21. You are given four pairs of congruent parts. Circle the additional information you need to prove the triangles congruent.

A third pair of congruent sides	A second pair of congruent angles	A third pair of congruent angles

22. Complete the steps of the proof.

1) $\overline{AE} \cong$ [ ], $\overline{EB} \cong$ [ ], $\overline{BA} \cong$ [ ]   1) Given

2) $\angle A \cong$ [ ]   2) Given

3) $\angle ABE \cong$ [ ]   3) Vertical angles are congruent.

4) $\angle E \cong$ [ ]   4) Third Angles Theorem

5) $\triangle AEB \cong$ [ ]   5) Definition of $\cong$ triangles

Lesson Check • Do you UNDERSTAND?

If each angle in one triangle is congruent to its corresponding angle in another triangle, are the two triangles congruent? Explain.

23. Underline the correct word to complete the sentence.

To disprove a conjecture, you need one / two / many counterexample(s).

24. An equilateral triangle has three congruent sides and three 60° angles. Circle the equilateral triangles below.

25. Use your answers to Exercise 24 to answer the question.

_____

_____

Math Success

Check off the vocabulary words that you understand.

☐ congruent   ☐ polygons

Rate how well you can *identify congruent polygons.*

Need to review 0   2   4   6   8   10   Now I get it!

Lesson 4-1

Vocabulary

● Review

1. Use the diagram at the right. Find each.

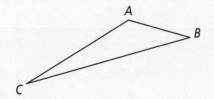

included angle between $\overline{AB}$ and $\overline{CA}$

included side between $\angle A$ and $\angle C$

included angle between $\overline{BC}$ and $\overline{CA}$

included side between $\angle B$ and $\angle C$

included angle between $\overline{BC}$ and $\overline{AB}$

included side between $\angle B$ and $\angle A$

● Vocabulary Builder

postulate (noun) PAHS **chuh lit**

Definition: A **postulate** is a statement that is accepted as true without being proven true.

Main Idea: In geometry, you use what you know to be true to prove new things true. The statements that you accept as true without proof are called **postulates** or axioms.

● Use Your Vocabulary

2. Underline the correct word to complete the sentence.

You can use properties, *postulates*, and previously proven theorems as reasons / statements in a proof.

3. **Multiple Choice** What is a *postulate*?

Ⓐ a convincing argument using deductive reasoning

Ⓑ a conjecture or statement that you can prove true

Ⓒ a statement accepted as true without being proven true

Ⓓ a conclusion reached by using inductive reasoning

Postulate 4–1   Side-Side-Side (SSS) Postulate

Postulate 4-1 Side-Side-Side (SSS) Postulate

If the three sides of one triangle are congruent to the three sides of another triangle, then the two triangles are congruent.

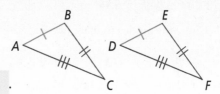

4. Use the figures at the right to complete the sentence.

If $\overline{AB} \cong \overline{DE}$, $\overline{BC} \cong \overline{EF}$, and $\overline{AC} \cong$ [ ], then $\triangle ABC \cong \triangle$ [ ].

Problem 1   Using SSS

Got It? Given: $\overline{BC} \cong \overline{BF}$, $\overline{CD} \cong \overline{FD}$
Prove: $\triangle BCD \cong \triangle BFD$

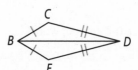

5. You know two pairs of sides that are congruent. What else do you need to prove the triangles congruent by SSS?

_____

6. The triangles share side [ ].

7. Complete the steps of the proof.

Statement	Reason
1) $\overline{BC} \cong$ [ ]	1) Given
2) $\overline{CD} \cong$ [ ]	2) Given
3) $\overline{BD} \cong$ [ ]	3) Reflexive Property of $\cong$
4) $\triangle BCD \cong$ [ ]	4) SSS

Postulate 4–2   Side-Angle-Side (SAS) Postulate

Postulate 4–2 Side-Angle-Side (SAS) Postulate

If two sides and the included angle of one triangle are congruent to two sides and the included angle of another triangle, then the two triangles are congruent.

Use the figures below to complete each statement.

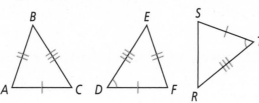

8. $\triangle DEF \cong$ [ ] by SAS.

9. $\triangle ABC \cong$ [ ] by SSS.

Lesson 4-2

Problem 2 Using SAS

Got It? What other information do you need to prove
△LEB ≅ △BNL by SAS?

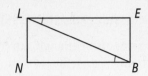

10. Circle the angles that are marked congruent in the diagram.

∠EBL   ∠ELB   ∠NBL   ∠NLB

11. Circle the sides that form the angles that are marked congruent in the diagram.

$\overline{BE}$ $\overline{BL}$ $\overline{BN}$ $\overline{LB}$ $\overline{LE}$ $\overline{LN}$

12. Complete each congruence statements.

$\overline{LB}$ ≅ ⬚   ∠BLE ≅ ⬚

Underline the correct word(s) to complete each sentence.

13. Proving △LEB ≅ △BNL by SAS requires one / two pair(s) of congruent sides and
one / two pair(s) of congruent angles.

14. The diagram shows congruency of zero / one / two pair(s) of congruent sides and
zero / one / two pair(s) of congruent angles.

15. To prove the triangles congruent by SAS, you still need zero / one / two pair(s) of
congruent sides and zero / one / two pair(s) of congruent angles .

16. To prove the triangles congruent, you need to prove ⬚ and ⬚ congruent.

Problem 3 Identifying Congruent Triangles

Got It? Would you use SSS or SAS to prove the triangles below congruent? Explain.

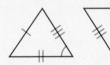

Complete each statement with *SSS* or *SAS*.

17. Use ___?___ if you have three pairs of sides congruent.   _____

18. Use ___?___ if you have two pairs of sides and the included angle congruent.   _____

Write T for *true* or F for *false*.

_____ **19.** The diagram shows congruence of three sides.

_____ **20.** In the triangle on the left, the marked angle is the included angle of the side
with two marks and the side with three marks.

_____ **21.** In the triangle on the right, the marked angle is the included angle of the side
with two marks and the side with three marks.

22. Would you use SSS or SAS to prove the triangles congruent? Explain.

_____

_____

_____

_____

Lesson Check • Do you UNDERSTAND?

Error Analysis Your friend thinks that the triangles below are congruent by SAS. Is your friend correct? Explain.

23. Are two pairs of corresponding sides congruent? | Yes / No

24. Is there a pair of congruent angles? | Yes / No

25. Are the congruent angles the included angles between the corresponding congruent sides? | Yes / No

26. Are the triangles congruent by SAS? Explain.

_____

_____

_____

_____

Math Success

Check off the vocabulary words that you understand.

☐ congruent   ☐ corresponding

Rate how well you can *use SSS and SAS to prove triangles congruent.*

Need to review 0   2   4   6   8   10   Now I get it!

4-3 Triangle Congruence by ASA and AAS

Vocabulary

● Review

1. Cross out the figure(s) that are NOT *triangle*(s).

2. A *triangle* is a polygon with ⬚ sides.

3. A *triangle* with a right angle is called a(n)

obtuse / right / scalene *triangle*.

● Vocabulary Builder

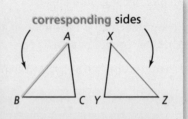

corresponding sides

corresponding (adjective) **kawr uh SPAHN ding**

Other Word Forms: correspond (verb); correspondence (noun)

Definition: Corresponding means similar in position, purpose, or form.

Math Usage: Congruent figures have congruent **corresponding** parts.

● Use Your Vocabulary

Draw a line from each part of △*ABC* in Column A to the *corresponding* part of △*XYZ* in Column B.

Column A	Column B
4. $\overline{BC}$	∠Z
5. ∠A	∠Y
6. $\overline{AB}$	$\overline{YZ}$
7. ∠C	∠X
8. $\overline{AC}$	$\overline{XY}$
9. ∠B	$\overline{XZ}$

Postulate 4–3   Angle-Side-Angle (ASA) Postulate

Postulate	If . . .	Then . . .
If two angles and the included side of one triangle are congruent to two angles and the included side of another triangle, then the two triangles are congruent.	$\angle A \cong \angle D$, $\overline{AC} \cong \overline{DF}$, $\angle C \cong \angle F$ 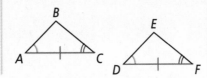	$\triangle ABC \cong \triangle DEF$

10. Explain how the ASA Postulate is different from the SAS Postulate.

_____

_____

_____

 Problem 1   Using ASA

Got It? Which two triangles are congruent by ASA? Explain.

11. Name the triangles. List the vertices in corresponding order: list the vertex with the one arc first, the vertex with the two arcs second, and the third vertex last.

[   ]   [   ]   [   ]

12. $\angle G \cong \angle$ [   ] $\cong \angle$ [   ]

13. $\angle H \cong \angle$ [   ] $\cong \angle$ [   ]

14. $\overline{HG} \cong$ [   ] $\cong$ [   ]

15. The congruent sides that are included between congruent angles are

[   ] and [   ].

16. Write a congruence statement. Justify your reasoning.

△ [   ] $\cong$ △ [   ]

_____

_____

Problem 2 Writing a Proof Using ASA

Got It? Given: $\angle CAB \cong \angle DAE$, $\overline{BA} \cong \overline{EA}$, $\angle B$ and $\angle E$ are right angles
Prove: $\triangle ABC \cong \triangle AED$

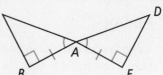

17. Complete the flow chart to prove $\triangle ABC \cong \triangle AED$.

Given	Given	Given
$\angle B$ and $\angle$ ☐ are right angles.	$\overline{BA} \cong$ ☐	$\angle CAB \cong \angle$ ☐

All right angles are congruent.

$\angle B \cong$ ☐

ASA Postulate

$\triangle ABC \cong$ ☐

---

take note

Theorem 4–2   Angle-Angle-Side (AAS) Theorem

Theorem	If . . .	Then . . .
If two angles and a nonincluded side of one triangle are congruent to two angles and the corresponding nonincluded side of another triangle, then the two triangles are congruent.	$\angle A \cong \angle D$, $\angle B \cong \angle E$, $\overline{AC} \cong \overline{DF}$ 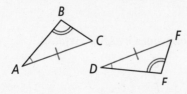	$\triangle ABC \cong \triangle DEF$

18. The nonincluded congruent sides of $\triangle ABC$ and $\triangle DEF$ are ☐ and ☐ .

Problem 3 Writing a Proof Using AAS

Got It? Given: $\angle S \cong \angle Q$, $\overline{RP}$ bisects $\angle SRQ$
Prove: $\triangle SRP \cong \triangle QRP$

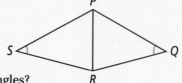

19. How do you know which angles in the diagram are corresponding angles?

_____

_____

20. Complete the statements to prove $\triangle SRP \cong \triangle QRP$.

Statements	Reasons
1) $\angle S \cong$ ☐	1) Given
2) $\overline{RP}$ bisects ☐	2) Given
3) $\angle SRP \cong$ ☐	3) Definition of an angle bisector
4) $\overline{RP} \cong$ ☐	4) Reflexive Property of Congruence
5) $\triangle SRP \cong$ ☐	5) AAS

Problem 4 Determining Whether Triangles Are Congruent

Got It? Are △PAR and △SIR congruent? Explain.

21. The congruence marks show that ∠A ≅ ☐ and $\overline{PR}$ ≅ ☐ .

22. What other corresponding congruent parts exist? Explain.

_____

23. Are △PAR and △SIR congruent? If so, what theorem proves them congruent?

_____

 ## Lesson Check • Do you UNDERSTAND?

Reasoning Suppose ∠E ≅ ∠I and $\overline{FE}$ ≅ $\overline{GI}$. What else must you know in order to prove △FDE and △GHI are congruent by ASA? By AAS?

24. Label the diagram at the right.

25. To prove the triangles congruent by ASA, what do you need?

_____

_____

26. To prove the triangles congruent by AAS, what do you need?

_____

_____

27. If you want to use ASA, ∠ ☐ and ∠ ☐ must also be congruent.

28. If you want to use AAS, ∠ ☐ and ∠ ☐ must also be congruent.

 ## Math Success

Check off the vocabulary words that you understand.

☐ included   ☐ nonincluded   ☐ corresponding

Rate how well you can *use ASA and AAS*.

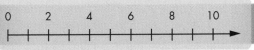

Lesson 4-3

Vocabulary

● Review

Underline the correct word(s) to complete each sentence.

1. The *Reflexive* Property of Congruence states that any geometric figure is
congruent / similar to itself.

2. The *Reflexive* Property of Equality states that any quantity is
equal to / greater than / less than itself.

3. Circle the expressions that illustrate the *Reflexive* Property of Equality.

$$a = a \qquad\qquad \text{If } AB = 2, \text{ then } 2 = AB.$$
$$3(x + y) = 3x + 3y \qquad\qquad 5 + c = 5 + c$$

4. Circle the expressions that illustrate the *Reflexive* Property of Congruence.

$$\text{If } \angle A \cong \angle B, \text{ then } \angle B \cong \angle A. \qquad \text{If } \overline{CD} \cong \overline{LM} \text{ and } \overline{LM} \cong \overline{XY}, \text{ then } \overline{CD} \cong \overline{XY}.$$
$$\angle ABC \cong \angle ABC \qquad\qquad \overline{CD} \cong \overline{CD}$$

● Vocabulary Builder

proof (noun) **proof**

Related Word: prove (verb)

Definition: A **proof** is convincing evidence that a statement or theory is true.

Math Usage: A **proof** is a convincing argument that uses deductive reasoning.

● Use Your Vocabulary

Complete each statement with *proof* or *prove*.

5. In geometry, a _?_ uses definitions, postulates, and theorems to
prove theorems.

6. No one can _?_ how our universe started.

7. He can _?_ when he bought the computer because he has a receipt.

8. Complete the steps in the *proof.*

Given: $\overline{AB} \cong \overline{AD}$, $\overline{BC} \cong \overline{DC}$,
$\angle D \cong \angle B$, $\angle DAC \cong \angle BAC$

Prove: $\triangle ABC \cong \triangle ADC$

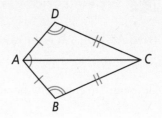

Statements	Reasons
1) $\overline{AB} \cong$ ▢ $\overline{BC} \cong$ ▢	1) Given
2) $\overline{AC} \cong$ ▢	2) Reflexive Property of $\cong$
3) $\angle D \cong$ ▢ $\angle DAC \cong$ ▢	3) Given
4) $\angle DCA \cong$ ▢	4) Third Angles Theorem
5) $\triangle ABC \cong$ ▢	5) Definition of $\cong$ triangles

 Problem 1 **Proving Parts of Triangles Congruent**

Got It? **Given:** $\overline{BA} \cong \overline{DA}$, $\overline{CA} \cong \overline{EA}$

Prove: $\angle C \cong \angle E$

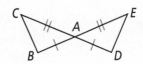

9. Name four ways you can use congruent parts of two triangles to prove that the triangles are congruent.

▢ ▢

▢ ▢

10. To prove triangles are congruent when you know two pairs of congruent corresponding sides, you can use ▢ or ▢ .

Underline the correct word to complete the sentence.

11. The *Given* states and the diagram shows that there are one / two / three pairs of congruent sides.

12. Give a reason for each statement of the proof.

Statements	Reasons
1) $\overline{BA} \cong \overline{DA}$	1)
2) $\overline{CA} \cong \overline{EA}$	2)
3) $\angle CAB \cong \angle EAD$	3)
4) $\triangle CAB \cong \triangle EAD$	4)
5) $\angle C \cong \angle E$	5)

Lesson 4-4

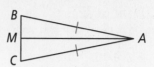

Problem 2 Proving Triangle Parts Congruent to Measure Distance

Got It? Given: $\overline{AB} \cong \overline{AC}$, M is the midpoint of $\overline{BC}$

Prove: $\angle AMB \cong \angle AMC$

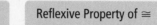

13. Use the flow chart to complete the proof.

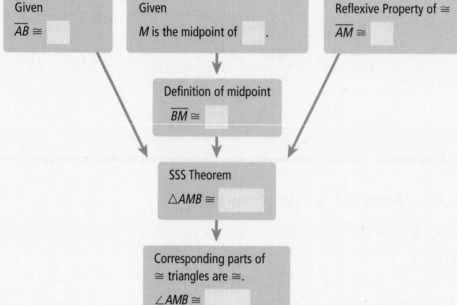

Given	Given	Reflexive Property of $\cong$
$\overline{AB} \cong$ ☐	M is the midpoint of ☐.	$\overline{AM} \cong$ ☐

Definition of midpoint
$\overline{BM} \cong$ ☐

SSS Theorem
$\triangle AMB \cong$ ☐

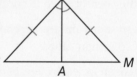

Corresponding parts of
$\cong$ triangles are $\cong$.
$\angle AMB \cong$ ☐

Lesson Check • **Do you know HOW?**

Name the postulate or theorem that you can use to show the triangles are congruent. Then explain why $\overline{EA} \cong \overline{MA}$.

14. Circle the angles that are marked congruent.

$\angle E$ $\angle ETA$ $\angle M$ $\angle EAT$ $\angle MTA$

15. Circle the sides that are marked congruent.

$\overline{ET}$ $\overline{MT}$ $\overline{EA}$ $\overline{MA}$ $\overline{AT}$

16. Circle the sides that are congruent by the Reflexive Property of Congruence.

$\overline{ET}$ and $\overline{MT}$ $\overline{EA}$ and $\overline{MA}$ $\overline{AT}$ and $\overline{AT}$

17. Underline the correct postulate or theorem to complete the sentence.

$\triangle EAT \cong \triangle MAT$ by SAS / AAS / ASA / SSS .

18. Now explain why $\overline{EA} \cong \overline{MA}$.

_____

Lesson Check • **Do you UNDERSTAND?**

Error Analysis Find and correct the error(s) in the proof.

Given: $\overline{KH} \cong \overline{NH}$, $\angle L \cong \angle M$ **Prove:** H is the midpoint of $\overline{LM}$.

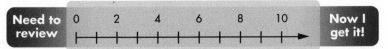

Proof: $\overline{KH} \cong \overline{NH}$ because it is given. $\angle L \cong \angle M$ because it is given. $\angle KHL \cong \angle NHM$ because vertical angles are congruent. So, $\triangle KHL \cong \triangle MHN$ by ASA Postulate. Since corresponding parts of congruent triangles are congruent, $\overline{LH} \cong \overline{MH}$. By the definition of midpoint, H is the midpoint of $\overline{LM}$.

Place a ✓ in the box if the statement is correct. Place an ✗ if it is incorrect.

19. $\angle KHL \cong \angle NHM$ because vertical angles are congruent.

20. $\triangle KHL \cong \triangle MHN$ by ASA Postulate.

Underline the correct word to complete each sentence.

21. When you name congruent triangles, you must name corresponding vertices in

a different / the same order.

22. To use the ASA Postulate, you need two pairs of congruent angles and a pair of

included / nonincluded congruent sides.

23. To use the AAS Theorem, you need two pairs of congruent angles and a pair of

included / nonincluded congruent sides.

24. Identify the error(s) in the proof.

_____

_____

_____

25. Correct the error(s) in the proof.

_____

_____

 Math Success

Check off the vocabulary words that you understand.

☐ congruent   ☐ corresponding   ☐ proof

Rate how well you can *use congruent triangles*.

Need to review 0 2 4 6 8 10 Now I get it!

Lesson 4-4

Vocabulary

● Review

Underline the correct word to complete each sentence.

1. An *equilateral* triangle has two/ three congruent sides.

2. An *equilateral* triangle has acute / obtuse angles.

3. Circle the *equilateral* triangle.

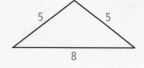

● Vocabulary Builder

isosceles (adjective) **eye** SAHS **uh leez**

Related Words: equilateral, scalene

Definition A triangle is **isosceles** if it has two congruent sides.

Main Idea: The angles and sides of **isosceles** triangles have special relationships.

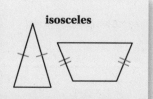

isosceles

● Use Your Vocabulary

4. Use the triangles below. Write the letter of each triangle in the correct circle(s) at the right.

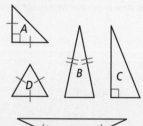

Equilateral	Isosceles	Right

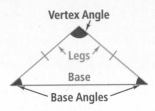

Theorems 4–3, 4–4, 4–5

Theorem 4-3 Isosceles Triangle Theorem

If two sides of a triangle are congruent, then the angles opposite those sides are congruent.

Theorem 4-4 Converse of Isosceles Triangle Theorem

If two angles of a triangle are congruent, then the sides opposite those angles are congruent.

Theorem 4-5

If a line bisects the vertex angle of an isosceles triangle, then the line is also the perpendicular bisector of the base.

5. If $\overline{PQ} \cong \overline{RQ}$ in $\triangle PQR$, then $\angle$ ⬚ $\cong \angle$ ⬚ .

6. Underline the correct theorem number to complete the sentence.

The theorem illustrated below is Theorem 4–3 / 4–4 / 4–5 .

Problem 1 **Using the Isosceles Triangle Theorems**

Got It? Is $\angle WVS$ congruent to $\angle S$? Is $\overline{TR}$ congruent to $\overline{TS}$? Explain.

7. The markings show that $\overline{WV} \cong$ ⬚ .

8. Is $\angle WVS \cong \angle S$? Explain.

_____

_____

9. Is $\angle R \cong \angle S$? Explain.

_____

_____

10. Is $\overline{TR} \cong \overline{TS}$? Explain.

_____

_____

Problem 2 **Using Algebra**

Got It? Suppose $m\angle A = 27$. What is the value of x?

11. Since $\overline{CB} \cong$ [____], $\triangle ABC$ is isosceles.

12. Since $\triangle ABC$ is isosceles, $m\angle A = m\angle$ [____] = [____].

13. Since $\overline{BD}$ bisects the vertex of an isosceles triangle, $\overline{BD} \perp$ [____]

    and $m\angle BDC =$ [____].

14. Use the justifications below to find the value of x.

$$m\angle \;[\ ] + m\angle BDC + x = 180 \qquad \text{Triangle Angle-Sum Theorem}$$
$$[\ ] + [\ ] + x = 180 \qquad \text{Substitute.}$$
$$[\ ] + x = 180 \qquad \text{Simplify.}$$
$$x = [\ ] \qquad \text{Subtract 117 from each side.}$$

Corollaries to Theorems 4–3 and 4–4

Corollary to Theorem 4-3

If a triangle is equilateral, then the triangle is equiangular.

Corollary to Theorem 4-4

If a triangle is equiangular, then the triangle is equilateral.

15. Underline the correct number to complete the sentence.

    The corollary illustrated below is Corollary to Theorem 4-3 / 4-4 .

    If . . . Then . . .

 Problem 3 **Finding Angle Measures**

Got It? Suppose the triangles at the right are isosceles triangles, where $\angle ADE$, $\angle DEC$, and $\angle ECB$ are vertex angles. If the vertex angles each have a measure of 58, what are $m\angle A$ and $m\angle BCD$?

16. Which triangles are congruent by the Side-Angle-Side Theorem?

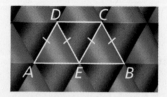

17. Which angles are congruent by the Isosceles Triangle Theorem?

18. By the Triangle Angle-Sum Theorem, $m\angle A + 58 + m\angle DEA = $ ◻.

19. Solve for $m\angle A$.

20. Since ◻ $\cong \angle ECD$, $m\angle ECD = $ ◻.

21. Using the Angle Addition Postulate, $m\angle BCD = 58 + m\angle ECD = $ ◻.

Lesson Check • Do you UNDERSTAND?

What is the relationship between sides and angles for each type of triangle?

isosceles   equilateral

Complete.

22. An isosceles triangle has ◻ congruent sides.

23. An equilateral triangle has ◻ congruent sides.

Complete each statement with *congruent, isosceles,* or *equilateral*.

24. The Isosceles Triangle Theorem states that the angles opposite the congruent sides are __?__.

25. Equilateral triangles are also __?__ triangles.

26. The sides and angles of an __?__ triangle are __?__.

Math Success

Check off the vocabulary words that you understand.

☐ corollary   ☐ legs of an isosceles triangle   ☐ base of an isosceles triangle

☐ vertex angle of an isosceles triangle   ☐ base angles of an isosceles triangle

Rate how well you understand *isosceles and equilateral triangles.*

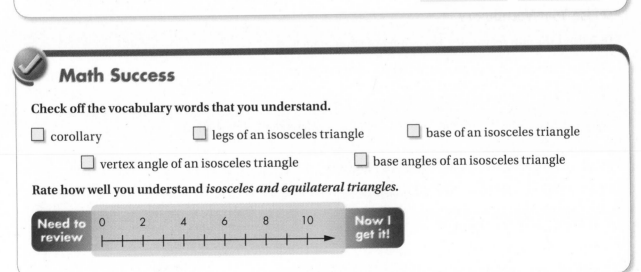

| Need to review | 0 | 2 | 4 | 6 | 8 | 10 | Now I get it! |

Lesson 4-5

Vocabulary

● Review

Write T for *true* or F for *false*.

_____ **1.** Segments that are *congruent* have the same length.

_____ **2.** Polygons that are *congruent* have the same shape but are not always the same size.

_____ **3.** In *congruent* figures, corresponding angles have the same measure.

● Vocabulary Builder

hypotenuse (noun) **hy PAH tuh noos**

Related Word: leg

Definition: The **hypotenuse** is the side opposite the right angle in a right triangle.

Main Idea: The **hypotenuse** is the longest side in a right triangle.

● Use Your Vocabulary

Underline the correct word(s) to complete each sentence.

4. One side of a right triangle is / is not a *hypotenuse*.

5. A right triangle has one / two / three *legs*.

6. The length of the *hypotenuse* is always equal to / greater than / less than the lengths of the *legs*.

Use the triangles at the right for Exercises 7 and 8.

7. Cross out the side that is NOT a *hypotenuse*.

$\overline{BC}$ $\qquad$ $\overline{AB}$ $\qquad$ $\overline{GH}$ $\qquad$ $\overline{FD}$

8. Circle the *leg(s)*.

$\overline{AC}$ $\qquad$ $\overline{AB}$ $\qquad$ $\overline{HI}$ $\qquad$ $\overline{ED}$

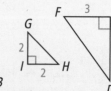

You can prove that two triangles are congruent without having to show that *all* corresponding parts are congruent. In this lesson, you will prove right triangles congruent by using one pair of right angles, a pair of hypotenuses, and a pair of legs.

take note

Theorem 4-6 Hypotenuse-Leg (HL) Theorem and Conditions

Theorem	**If . . .**	**Then . . .**
If the hypotenuse and a leg of one right triangle are congruent to the hypotenuse and leg of another right triangle, then the triangles are congruent.	$\triangle PQR$ and $\triangle XYZ$ are right triangles, $\overline{PR} \cong \overline{XZ}$, and $\overline{PQ} \cong \overline{XY}$	$\triangle PQR \cong \triangle XYZ$

9. To use the HL Theorem, the triangles must meet three conditions. Complete each sentence with *right* or *congruent*.

   There are two __?__ triangles.

   The triangles have __?__ hypotenuses.

   There is one pair of __?__ legs.

Use the information in the Take Note for Exercises 10–12.

10. How do the triangles in the Take Note meet the first condition in Exercise 9? Explain.

11. How do the triangles in the Take Note meet the second condition in Exercise 9? Explain.

12. How do the triangles in the Take Note meet the third condition in Exercise 9? Explain.

Lesson 4-6

Problem 1 Using the HL Theorem

Got It? Given: ∠*PRS* and ∠*RPQ* are right angles, $\overline{SP} \cong \overline{QR}$
Prove: △*PRS* ≅ △*RPQ*

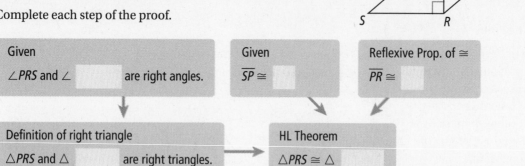

13. Complete each step of the proof.

Given	Given	Reflexive Prop. of ≅
∠*PRS* and ∠ [ ] are right angles.	$\overline{SP} \cong$ [ ]	$\overline{PR} \cong$ [ ]

Definition of right triangle	HL Theorem
△*PRS* and △ [ ] are right triangles.	△*PRS* ≅ △ [ ]

 Problem 2 Writing a Proof Using the HL Theorem

Got It? Given: $\overline{CD} \cong \overline{EA}$, $\overline{AD}$ is the perpendicular bisector of $\overline{CE}$
Prove: △*CBD* ≅ △*EBA*

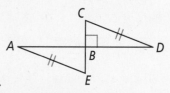

14. Circle what you know because $\overline{AD}$ is the perpendicular bisector of $\overline{CE}$.

∠*CBD* and ∠*EBA* are right angles.   ∠*CBD* and ∠*EBA* are acute angles.

   B is the midpoint of $\overline{AD}$.   *B* is the midpoint of $\overline{CE}$.

15. Circle the congruent legs.

$\overline{AB}$ $\overline{CB}$ $\overline{DB}$ $\overline{EB}$

16. Write the hypotenuse of each triangle.

△*CBD* [ ]   △*EBA* [ ]

17. Complete the proof.

Statements	**Reasons**
1) $\overline{CD} \cong$ [ ]	1) Given
2) ∠*CBD* and ∠ [ ] are right ∠s.	2) Definition of ⊥ bisector
3) △*CBD* and △ [ ] are right △s.	3) Definition of right △
4) $\overline{CB} \cong$ [ ]	4) Definition of ⊥ bisector
5) △*CBD* ≅ [ ]	5) HL Theorem

Lesson Check • Do you UNDERSTAND?

Error Analysis Your classmate says that there is not enough information to determine whether the two triangles at the right are congruent. Is your classmate correct? Explain.

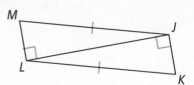

Write T for *true* or F for *false*.

_____ **18.** There are three right angles.

_____ **19.** There are two right triangles.

_____ **20.** There are two congruent hypotenuses.

_____ **21.** There are no congruent legs.

_____ **22.** You need to use the Reflexive Property of Congruence.

_____ **23.** $\overline{LJ} \cong \overline{LJ}$ is given.

24. Do you always need three congruent corresponding parts to prove triangles congruent? Explain.

_____

_____

25. Is your classmate correct? Explain.

_____

_____

_____

Math Success

Check off the vocabulary words that you understand.

☐ hypotenuse   ☐ legs of a right triangle

Rate how well you can *use the Hypotenuse-Leg (HL) Theorem.*

| Need to review | 0 | 2 | 4 | 6 | 8 | 10 | Now I get it! |

Lesson 4-6

Vocabulary

● Review

1. Circle the *common* side of △ABC and △ADC.

$\overline{AB}$ $\overline{AC}$ $\overline{AD}$ $\overline{BC}$

2. Circle the *common* side of △XWZ and △YWZ.

$\overline{WZ}$ $\overline{WX}$ $\overline{WY}$ $\overline{ZY}$

3. Circle the *common* side of △RST and △RPT.

$\overline{RP}$ $\overline{RS}$ $\overline{RT}$ $\overline{ST}$

● Vocabulary Builder

overlapping (adjective) **oh vur LAP ing**

Other Word Form: overlap (noun)

Definition: Overlapping events or figures have parts in common.

Math Usage: Two or more figures with common regions are **overlapping** figures.

● Use Your Vocabulary

**Circle the common regions of the *overlapping*
figures in the diagram at the right.**

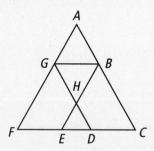

4. △FGD and △CBE

    △ABG   △ACF   △EHD   △GHB

5. △BEC and △HED

    △BEC   △GBH   △GDF   △HED

6. △ACF and △ABG

    △ABG   △ACF   △GBH   △EHD

7. △ACF and △GBH

    △ABG   △ACF   △GBH   △HED

Problem 1 Identifying Common Parts

Got It? What is the common side in △ABD and △DCA?

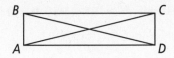

8. Separate and redraw △ABD and △DCA.

9. You drew [ ] twice, so the common side is [ ].

Problem 2 Using Common Parts

Got It? Given: △ACD ≅ △BDC

Prove: $\overline{CE} \cong \overline{DE}$

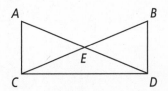

10. Use the information in the problem to complete the problem-solving model below.

Know	Need	Plan

11. Use the justifications below to complete each statement.

Statements

1) △ACD ≅ [ ]

2) $\overline{AC}$ ≅ [ ]

3) ∠A ≅ [ ]

4) [ ] ≅ ∠BED

5) [ ] ≅ △BED

6) $\overline{CE}$ ≅ [ ]

Reasons

1) Given

2) Corresponding parts of ≅ triangles are ≅.

3) Corresponding parts of ≅ triangles are ≅.

4) Vertical angles are congruent.

5) Angle-Angle-Side (AAS) Theorem

6) Corresponding parts of ≅ triangles are ≅.

12. How could you use the Converse of the Isosceles Triangle Theorem to prove $\overline{CE} \cong \overline{DE}$?

Lesson 4-7

Got It? Given: $\overline{PS} \cong \overline{RS}$, $\angle PSQ \cong \angle RSQ$

Prove: $\triangle QPT \cong \triangle QRT$

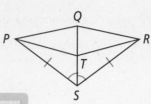

13. Give the reason for each statement in the proof.

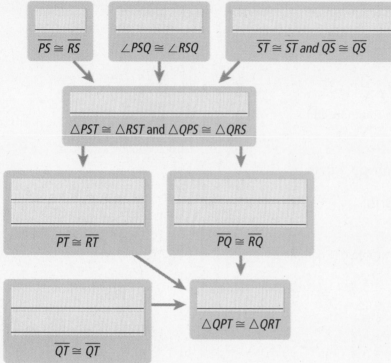

$\overline{PS} \cong \overline{RS}$ $\angle PSQ \cong \angle RSQ$ $\overline{ST} \cong \overline{ST}$ and $\overline{QS} \cong \overline{QS}$

$\triangle PST \cong \triangle RST$ and $\triangle QPS \cong \triangle QRS$

$\overline{PT} \cong \overline{RT}$ $\overline{PQ} \cong \overline{RQ}$

$\overline{QT} \cong \overline{QT}$ $\triangle QPT \cong \triangle QRT$

Got It? Given: $\angle CAD \cong \angle EAD$, $\angle C \cong \angle E$

Prove: $\overline{BD} \cong \overline{FD}$

14. Circle the angles that are vertical angles.

$\angle ADB$	$\angle ADC$	$\angle ADE$	$\angle ADF$	$\angle BDC$	$\angle FDE$

15. Mark the angles that you know are congruent in each pair of separated triangles below.

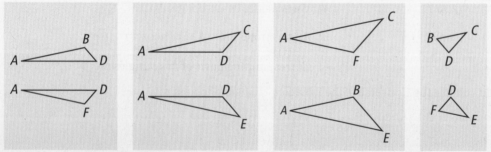

16. Which triangles are congruent by AAS? Explain.

17. Which triangles are congruent by ASA? Explain.

_____

_____

_____

18. How can you prove $\overline{BD} \cong \overline{FD}$?

_____

_____

_____

Lesson Check • Do you UNDERSTAND?

In the figure at the right, which pair of triangles could you prove congruent first in order to prove that $\triangle ACD \cong \triangle CAB$? Explain.

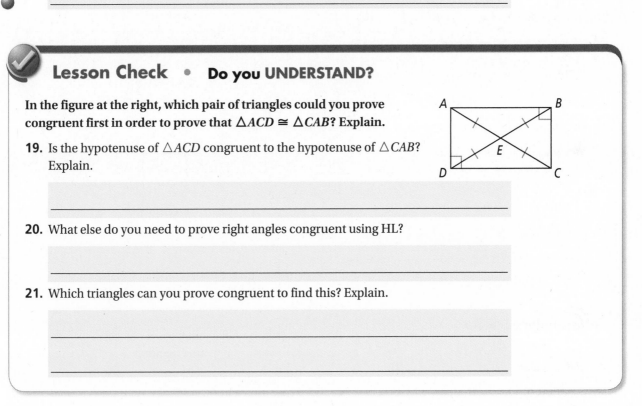

19. Is the hypotenuse of $\triangle ACD$ congruent to the hypotenuse of $\triangle CAB$? Explain.

_____

_____

20. What else do you need to prove right angles congruent using HL?

_____

_____

21. Which triangles can you prove congruent to find this? Explain.

_____

_____

_____

Math Success

Check off the vocabulary words that you understand.

☐ congruent   ☐ corresponding   ☐ overlapping

Rate how well you can *identify congruent overlapping triangles*.

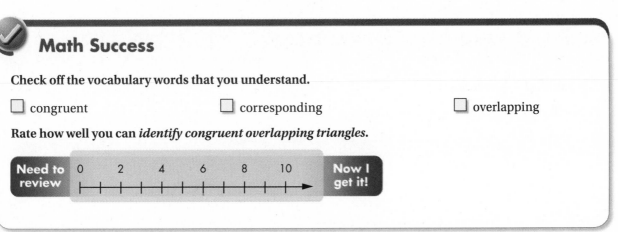

5-1 Midsegments of Triangles

Vocabulary

● Review

Use the number line at the right for Exercises 1–3.

A   B   C   D   E

−4 −3 −2 −1   0   1   2   3   4

1. Point ⬚ is the *midpoint* of $\overline{AE}$.

2. Point ⬚ is the *midpoint* of $\overline{CE}$.

3. Point ⬚ is the *midpoint* of $\overline{AC}$.

Use the graph at the right for Exercises 4–6. Name each *segment*.

4. a *segment* that lies on the *x*-axis

5. a *segment* that contains the point (0, 4)

6. a *segment* whose endpoints both have *x*-coordinate 3

● Vocabulary Builder

midsegment (noun) MID **seg munt**

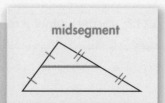

midsegment

Related Words: midpoint, segment

Definition: A **midsegment** of a triangle is a segment connecting the midpoints of two sides of the triangle.

● Use Your Vocabulary

Circle the correct statement in each pair.

7. A *midsegment* connects the midpoints of two sides of a triangle.

   A *midsegment* connects a vertex of a triangle to the midpoint of the opposite side.

8. A triangle has exactly one *midsegment*.   A triangle has three *midsegments*.

Theorem 5-1 Triangle Midsegment Theorem

If a segment joins the midpoints of two sides of a triangle, then the segment is parallel to the third side and is half as long.

9. Use the triangle at the right to complete the table below.

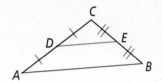

If	Then
☐ is the midpoint of $\overline{CA}$ and	☐ ∥ $\overline{AB}$
☐ is the midpoint of $\overline{CB}$	☐ = $\frac{1}{2}$ AB

Use the graph at the right for Exercises 10–11.

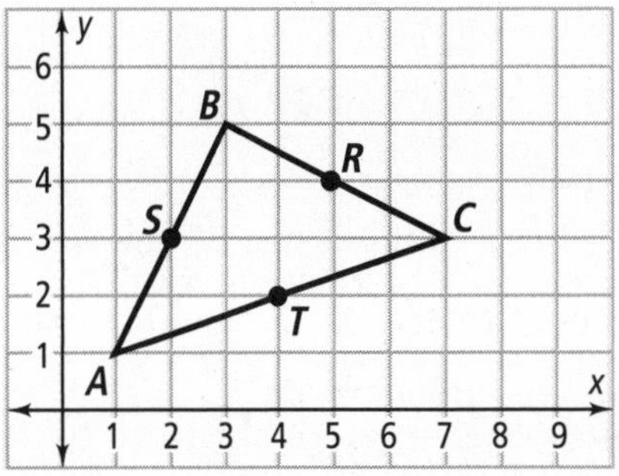

10. Draw $\overline{RS}$. Then underline the correct word or number to complete each sentence below.

$\overline{RS}$ is a midsegment of / parallel to $\triangle ABC$.

$\overline{RS}$ is a midsegment of / parallel to $\overline{AC}$.

11. Use the Triangle Midsegment Theorem to complete.

$RS = $ ☐ AC

12. Draw $\overline{ST}$. What do you know about $\overline{ST}$?

_____

✓ **Problem 1** **Identifying Parallel Segments**

Got It? In $\triangle XYZ$, A is the midpoint of $\overline{XY}$, B is the midpoint of $\overline{YZ}$, and C is the midpoint of $\overline{ZX}$. **What are the three pairs of parallel segments?**

13. Draw a diagram to illustrate the problem.

14. Write the segment parallel to each given segment.

$\overline{AB}$ ∥ ☐ $\overline{CB}$ ∥ ☐ $\overline{CA}$ ∥ ☐

Problem 2 Finding Lengths

Got It? In the figure below, $AD = 6$ and $DE = 7.5$. What are the lengths of $\overline{DC}$, $\overline{AC}$, $\overline{EF}$, and $\overline{AB}$?

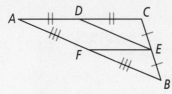

15. Complete the problem-solving model below.

Know	Need	Plan
$AD = 6$ and $DE = 7.5$. $CE = EB$, $AD = DC$, $BF = \boxed{}$		Use the Triangle Midsegment Theorem to find DC, AC, EF, and $\boxed{}$.

16. The diagram shows that $\overline{EF}$ and $\overline{DE}$ join the midpoints of two sides of $\triangle$ ▢.

By the Triangle Midsegment Theorem, $EF = \frac{1}{2} \cdot$ ▢ and $DE = \frac{1}{2} \cdot$ ▢.

Complete each statement.

17. $DC = AD = $ ▢

18. $AC = AD + $ ▢ $ = $ ▢ $ + $ ▢ $ = $ ▢

19. $EF = $ ▢ $\cdot AC = $ ▢ $\cdot$ ▢ $ = 6$

20. $CB = $ ▢ $\cdot DE = $ ▢ $\cdot$ ▢ $ = 15$

Problem 3 Using the Midsegment of a Triangle

Got It? $\overline{CD}$ is a bridge being built over a lake, as shown in the figure at the right. What is the length of the bridge?

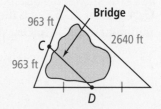

21. Complete the flow chart to find the length of the bridge.

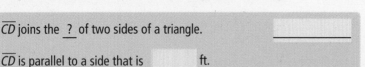

$\overline{CD}$ joins the __?__ of two sides of a triangle.

$\overline{CD}$ is parallel to a side that is ▢ ft.

Use the Triangle __?__ Theorem.

$CD = \frac{1}{2} \cdot$ ▢

$CD = $ ▢

22. The length of the bridge is ▢ ft.

Lesson Check • Do you know HOW?

If $JK = 5x + 20$ and $NO = 20$, what is the value of x?

Complete each statement.

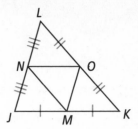

23. ⬚ is the midpoint of $\overline{LJ}$.

24. ⬚ is the midpoint of $\overline{LK}$.

25. $\overline{NO}$ is a __?__ of $\triangle JKL$, so $NO = \frac{1}{2} JK$. _____

26. Substitute the given information into the equation in Exercise 25 and solve for x.

Lesson Check • Do you UNDERSTAND?

Reasoning If two noncollinear segments in the coordinate plane have slope 3, what can you conclude?

27. Place a ✓ in the box if the response is correct. Place an ✗ if it is incorrect.

⬚ If two segments in a plane are parallel, then they have the same slope.

⬚ If two segments lie on the same line, they are parallel.

28. Now answer the question.

_____

_____

Math Success

Check off the vocabulary words that you understand.

☐ midsegment ☐ midpoint ☐ segment

Rate how well you can *use properties of midsegments.*

Need to review 0 2 4 6 8 10 Now I get it!

Lesson 5-1

Perpendicular and Angle Bisectors

Vocabulary

● Review

Complete each statement with *bisector* or *bisects*.

1. $\overrightarrow{BD}$ is the __?__ of $\angle ABC$.

2. BD __?__ $\angle ABC$.

Write T for *true* or F for *false*.

_____ 3. Two *perpendicular* segments intersect to form four right angles.

_____ 4. You can draw more than one line *perpendicular* to a given line through a point not on the line.

● Vocabulary Builder

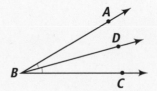

equidistant (adjective) **ee kwih DIS tunt**

Related Words: equal, distance

Definition: **Equidistant** means at an equal distance from a single point or object.

● Use Your Vocabulary

Use to the number line at the right for Exercises 5 and 6.

5. Circle two points *equidistant* from zero.

6. Name points that are *equidistant* from point C.

   _____ and _____

Use to the diagram at the right for Exercises 7 and 8.

7. Circle two points *equidistant* from point Q.

8. Name four segments that are *equidistant* from the origin.

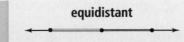

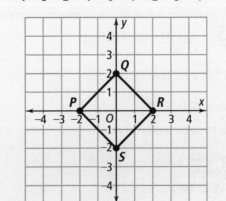

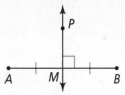

Theorem 5-2 Perpendicular Bisector Theorem

If a point is on the perpendicular bisector of a segment, then it is equidistant from the endpoints of the segment.

9. Use the diagrams below to complete the hypothesis and the conclusion.

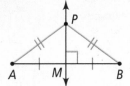

If

$\overleftrightarrow{PM} \perp \overline{AB}$ and $AM = $ ▭

Then

$PA = $ ▭

Theorem 5-3 Converse of the Perpendicular Bisector Theorem

10. Complete the converse of Theorem 5-2.

If a point is equidistant from the endpoints of a segment, then it is on the __?__ of the segment.

_____

11. Complete the diagram at the right to illustrate Theorem 5-3.

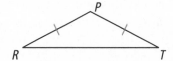

Problem 1 Using the Perpendicular Bisector

Got It? Use the diagram at the right. What is the length of $\overline{QR}$?

12. Complete the reasoning model below.

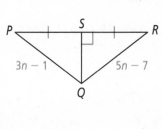

Think	Write
$\overline{QS}$ is the perpendicular bisector of $\overline{PR}$, so Q is equidistant from P and R by the Perpendicular Bisector Theorem.	$PQ = $ ▭ $3n - 1 = $ ▭
I need to solve for n.	$3n + 6 = $ ▭ $6 = $ ▭ ▭ $= n$
Now I can substitute for n to find QR.	$QR = 5n - 7$ $= 5($ ▭ $) - 7 = $ ▭

Lesson 5-2

Got It? If the director of the park at the right wants a T-shirt stand built at a point equidistant from the Spaceship Shoot and the Rollin' Coaster, by the Perpendicular Bisector Theorem he can place the stand anywhere along line ℓ. Suppose the park director wants the T-shirt stand to be equidistant from the paddle boats and the Spaceship Shoot. What are the possible locations?

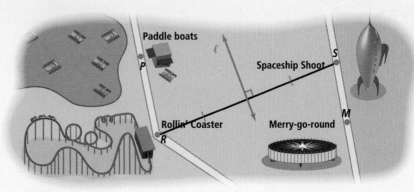

13. On the diagram, draw $\overline{PS}$.

14. On the diagram, sketch the points that are equidistant from the paddle boats and the Spaceship Shoot. Describe these points.

_____

_____

Got It? **Reasoning** Can you place the T-shirt stand so that it is equidistant from the paddle boats, the Spaceship Shoot, and the Rollin' Coaster? Explain.

15. Does the line you drew in Exercise 14 intersect line ℓ?   Yes / No

16. Where should the T-shirt stand be placed so that it is equidistant from the paddle boats, the Spaceship Shoot, and the Rollin Coaster? Explain.

_____

_____

_____

_____

The **distance from a point to a line** is the length of the perpendicular segment from the point to the line. This distance is also the length of the shortest segment from the point to the line.

Copyright © by Pearson Education, Inc. or its affiliates. All Rights Reserved.

---

take note

Theorems 5-4 and 5-5

Angle Bisector Theorem

If a point is on the bisector of an angle, then the point is equisdistant from the sides of the angle.

17. If point S is on the angle bisector of $\angle$ _____ , then $SP = $ ____ .

Converse of the Angle Bisector Theorem

If a point in the interior of an angle is equidistant from the sides of the angle, then the point is on the angle bisector.

18. Point S is in the interior of $\angle$ _____ .

19. If $SP = SR$, then S is on the __?__ of $\angle PQR$.   _____

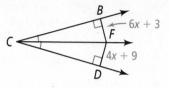

Problem 3 Using the Angle Bisector Theorem

Got It? What is the length of $\overline{FB}$?

20. The problem is solved below. Justify each step.

$FB = FD$	
$6x + 3 = 4x + 9$	
$6x = 4x + 6$	
$2x = 6$	
$x = 3$	
$FB = 6x + 3$	
$= 6(3) + 3 = 21$	

Lesson Check • Do you know HOW?

Use the figure at the right. What is the relationship between $\overline{AC}$ and $\overline{BD}$?

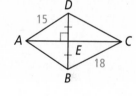

21. Underline the correct word or symbol to complete each sentence.

$\overline{AC}$ is parallel / perpendicular to $\overline{BD}$.

$\overline{AC}$ divides $\overline{BD}$ into two congruent / noncongruent segments.

$\overline{BD}$ divides $\overline{AC}$ into two congruent / noncongruent segments.

$\overline{AC}$ / $\overline{BD}$ is the perpendicular bisector of $\overline{AC}$ / $\overline{BD}$.

Math Success

Check off the vocabulary words that you understand.

☐ perpendicular bisector   ☐ equidistant   ☐ distance from a point to a line

Rate how well you can *understand bisectors.*

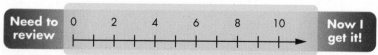

Lesson 5-2

5-3   Bisectors in Triangles

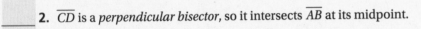

Vocabulary

● Review

Use the figure at the right. Write T for *true* or F for *false*.

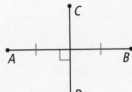

_____ **1.** $\overline{AB}$ is the *perpendicular bisector* of $\overline{CD}$.

_____ **2.** $\overline{CD}$ is a *perpendicular bisector*, so it intersects $\overline{AB}$ at its midpoint.

_____ **3.** Any point on $\overline{CD}$ is *equidistant* from points A and B.

● Vocabulary Builder

concurrent (adjective) **kun KUR unt**

Main Idea: **Concurrent** means occurring or existing at the same time.

Math Usage: When three or more lines intersect in one point, they are **concurrent**.

concurrent lines

● Use Your Vocabulary

Complete each statement with *concurrency, concurrent,* or *concurrently*.

4. Two classes are __?__ when they meet at the same time.

5. The point of __?__ of three streets is the intersections of the streets.

6. A person may go to school and hold a job __?__ .

Label each diagram below *concurrent* or *not concurrent*.

7.

8.

9.

_____   _____   _____

Theorem 5-6 Concurrency of Perpendicular Bisectors Theorem

The perpendicular bisectors of the sides of a triangle are concurrent at a point equidistant from the vertices.

Perpendicular bisectors $\overline{PX}$, $\overline{PY}$ and $\overline{PZ}$ are concurrent at P.

10. Mark $\triangle ABC$ to show all congruent segments.

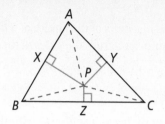

Problem 1 Finding the Circumcenter of a Triangle

Got It? What are the coordinates of the circumcenter of the triangle with vertices $A(2, 7)$, $B(10, 7)$, and $C(10, 3)$?

11. Draw $\triangle ABC$ on the coordinate plane.

12. Label the coordinates the midpoint of $\overline{AB}$ and the midpoint of $\overline{BC}$.

13. Draw the perpendicular bisector of $\overline{AB}$.

14. Draw the perpendicular bisector of $\overline{BC}$.

15. Label the coordinates of the point of intersection of the bisectors.

16. The circumcenter of $\triangle ABC$ is (,   ).

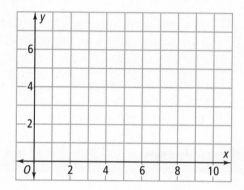

Problem 2 Using a Circumcenter

Got It? A town planner wants to place a bench equidistant from the three trees in the park. Where should he place the bench?

17. Complete the problem-solving model below.

Know	Need	Plan
The trees form the __?__ of a triangle.	Find the point of concurrency of the __?__ of the sides.	Find the __?__ of the triangle, which is equidistant from the three trees.

18. How can the town planner determine where to place the bench? Explain.

Lesson 5-3

Theorem 5-7 Concurrency of Angle Bisectors Theorem

The bisectors of the angles of a triangle are concurrent at a point equidistant from the sides of the triangle.

Angle bisectors $\overline{AP}$, $\overline{BP}$, and $\overline{CP}$ are concurrent at P.

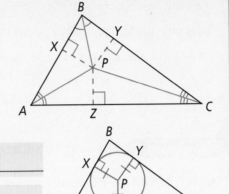

19. $PX =$ ☐ $=$ ☐

Complete each sentence with the appropriate word from the list.

incenter	inscribed	inside

20. The point of concurrency of the angle bisectors of a triangle is the __?__ of the triangle.

21. The point of concurrency of the angle bisectors of a triangle is always __?__ the triangle.

22. The circle is __?__ in △ABC.

Problem 3 **Identifying and Using the Incenter**

Got It? $QN = 5x + 36$ and $QM = 2x + 51$. What is QO?

23. Complete the reasoning model below.

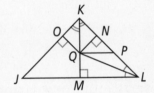

Think	Write
I know that Q is the point of concurrency of the angle bisectors.	Q is the incenter / midpoint of △JKL.
And I know that	the distance from Q to each side of △JKL is equal / unequal .
I can write an equation and solve for *x*.	$QO = $ ☐ $5x + 36 = $ ☐ $5x = $ ☐ $3x = $ ☐ $x = $ ☐

24. Use your answer to Exercise 23 to find QO.

Got It? Reasoning Is it possible for *QP* to equal 50? Explain.

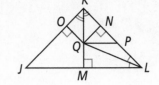

25. Drawn an inscribed circle in the diagram at the right.

26. [____] and [____] are two segments that have the same length as $\overline{QO}$.

27. Circle the correct relationship between *QO* and *QP*.

$QO < QP$ $\qquad\qquad$ $QO = QP$ $\qquad\qquad$ $QO > QP$

28. Given your answer to Exercise 27, is it possible for *QP* to equal 50? Explain.

_____

_____

Lesson Check • Do you UNDERSTAND?

Vocabulary A triangle's circumcenter is outside the triangle. What type of triangle is it?

29. Draw an example of each type of triangle on a coordinate plane below.

acute $\qquad\qquad$ obtuse $\qquad\qquad$ right

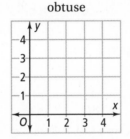
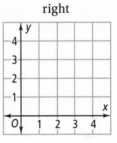

30. Circle the phrase that describes the circumcenter of a triangle.

| the point of concurrency of the angle bisectors | the point of concurrency of the perpendicular bisectors of the sides |

31. Underline the correct word to complete the sentence.

When a triangle's circumcenter is outside the triangle, the triangle is acute / obtuse / right .

Math Success

Check off the vocabulary words that you understand.

☐ concurrent $\quad$ ☐ circumscribed about $\quad$ ☐ incenter $\quad$ ☐ inscribed in $\quad$ ☐ bisector

Rate how well you can *use bisectors in triangles.*

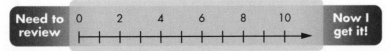

Lesson 5-3

5-4   Medians and Altitudes

Vocabulary

● Review

1. Are three diameters of a circle *concurrent*?   Yes / No

2. Are two diagonals of a rectangle *concurrent*?   Yes / No

3. Is point *C* at the right a point of *concurrency*?   Yes / No

● Vocabulary Builder

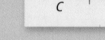

median (noun) MEE **dee un**

Related Words: median (adjective), middle (noun), midpoint (noun)

Definition: A **median** of a triangle is a segment whose endpoints are a vertex and the midpoint of the opposite side.

● Use Your Vocabulary

Write T for *true* or F for *false*.

_____ **4.** The *median* of a triangle is a segment that connects the midpoint of one side to the midpoint of an adjacent side.

_____ **5.** The point of concurrency of the *medians* of a triangle is where they intersect.

_____ **6.** A triangle has one median.

7. Circle the drawing that shows *median* $\overline{AD}$ of $\triangle ABC$.

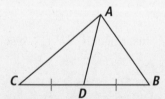   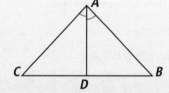

Theorem 5-8   Concurrency of Medians Theorem

The medians of a triangle are concurrent at a point (the centroid of the triangle) that is two thirds the distance from each vertex to the midpoint of the opposite side.

For any triangle, the centroid is always inside the triangle.

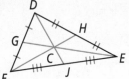

8. Complete each equation.

$DC = \frac{2}{3}$ ☐ $EC = \frac{2}{3}$ ☐ $FC =$ ☐

Problem 1 **Finding the Length of a Median**

Got It? In the diagram at the right, $ZA = 9$. What is the length of $\overline{ZC}$?

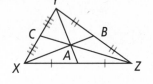

9. Point ☐ is the centroid of $\triangle XYZ$.

10. Use the justifications at the right to solve for ZC.

$ZA = $ ☐ $\cdot ZC$ Concurrency of Medians Theorem

☐ $=$ ☐ $\cdot ZC$ Substitute for ZA.

☐ $=$ ☐ $\cdot ZC$ Multiply each side by $\frac{3}{2}$.

☐ $= ZC$ Simplify.

11. ZC is ☐ , or ☐ .

An *altitude* of a triangle is the perpendicular segment from a vertex of the triangle to the line containing the opposite side.

Problem 2 **Identifying Medians and Altitudes**

Got It? For $\triangle ABC$, is each segment, $\overline{AD}$, $\overline{EG}$, and $\overline{CF}$, a *median*, an *altitude*, or *neither*? Explain.

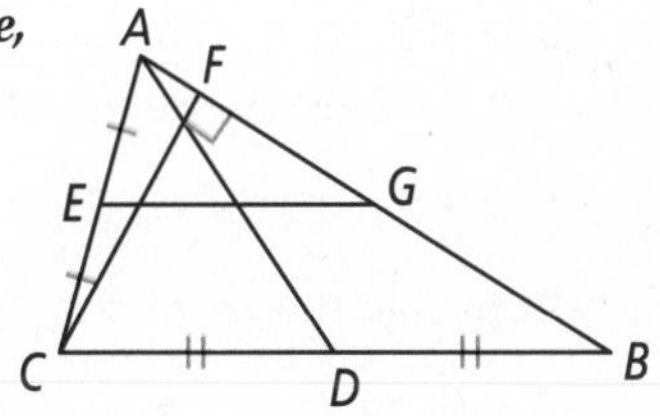

12. Read each statement. Then cross out the words that do NOT describe $\overline{AD}$.

$\overline{AD}$ is a segment that extends from vertex A to $\overline{CB}$, which is opposite A.

$\overline{AD}$ meets $\overline{CB}$ at point D, which is the midpoint of $\overline{CB}$ since $\overline{CD} \cong \overline{DB}$.

$\overline{AD}$ is not perpendicular to $\overline{CB}$.

| altitude | median | neither altitude nor median |

13. Circle the correct statement below.

| $\overline{AD}$ is a median. | $\overline{AD}$ is an altitude. | $\overline{AD}$ is neither a median nor an altitude. |

14. Read the statement. Then circle the correct description of $\overline{EG}$.

$\overline{EG}$ does not extend from a vertex.

| $\overline{EG}$ is a median. | $\overline{EG}$ is an altitude. | $\overline{EG}$ is neither a median nor an altitude. |

131   Lesson 5-4

15. Read each statement. Then circle the correct description of $\overline{CF}$.

$\overline{CF}$ is a segment that extends from vertex C to $\overline{AB}$, which opposite C.

$\overline{CF} \perp \overline{AB}$

$\overline{CF}$ is median. $\overline{CF}$ is an altitude. $\overline{CF}$ is neither a median nor an altitude.

---

take note

Theorem 5-9   Concurrency of Altitudes Theorem

The lines that contain the altitudes of a triangle are concurrent.

The point of concurrency is the *orthocenter of the triangle*. The orthocenter of a triangle can be inside, on, or outside the triangle.

16. Draw an example of each type of triangle on a coordinate plane below.

acute   obtuse   right

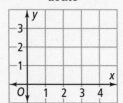   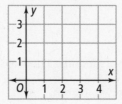   

Draw a line from the type of triangle in Column A to the location of its orthocenter in Column B.

Column A	Column B
17. acute	outside the triangle
18. right	inside the triangle
19. obtuse	at a vertex of the triangle

Problem 3   Finding the Orthocenter

Got It? $\triangle DEF$ has vertices $D(1, 2)$, $E(1, 6)$, and $F(4, 2)$. What are the coordinates of the orthocenter of $\triangle DEF$?

20. Graph $\triangle DEF$ on the coordinate plane.

Underline the correct word to complete each sentence.

21. $\triangle DEF$ is a(n) acute / right triangle, so the

orthocenter is at vertex D.

22. The altitude to $\overline{DF}$ is horizontal / vertical .

23. The altitude to $\overline{DE}$ is horizontal / vertical .

24. The coordinates of the orthocenter

of $\triangle DEF$ are (,   ).

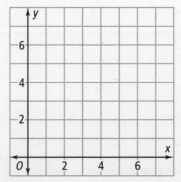

25. Use the words *altitudes, angle bisectors, medians,* and *perpendicular bisectors* to describe the intersecting lines in each triangle below.

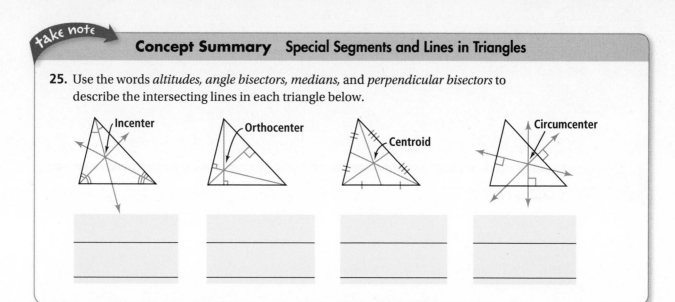

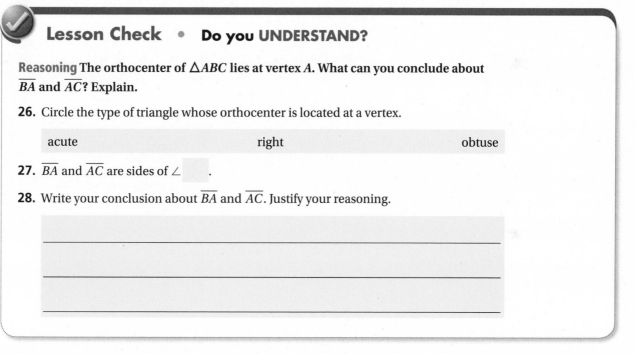

Lesson Check • Do you UNDERSTAND?

Reasoning The orthocenter of △*ABC* lies at vertex *A*. What can you conclude about $\overline{BA}$ and $\overline{AC}$? Explain.

26. Circle the type of triangle whose orthocenter is located at a vertex.

acute	right	obtuse

27. $\overline{BA}$ and $\overline{AC}$ are sides of ∠ ☐ .

28. Write your conclusion about $\overline{BA}$ and $\overline{AC}$. Justify your reasoning.

Math Success

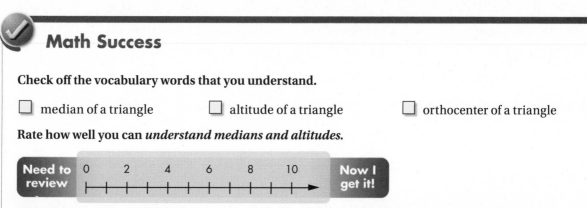

Check off the vocabulary words that you understand.

☐ median of a triangle ☐ altitude of a triangle ☐ orthocenter of a triangle

Rate how well you can *understand medians and altitudes.*

Need to review 0 2 4 6 8 10 Now I get it!

Vocabulary

● **Review**

Draw a line from each statement in Column A to one or more pictures that contradict it in Column B.

Column A	Column B

1. $x < y$

2. $x = y$

Radius = x   Radius = y

3. $x > y$

Ordered pair
(3, 3)

● **Vocabulary Builder**

indirect (adjective) **in duh** REKT

Definition: **Indirect** means not direct in course or action, taking a roundabout route to get to a point or idea.

Math Usage: In **indirect** reasoning, all possibilities are considered and then all but one are proved false. The remaining possibility must be true.

● **Use Your Vocabulary**

Write *indirect* or *indirectly* to complete each sentence.

4. The __?__ way home from school takes a lot more time. _____

5. By finding the negation of a statement false, you __?__ prove the statement true. _____

Key Concept   Writing an Indirect Proof

Step 1
State as a temporary assumption the opposite (negation) of what you want to prove.

Step 2
Show that this temporary assumption leads to a contradiction.

Step 3
Conclude that the temporary assumption must be false and what you want to prove must be true.

 **Problem 1**   **Writing the First Step of an Indirect Proof**

Got It? Suppose you want to write an indirect proof of the statement. As the first step of the proof, what would you assume?

△*BOX* is not acute.

6. What do you want to prove?

7. What is the opposite of what you want to prove?

8. The first step in the indirect proof is to write the following:

Assume temporarily that △*BOX* is __?__ .

Got It? Suppose you want to write an indirect proof of the statement. As the first step of the proof, what would you assume?

At least one of the items costs more than $25.

9. What do you want to prove?

For Exercises 10–11, use <, >, ≤, ≥, or = to complete each statement.
Let *n* = the cost of at least one of the items.

10. What do you want to prove?

n ☐ 25

11. What is the opposite of what you want to prove?

n ☐ 25

12. The first step in the indirect proof is to write the following:

Assume temporarily that at least one of the items costs __?__ $25.

Write the first step of the indirect proof of each statement.

13. Prove: *AB* = *CD*

14. Prove: The sun is shining.

Lesson 5-5

Problem 2 **Identifying Contradictions**

Got It? Which two statements contradict each other?

    I. △XYZ is acute.   II. △XYZ is scalene   III. △XYZ is equiangular

15. Use the words in the box at the right to complete the flow chart below.

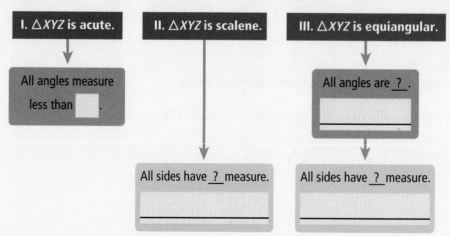

16. In the first row of the flow chart above, circle the two statements that contradict one another.

 Problem 3 **Writing an Indirect Proof**

Got It? Given: $7(x + y) = 70$ and $x \neq 4$.

      Prove: $y \neq 6$

17. Give the reason for each statement of the proof.

Statements	Reasons
1) Assume $y = 6$.	1)
2) $7(x + y) = 70$	2)
3) $7(x + 6) = 70$	3)
4) $7x + 42 = 70$	4)
5) $\quad\quad 7x = 28$	5)
6) $\quad\quad x = 4$	6)
7) $\quad\quad x \neq 4$	7)
8) $\quad\quad y \neq 6$	8)

Lesson Check • Do you know HOW?

Suppose you want to write an indirect proof of the following statement. As the first step of the proof, what would you assume?

Quadrilateral *ABCD* has four right angles.

18. Place a ✓ if the statement is the correct assumption to make as the first step in the indirect proof. Place an ✗ if it is not.

Quadrilateral *ABCD* is a rectangle.

Quadrilateral *ABCD* has four non-right angles.

Quadrilateral *ABCD* does *not* have four right angles.

Lesson Check • Do you UNDERSTAND?

Error Analysis A classmate began an indirect proof as shown at the right. Explain and correct your classmate's error.

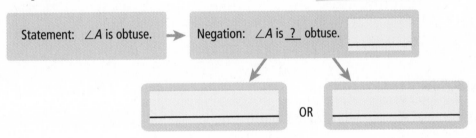

Given: △ABC
Prove: ∠A is obtuse.
Assume temporarily that ∠A is acute.

19. Complete the flow chart.

Statement: ∠A is obtuse. → Negation: ∠A is _?_ obtuse. ⬚

⬚ OR ⬚

20. Underline the correct words to complete the sentence.

The indirect proof has an incorrect conclusion / assumption because the opposite of

" ∠A is obtuse" is " ∠A is acute / not obtuse / right ."

Math Success

Check off the vocabulary words that you understand.

☐ indirect reasoning   ☐ indirect proof   ☐ contradiction

Rate how well you can *use indirect reasoning*.

Need to review   0   2   4   6   8   10   Now I get it!

Lesson 5-5

Vocabulary

● Review

1. Circle the labeled *exterior angle*.

2. Write the *Exterior Angle* Theorem as it relates to the diagram.

$m\angle = m\angle + m\angle $

3. Draw an *exterior angle* adjacent to ∠1 and label it ∠5.

Circle the statement that represents an *inequality* in each pair below.

4. $x \neq 32$

$x = 32$

5. The number of votes is equal to 10,000.

The number of votes is greater than 10,000.

Complete each statement with an inequality symbol.

6. y is less than or equal to z.

$y z$

7. The temperature t is at least 80 degrees.

$t 80°$

● Vocabulary Builder

compare (verb) **kum** PEHR	There are more letters in the word *comparison* than in the word *compare*.

Other Word Form: comparison (noun)

Definition: To **compare** is to examine two or more items, noting similarities and differences.

Math Usage: Use inequalities to **compare** amounts.

● Use Your Vocabulary

8. Complete each statement with the appropriate form of the word *compare*.

NOUN   By __?__ , a spider has more legs than a beetle.

VERB   You can __?__ products before deciding which to buy.

VERB   To __?__ quantities, you can write an equation or an inequality.

Property Comparison Property of Inequality

If $a = b + c$ and $c > 0$, then $a > b$.

9. Circle the group of values that satisfies the Comparison Property of Inequality.

$a = 5, b = 5,$ and $c = 0$ $a = 5, b = 2,$ and $c = 3$ $a = 8, b = 6,$ and $c = 1$

Corollary Corollary to the Triangle Exterior Angle Theorem

The measure of an exterior angle of a triangle is greater than the measure of each of its remote interior angles.

10. Circle the angles whose measures are always less than the measure of $\angle 1$.

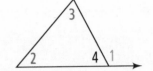

Problem 1   Applying the Corollary

Got It? Use the figure at the right. Why is $m\angle 5 > m\angle C$?

Write the justification for each statement.

11. $\angle 5$ is an exterior angle of $\triangle ADC$.

_____

12. $m\angle 5 > m\angle C$

_____

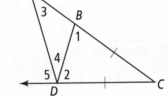

You can use the Corollary to the Triangle Exterior Angle Theorem to prove the following theorem.

Theorem 5-10 and Theorem 5-11

Theorem 5-10

If two sides of a triangle are not congruent, then the larger angle lies opposite the longer side.

If $XZ > XY$, then $m\angle Y > m\angle Z$.

13. Theorem 5-11 is related to Theorem 5-10. Write the text of Theorem 5-11 by exchanging the words "larger angle" and "longer side."

Theorem 5-11 If two sides of a triangle are not congruent, then

_____.

Lesson 5-6

Problem 3 Using Theorem 5-11

Got It? Reasoning In the figure at the right, $m\angle S = 24$ and $m\angle O = 130$. Which side of $\triangle SOX$ is the shortest side? Explain your reasoning.

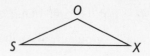

14. By the Triangle Angle-Sum Theorem, $m\angle S + m\angle O + m\angle X = 180$, so $m\angle X = \boxed{} - m\angle S - m\angle O$.

15. Use the given angle measures and the equation you wrote in Exercise 14 to find $m\angle X$.

$m\angle X = \boxed{} - \boxed{} - \boxed{} = \boxed{}$

16. Complete the table below.

angle			
angle measure	130	26	24
opposite side			

17. Which is the shortest side? Explain.

The shortest side is $\boxed{}$ because it is opposite the smallest angle, $\angle\boxed{}$.

Theorem 5-12   Triangle Inequality Theorem

The sum of the lengths of any two sides of a triangle is greater than the length of the third side.

18. Complete each inequality.

$XY + YZ > \boxed{}$ $YZ + ZX > \boxed{}$ $ZX + XY > \boxed{}$

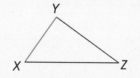

Problem 4 Using the Triangle Inequality Theorem

Got It? Can a triangle have sides with lengths 2 m, 6 m, and 9 m? Explain.

19. Complete the reasoning model below.

Think	Write
The sum of the lengths of any two sides must be greater than the length of the third side.	$2 + 6 = 8$ $6 + 9 = 15$ $2 + 9 = 11$
I need to write three sums and three inequalities.	$8 \boxed{} 9$ $15 \boxed{} 2$ $11 \boxed{} 6$
One of those sums is greater / not greater than the length of the third side.	It is / is not possible for a triangle to have sides with lengths 2 m, 6 m, and 9 m.

Got It? A triangle has side lengths of 4 in. and 7 in. What is the range of possible lengths for the third side?

20. Let x = the length of the third side. Use the Triangle Inequality Theorem to write and solve three inequalities.

$x + 4 > \boxed{}$ $x + 7 > \boxed{}$ $7 + 4 > \boxed{}$

$x > \boxed{}$ $x > \boxed{}$ $11 > \boxed{}$

21. Underline the correct word to complete each sentence.

Length is always / sometimes / never positive.

The first / second / third inequality pair is invalid in this situation.

22. Write the remaining inequalities as the compound inequality $\boxed{} < x < \boxed{}$.

23. The third side must be longer than $\boxed{}$ in. and shorter than $\boxed{}$ in.

Lesson Check • Do you UNDERSTAND?

Error Analysis A friend tells you that she drew a triangle with perimeter 16 and one side of length 8. How do you know she made an error in her drawing?

24. If one side length is 8 and the perimeter is 16, then the sum of the lengths of the two remaining sides must be $16 - 8 = \boxed{}$.

25. Underline the correct words or number to complete each sentence.

By the Triangle Inequality Theorem, the sum of the lengths of two sides of a triangle must be equal to / greater than / less than the length of the third side.

By the Triangle Inequality Theorem, the sum of the lengths of the two unknown sides must be equal to / greater than / less than the length 8 / 16 .

But 8 is *not* equal to / greater than 8, so there must be an error in the drawing.

Math Success

Check off the vocabulary words that you understand.

☐ exterior angle   ☐ comparison property of inequality

Rate how well you can *use the Triangle Inequality Theorem.*

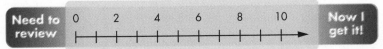

     Lesson 5-6

5-7 Inequalities in Two Triangles

Vocabulary

● Review

Circle the *included angles* in each diagram.

1.

2.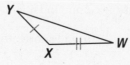

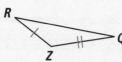

In Exercises 3–5, cross out the group of values that does not satisfy the *Comparison Property of Inequality*.

3. $a = 3, b = 3, c = 0$
   $a = 6, b = 4, c = 2$

4. $a = 11, b = 3, c = 8$
   $a = 1, b = 2, c = 3$

5. $a = 8, b = 3, c = 5$
   $a = 8, b = 5, c = 4$

Write a number so that each group satisfies the *Comparison Property of Inequality*.

6. $a = \boxed{}, b = 0, c = 2$ 7. $a = 9, b = \boxed{}, c = 1$ 8. $a = 3, b = \boxed{}, c = 2$

● Vocabulary Builder

hinge (noun, verb) <u>hinj</u>

Definition (noun): A **hinge** is a device on which something else depends or turns.

Definition (verb): To **hinge** upon means to depend on.

● Use Your Vocabulary

Circle the correct form of the word *hinge*.

9. Everything *hinges* on his decision.   Noun / Verb

10. The *hinge* on a gate allows it to swing open or closed.   Noun / Verb

11. Your plan *hinges* on your teacher's approval.   Noun / Verb

12. The lid was attached to the jewelry box by two *hinges*.   Noun / Verb

Chapter 5

142

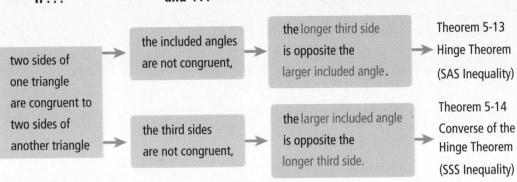

Theorems 5-13 and 5-14   The Hinge Theorem and its Converse

If ...	and ...	then ...	
two sides of one triangle are congruent to two sides of another triangle	the included angles are not congruent,	the longer third side is opposite the larger included angle.	Theorem 5-13 Hinge Theorem (SAS Inequality)
	the third sides are not congruent,	the larger included angle is opposite the longer third side.	Theorem 5-14 Converse of the Hinge Theorem (SSS Inequality)

13. Use the triangles at the right to complete the table.

Theorem	If...	Then...
5-13: Hinge Theorem	$m\angle A > m\angle X$	BC ⬚ YZ
5-14: Converse of the Hinge Theorem	$BC >$ ⬚	$m\angle A >$ ⬚

14. Explain why Theorems 5–13 and 5–14 are also called the SAS and SSS Inequality Theorems.

_____

_____

_____

Problem 1   Using the Hinge Theorem

Got It? What inequality relates *LN* and *OQ* in the figure at the right?

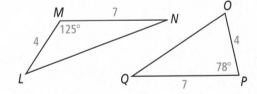

15. Use information in the diagram to complete each statement.

The included angle in △*LMN* is ∠ ⬚ .

The included angle in △*OPQ* is ∠ ⬚ .

16. Circle the side opposite the included angle in △*LMN*. Underline the side opposite the included angle in △*OPQ*.

$\overline{LM}$		$\overline{LN}$		$\overline{MN}$
	$\overline{QO}$		$\overline{QP}$	$\overline{OP}$

17. Use the Hinge Theorem to complete the statement below

$m\angle$ ⬚ $> m\angle$ ⬚ , so $LN >$ ⬚ .

Lesson 5-7

Problem 3 Using the Converse of the Hinge Theorem

Got It? What is the range of possible values for x in the figure at the right?

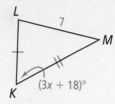
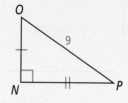

18. From the diagram you know that the triangles have two pairs of congruent corresponding sides, that

   $LM <$ [____] , and that $m\angle N =$ [____] .

Complete the steps and justifications to find upper and lower limits on x.

19. $m\angle K <$ [____]   Converse of the Hinge Theorem

   $3x + 18 <$ [____]   Substitute.

   $3x <$ [____]   Subtract [____] from each side.

   $x <$ [____]   Divide each side by [____].

20. $m\angle K >$ [____]   The measure of an angle of a triangle is greater than 0.

   $3x + 18 >$ [____]   Substitute.

   $3x >$ [____]   Subtract [____] from each side.

   $x >$ [____]   Divide each side by [____].

21. Write the two inequalities as the compound inequality [____] $< x <$ [____].

Problem 4 Proving Relationships in Triangles

Got It? Given: $m\angle MON = 80$; O is the midpoint of $\overline{LN}$.

   Prove: $LM > MN$

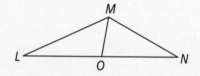

22. Write a justification for each statement.

Statements	Reasons
1) $m\angle MON = 80$	1) _____
2) $m\angle MON + m\angle MOL = 180$	2) _____
3) $80 + m\angle MOL = 180$	3) _____
4) $m\angle MOL = 100$	4) _____
5) $\overline{LO} \cong \overline{ON}$	5) _____
6) $\overline{MO} \cong \overline{MO}$	6) _____
7) $m\angle MOL > m\angle MON$	7) _____
8) $LM > MN$	8) _____

Lesson Check • Do you know HOW?

Write an inequality relating *FD* and *BC*.

In Exercises 23–26, circle the correct statement in each pair.

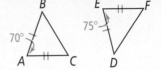

23. $\overline{AC} \cong \overline{EF}$ $\qquad AC > EF$ **24.** $AB > ED$ $\qquad \overline{AB} \cong \overline{ED}$

25. $m\angle BAC > m\angle FED$ $\qquad m\angle BAC < m\angle FED$

26. By the Hinge Theorem, you can relate *FD* and *BC*.

By the Converse of Hinge Theorem, you can relate *FD* and *BC*.

27. Write an inequality relating *FD* and *BC*.

$FD \quad \boxed{} \quad BC$

Lesson Check • Do you UNDERSTAND?

Error Analysis From the figure at the right, your friend concludes that $m\angle BAD > m\angle BCD$. How would you correct your friend's mistake?

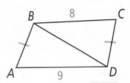

Write T for *true* or F for *false*.

____ **28.** $AB = CD$ $\qquad$ ____ **29.** $AD = CB$ $\qquad$ ____ **30.** $BD = BD$

31. Your friend should compare $\boxed{}$ and $\boxed{}$.

32. The longer of the two sides your friend should compare is $\boxed{}$.

33. How would you correct your friend's mistake? Explain.

_____

_____

Math Success

Check off the vocabulary words that you understand.

☐ exterior angle $\qquad$ ☐ comparison property of inequality $\qquad$ ☐ Hinge Theorem

Rate how well you can *use triangle inequalities.*

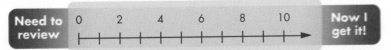

Lesson 5-7

6-1 The Polygon Angle-Sum Theorems

Vocabulary

● Review

1. Underline the correct word to complete the sentence.

   In a *convex* polygon, no point on the lines containing the sides of the polygon is in the interior / exterior of the polygon.

2. Cross out the polygon that is NOT *convex*.

● Vocabulary Builder

| regular polygon (noun) REG yuh lur PAHL ih gahn |

Definition: A **regular polygon** is a polygon that is both equilateral and equiangular.

Example: An equilateral triangle is a **regular polygon** with three congruent sides and three congruent angles.

● Use Your Vocabulary

Underline the correct word(s) to complete each sentence.

3. The sides of a *regular polygon* are congruent / scalene .

4. A right triangle is / is not a *regular polygon*.

5. An isosceles triangle is / is not always a *regular polygon*.

Write *equiangular, equilateral,* or *regular* to identify each hexagon. Use each word once.

6.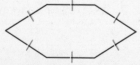

7.

8.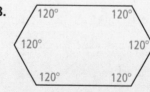

_____   _____   _____

Theorem 6-1 Polygon Angle-Sum Theorem and Corollary

Theorem 6-1 The sum of the measures of the interior angles of an *n*-gon is $(n - 2)180$.

Corollary The measure of each interior angle of a regular *n*-gon is $\dfrac{(n - 2)180}{n}$.

9. When $n - 2 = 1$, the polygon is a(n) __?__ .

10. When $n - 2 = 2$, the polygon is a(n) __?__ .

 Problem 1 **Finding a Polygon Angle Sum**

Got It? What is the sum of the interior angle measures of a 17-gon?

11. Use the justifications below to find the sum.

$$\text{sum} = \left(\boxed{} - 2\right)180 \qquad \text{Polygon Angle-Sum Theorem}$$

$$= \left(\boxed{} - 2\right)180 \qquad \text{Substitute for } n.$$

$$= \boxed{} \cdot 180 \qquad \text{Subtract.}$$

$$= \boxed{} \qquad \text{Simplify.}$$

12. Draw diagonals from vertex A to check your answer.

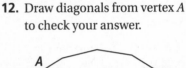

13. The sum of the interior angle measures of a 17-gon is $\boxed{}$.

 Problem 2 **Using the Polygon Angle-Sum Theorem**

Got It? What is the measure of each interior angle in a regular nonagon?

Underline the correct word or number to complete each sentence.

14. The interior angles in a regular polygon are congruent / different .

15. A regular nonagon has 7 / 8 / 9 congruent sides.

16. Use the Corollary to the Polygon Angle-Sum Theorem to find the measure of each interior angle in a regular nonagon.

$$\text{Measure of an angle} = \frac{\left(\boxed{} - 2\right)180}{\boxed{}}$$

$$= \frac{\left(\boxed{}\right)180}{\boxed{}}$$

$$= \boxed{}$$

17. The measure of each interior angle in a regular nonagon is $\boxed{}$.

Lesson 6-1

Problem 3 Using the Polygon Angle-Sum Theorem

Got It? What is $m\angle G$ in quadrilateral *EFGH*?

18. Use the Polygon Angle-Sum Theorem to find $m\angle G$ for $n = 4$.

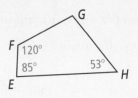

$$m\angle E + m\angle F + m\angle G + m\angle H = (n - 2)180$$

$$m\angle E + m\angle F + m\angle G + m\angle H = \left(\boxed{} - 2\right)180$$

$$\boxed{} + \boxed{} + \boxed{} + \boxed{} = \boxed{} \cdot 180$$

$$m\angle G + \boxed{} = \boxed{}$$

$$m\angle G = \boxed{}$$

19. $m\angle G$ in quadrilateral *EFGH* is $\boxed{}$.

Theorem 6-2 Polygon Exterior Angle-Sum Theorem

The sum of the measures of the exterior angles of a polygon, one at each vertex, is 360.

20. In the pentagon below, $m\angle 1 + m\angle 2 + m\angle 3 + m\angle 4 + m\angle 5 = \boxed{}$.

Use the Polygon Exterior Angle-Sum Theorem to find each measure.

21.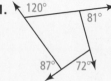

$$120 + 81 + \boxed{} + 87 = 360$$

22.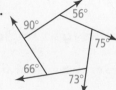

$$90 + \boxed{} + 75 + 73 + 66 = \boxed{}$$

Problem 4 Finding an Exterior Angle Measure

Got It? What is the measure of an exterior angle of a regular nonagon?

Underline the correct number or word to complete each sentence.

23. Since the nonagon is regular, its interior angles are congruent / right .

24. The exterior angles are complements / supplements of the interior angles.

25. Since the nonagon is regular, its exterior angles are congruent / right .

26. The sum of the measures of the exterior angles of a polygon is 180 / 360 .

27. A regular nonagon has 7 / 9 / 12 sides.

28. What is the measure of an exterior angle of a regular nonagon? Explain.

_____

_____

Lesson Check • Do you UNDERSTAND?

Error Analysis Your friend says that she measured an interior angle of a regular polygon as 130. Explain why this result is impossible.

29. Use indirect reasoning to find a contradiction.

Assume temporarily that a regular n-gon has a $130°$ interior angle.

angle sum = [ ] · n	A regular n-gon has n congruent angles.
angle sum = ([ ])180	Polygon Angle-Sum Theorem
[ ] = ([ ])180	Use the Transitive Property of Equality.
[ ] = [ ] − [ ]	Use the Distributive Property.
[ ] = [ ]	Subtract $180n$ from each side.
n = [ ]	Divide each side by -50.
$n \neq$ [ ]	The number of sides in a polygon is a whole number ≥ 3.

30. Explain why your friend's result is impossible.

_____

_____

_____

_____

Math Success

Check off the vocabulary words that you understand.

☐ equilateral polygon   ☐ equiangular polygon   ☐ regular polygon

Rate how well you can *find angle measures of polygons.*

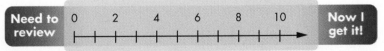

Need to review   0   2   4   6   8   10   Now I get it!

Properties of Parallelograms

Vocabulary

● Review

1. Supplementary angles are two angles whose measures sum to [   ].

2. Suppose $\angle X$ and $\angle Y$ are *supplementary*. If $m\angle X = 75$, then $m\angle Y =$ [   ].

Underline the correct word to complete each sentence.

3. A linear pair is complementary / *supplementary*.

4. $\angle AFB$ and $\angle EFD$ at the right are complementary / *supplementary*.

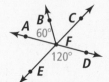

● Vocabulary Builder

consecutive (adjective) **kun SEK yoo tiv**

Definition: **Consecutive** items follow one after another in uninterrupted order.

Math Usage: **Consecutive** angles of a polygon share a common side.

Examples: The numbers $-3, -2, -1, 0, 1, 2, 3, \ldots$ are **consecutive** integers.

Non-Example: The letters A, B, C, F, P, . . . are NOT **consecutive** letters of the alphabet.

● Use Your Vocabulary

Use the diagram at the right. Draw a line from each angle in Column A to a *consecutive* angle in Column B.

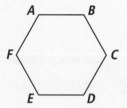

Column A	Column B
5. $\angle A$	$\angle F$
6. $\angle C$	$\angle E$
7. $\angle D$	$\angle D$

Write the next two *consecutive* months in each sequence.

8. January, February, March, April, _____, _____

9. December, November, October, September, _____, _____

Theorems 6-3, 6-4, 6-5, 6-6

Theorem 6-3 If a quadrilateral is a parallelogram, then its opposite sides are congruent.

Theorem 6-4 If a quadrilateral is a parallelogram, then its consecutive angles are supplementary.

Theorem 6-5 If a quadrilateral is a parallelogram, then its opposite angles are congruent.

Theorem 6-6 If a quadrilateral is a parallelogram, then its diagonals bisect each other.

Use the diagram at the right for Exercises 10–12.

10. Mark parallelogram *ABCD* to model Theorem 6-3 and Theorem 6-5.

11. $\overline{AE} \cong$ ▢

12. $\overline{BE} \cong$ ▢

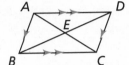

Problem 1 **Using Consecutive Angles**

Got It? Suppose you adjust the lamp so that $m\angle S$ is 86. What is $m\angle R$ in $\square PQRS$?

Underline the correct word or number to complete each statement.

13. $\angle R$ and $\angle S$ are adjacent / consecutive angles, so they are supplementary.

14. $m\angle R + m\angle S =$ 90 / 180

15. Now find $m\angle R$.

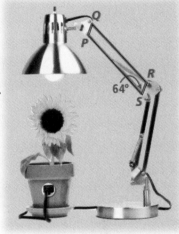

16. $m\angle R =$ ▢ .

Problem 2 **Using Properties of Parallelograms in a Proof**

Got It? Use the diagram at the right.

    Given: $\square ABCD, \overline{AK} \cong \overline{MK}$ **Prove:** $\angle BCD \cong \angle CMD$

17. Circle the classification of $\triangle AKM$.

    equilateral   isosceles   right

18. Complete the proof. The reasons are given.

Statements	Reasons
1) $\overline{AK} \cong$ ▢	1) Given
2) $\angle DAB \cong$ ▢	2) Angles opposite congruent sides of a triangle are congruent.
3) $\angle BCD \cong$ ▢	3) Opposite angles of a parallelogram are congruent.
4) $\angle BCD \cong$ ▢	4) Transitive Property of Congruence

Lesson 6-2

Got It? Find the values of *x* and *y* in ▱*PQRS* at the right. What are *PR* and *SQ*?

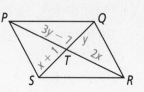

19. Circle the reason $\overline{PT} \cong \overline{TR}$ and $\overline{ST} \cong \overline{TQ}$.

| Diagonals of a parallelogram bisect each other. | Opposite sides of a parallelogram are congruent. | $\overline{PR}$ is the perpendicular bisector of $\overline{QS}$. |

20. Cross out the equation that is NOT true.

$3(x + 1) - 7 = 2x$ $y = x + 1$ $3y - 7 = x + 1$ $3y - 7 = 2x$

21. Find the value of *x*.

22. Find the value of *y*.

23. Find *PT*.

$PT = 3$ ▢ $- 7$

$PT = $ ▢ $- 7$

$PT = $ ▢

24. Find *ST*.

$ST = $ ▢ $+ 1$

$ST = $ ▢

25. Find *PR*.

$PR = 2($ ▢ $)$

$PR = $ ▢

26. Find *SQ*.

$SQ = 2($ ▢ $)$

$SQ = $ ▢

27. Explain why you do not need to find *TR* and *TQ* after finding *PT* and *ST*.

_____

_____

take note

Theorem 6-7

If three (or more) parallel lines cut off congruent segments on one transversal, then they cut off congruent segments on every transversal.

Use the diagram at the right for Exercises 28 and 29.

28. If $\overleftrightarrow{AB} \parallel \overleftrightarrow{CD} \parallel \overleftrightarrow{EF}$ and $\overline{AC} \cong \overline{CE}$, then $\overline{BD} \cong$ ▢ .

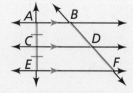

29. Mark the diagram to show your answer to Exercise 28.

Got It? In the figure at the right, $\overleftrightarrow{AE} \parallel \overleftrightarrow{BF} \parallel \overleftrightarrow{CG} \parallel \overleftrightarrow{DH}$. If $EF = FG = GH = 6$ and $AD = 15$, what is CD?

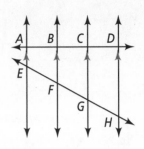

30. You know that the parallel lines cut off congruent segments on transversal ▢ .

31. By Theorem 6-7, the parallel lines also cut off congruent segments on ▢ .

32. $AD = AB + BC + $ ▢ by the Segment Addition Postulate.

33. $AB = $ ▢ $= CD$, so $AD = $ ▢ $\cdot CD$. Then $CD = $ ▢ $\cdot AD$.

34. You know that $AD = 15$, so $CD = $ ▢ $\cdot 15 = $ ▢ .

Lesson Check • Do you UNDERSTAND?

Error Analysis Your classmate says that $QV = 10$. Explain why the statement may not be correct.

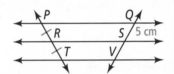

35. Place a ✓ in the box if you are given the information. Place an ✗ if you are not given the information.

▢ three lines cut by two transversals

▢ three parallel lines cut by two transversals

▢ congruent segments on one transversal

36. What needs to be true for QV to equal 10?

_____

37. Explain why your classmate's statement may not be correct.

_____

Math Success

Check off the vocabulary words that you understand.

☐ parallelogram   ☐ opposite sides   ☐ opposite angles   ☐ consecutive angles

Rate how well you *understand parallelograms*.

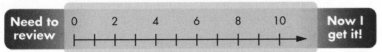

Vocabulary

● Review

1. Does a pentagon have *opposite sides*?   Yes / No

2. Does an *n*-gon have *opposite sides* if *n* is an odd number?   Yes / No

Draw a line from each side in Column A to the *opposite side* in Column B.

Column A	Column B
3. $\overline{AB}$	$\overline{BC}$
4. $\overline{AD}$	$\overline{DC}$

● Vocabulary Builder

parallelogram (noun) **pa ruh LEL uh gram**

Definition: A **parallelogram** is a quadrilateral with two pairs of opposite sides parallel. Opposite sides may include arrows to show the sides are parallel.

Related Words: square, rectangle, rhombus

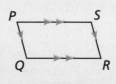

parallelogram

● Use Your Vocabulary

Write P if the statement describes a *parallelogram* or NP if it does not.

_____ **5.** octagon   _____ **6.** five congruent sides   _____ **7.** regular quadrilateral

Write P if the figure appears to be a *parallelogram* or NP if it does not.

_____ **8.**   _____ **9.**   _____ **10.**

Theorems 6-8 through 6-12

Theorem 6-8 If both pairs of opposite sides of a quadrilateral are congruent, then the quadrilateral is a parallelogram.

Theorem 6-9 If an angle of a quadrilateral is supplementary to both of its consecutive angles, then the quadrilateral is a parallelogram.

Theorem 6-10 If both pairs of opposite angles of a quadrilateral are congruent, then the quadrilateral is a parallelogram.

Theorem 6-11 If the diagonals of a quadrilateral bisect each other, then the quadrilateral is a parallelogram.

Theorem 6-12 If one pair of opposite sides of a quadrilateral is both congruent and parallel, then the quadrilateral is a parallelogram.

Use the diagram at the right and Theorems 6-8 through 6–12 for Exercises 11–16.

11. If $\overline{AB} \cong$ ☐ , and $\overline{BC} \cong$ ☐ , then *ABCD* is a ▱.

12. If $m\angle A + m\angle B =$ ☐ and $m\angle$ ☐ $+ m\angle D = 180$, then *ABCD* is a ▱.

13. If $\angle A \cong \angle$ ☐ and $\angle$ ☐ $\cong \angle D$, then *ABCD* is a ▱.

14. If $\overline{AE} \cong$ ☐ and $\overline{BE} \cong$ ☐ , then *ABCD* is a ▱.

15. If $\overline{BC} \cong$ ☐ and $\overline{BC} \parallel$ ☐ , then *ABCD* is a ▱.

16. If $\overline{CD} \cong$ ☐ and $\overline{CD} \parallel$ ☐ , then ABCD is a ▱.

✓ **Problem 1** **Finding Values for Parallelograms**

Got It? Use the diagram at the right. For what values of *x* and *y* must *EFGH* be a parallelogram?

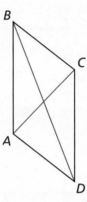

17. Circle the equation you can use to find the value of *y*. Underline the equation you can use to find the value of *x*.

| $y + 10 = 3y - 2$ | $y + 10 = 4x + 13$ | $(y + 10) + (3y - 2) = 180$ |

18. Find *y*.   **19.** Find *x*.

20. What equation could you use to find the value of *x* first? ☐

21. *EFGH* must be a parallelogram for $x =$ ☐ and $y =$ ☐ .

Copyright © by Pearson Education, Inc. or its affiliates. All Rights Reserved.

Deciding Whether a Quadrilateral Is a Parallelogram

Got It? Can you prove that the quadrilateral is a parallelogram based on the given information? Explain.

Given: $\overline{EF} \cong \overline{GD}$, $\overline{DE} \parallel \overline{FG}$

Prove: *DEFG* is a parallelogram.

22. Circle the angles that are consecutive with ∠G.

∠D	∠E	∠F

23. Underline the correct word to complete the sentence.

Same-side interior angles formed by parallel lines cut by a transversal are

complementary / congruent / supplementary .

24. Circle the interior angles on the same side of transversal $\overline{DG}$. Underline the interior angles on the same side of transversal $\overline{EF}$.

∠D	∠E	∠F	∠G

25. Can you prove *DEFG* is a parallelogram? Explain.

_____

_____

_____

Identifying Parallelograms

Got It? **Reasoning** A truck sits on the platform of a vehicle lift. Two moving arms raise the platform. What is the maximum height that the vehicle lift can elevate the truck? Explain.

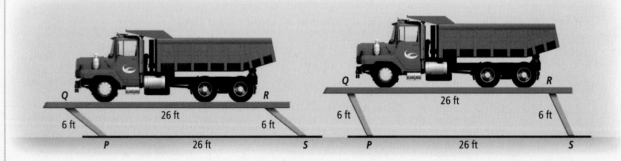

26. Do the lengths of the opposite sides change as the truck is lifted?   Yes / No

27. The least and greatest possible angle measures for ∠P and ∠Q are   and   .

28. The greatest possible height is when $m\angle P$ and $m\angle Q$ are   .

29. What is the maximum height that the vehicle lift can elevate the truck? Explain.

_____

_____

_____

Lesson Check • Do you UNDERSTAND?

Compare and Contrast How is Theorem 6-11 in this lesson different from Theorem 6-6 in the previous lesson? In what situations should you use each theorem? Explain.

For each theorem, circle the hypothesis and underline the conclusion.

30. Theorem 6-6

If a quadrilateral is a parallelogram, then its diagonals bisect each other.

31. Theorem 6-11

If the diagonals of a quadrilateral bisect each other, then the quadrilateral is a parallelogram.

Draw a line from each statement in Column A to the corresponding diagram in Column B.

Column A	Column B

32. A quadrilateral is a parallelogram.

33. The diagonals of a quadrilateral bisect each other.

34. Circle the word that describes how Theorem 6-6 and Theorem 6-11 are related.

contrapositive   converse   inverse

35. In which situations should you use each theorem? Explain.

_____

_____

_____

Math Success

Check off the vocabulary words that you understand.

☐ diagonal   ☐ parallelogram   ☐ quadrilateral

Rate how well you can _prove that a quadrilateral is a parallelogram_.

Need to review   0   2   4   6   8   10   Now I get it!

Lesson 6-3

6-4 | Properties of Rhombuses, Rectangles, and Squares

Vocabulary

● Review

1. Circle the segments that are *diagonals*.

$\overline{AG}$ $\overline{AC}$ $\overline{HD}$ $\overline{GC}$

$\overline{BF}$ $\overline{AE}$ $\overline{EG}$ $\overline{EF}$

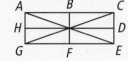

2. Is a *diagonal* ever a line or a ray?   Yes / No

3. The *diagonals* of quadrilateral *JKLM* are ☐ and ☐ .

● Vocabulary Builder

rhombus

rhombus (noun) RAHM **bus**

Definition: A **rhombus** is a parallelogram with four congruent sides.

Main Idea: A **rhombus** has four congruent sides but not necessarily four right angles.

Examples: diamond, square

● Use Your Vocabulary

Complete each statement with *always*, *sometimes*, or *never*.

4. A *rhombus* is __?__ a parallelogram.

5. A parallelogram is __?__ a *rhombus*.

6. A rectangle is __?__ a *rhombus*.

7. A square is __?__ a *rhombus*.

8. A *rhombus* is __?__ a square.

9. A *rhombus* is __?__ a hexagon.

Key Concept Special Parallelograms

A *rhombus* is a parallelogram with four congruent sides.

A *rectangle* is a parallelogram with four right angles.

A *square* is a parallelogram with four congruent sides and four right angles.

10. Write the words *rectangles*, *rhombuses*, and *squares* in the Venn diagram below to show that one special parallelogram has the properties of the other two.

Special Parallelograms

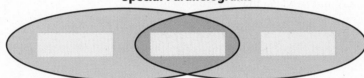

✓ **Problem 1** **Classifying Special Parallelograms**

Got It? Is □*EFGH* a *rhombus*, a *rectangle*, or a *square*? Explain.

11. Circle the number of sides marked congruent in the diagram.

| 1 | 2 | 3 | 4 |

12. Are any of the angles right angles?   Yes / No

13. Is □*EFGH* a rhombus, a rectangle, or a square? Explain.

_____

_____

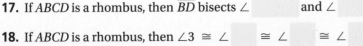

Theorems 6-13 and 6-14

Theorem 6-13 If a parallelogram is a rhombus, then its diagonals are perpendicular.

Theorem 6-14 If a parallelogram is a rhombus, then each diagonal bisects a pair of opposite angles.

Use the diagram at the right for Exercises 14–18.

14. If *ABCD* is a rhombus, then $\overline{AC} \perp$ ▢ .

15. If *ABCD* is a rhombus, then $\overline{AC}$ bisects ∠ ▢ and ∠ ▢ .

16. If *ABCD* is a rhombus, then ∠1 ≅ ∠2 ≅ ∠ ▢ ≅ ∠ ▢ .

17. If *ABCD* is a rhombus, then $\overline{BD}$ bisects ∠ ▢ and ∠ ▢ .

18. If *ABCD* is a rhombus, then ∠3 ≅ ∠ ▢ ≅ ∠ ▢ ≅ ∠ ▢ .

Lesson 6-4

Problem 2 **Finding Angle Measures**

Got It? What are the measures of the numbered angles in rhombus *PQRS*?

19. Circle the word that describes △*PQR* and △*RSP*.

equilateral   isosceles   right

20. Circle the congruent angles in △*PQR*. Underline the congruent angles in △*RSP*.

∠1   ∠2   ∠3   ∠4   ∠Q   ∠S

21. $m\angle 1 + m\angle 2 + 104 =$ ☐   **22.** $m\angle 1 + m\angle 2 =$ ☐   **23.** $m\angle 1 =$ ☐

24. Each diagonal of a rhombus __?__ a pair of opposite angles. _____

25. Circle the angles in rhombus *PQRS* that are congruent.

∠1   ∠2   ∠3   ∠4

26. $m\angle 1 =$ ☐ , $m\angle 2 =$ ☐ , $m\angle 3 =$ ☐ , and $m\angle 4 =$ ☐ .

 Theorem 6-15

Theorem 6-15 If a parallelogram is a rectangle, then its diagonals are congruent.

27. If *RSTU* is a rectangle, then $\overline{RT} \cong$ ☐ .

 Problem 3 **Finding Diagonal Length**

Got It? If *LN* = 4*x* − 17 and *MO* = 2*x* + 13, what are the lengths of the diagonals of rectangle *LMNO*?

Underline the correct word to complete each sentence.

28. *LMNO* is a rectangle / rhombus .

29. The diagonals of this figure are congruent / parallel .

30. Complete.

LN = ☐ , so 4*x* − 17 = ☐ .

31. Write and solve an equation to find the value of *x*.

32. Use the value of *x* to find the length of $\overline{LN}$.

33. The diagonals of a rectangle are congruent, so the length of each diagonal is ☐ .

Error Analysis Your class needs to find the value of x for which $\square DEFG$ is a rectangle. A classmate's work is shown below. What is the error? Explain.

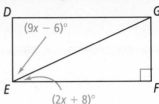

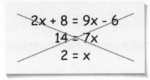

$2x + 8 = 9x - 6$

$14 = 7x$

$2 = x$

Write T for *true* or F for *false*.

_____ **34.** If a parallelogram is a rectangle, then each diagonal bisects a pair of opposite angles.

_____ **35.** If a parallelogram is a rhombus, then each diagonal bisects a pair of opposite angles.

36. If *DEFG* is a rectangle, $m\angle D = m\angle$ ____ $= m\angle$ ____ $= m\angle$ ____ .

37. $m\angle F =$ ____ .

38. What is the error? Explain.

_____

_____

_____

39. Find the value of x for which $\square DEFG$ is a rectangle.

40. The value of x for which $\square DEFG$ is a rectangle is ____ .

Math Success

Check off the vocabulary words that you understand.

☐ parallelogram   ☐ rhombus   ☐ rectangle   ☐ square   ☐ diagonal

Rate how well you can *find angles and diagonals of special parallelograms*.

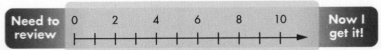

Lesson 6-4

Vocabulary

● Review

1. A *quadrilateral* is a polygon with ⬚ sides.

2. Cross out the figure that is NOT a *quadrilateral*.

● Vocabulary Builder

diagonal (noun) **dy AG uh nul**

Definition: A **diagonal** is a segment with endpoints at two nonadjacent vertices of a polygon.

Word Origin: The word **diagonal** comes from the Greek prefix *dia-*, which means "through," and *gonia*, which means "angle" or "corner."

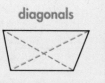

diagonals

● Use Your Vocabulary

3. Circle the polygon that has no *diagonal*.

triangle   quadrilateral   pentagon   hexagon

4. Circle the polygon that has two *diagonals*.

triangle   quadrilateral   pentagon   hexagon

5. Draw the *diagonals* from one vertex in each figure.

6. Write the number of diagonals you drew in each of the figures above.

pentagon: ⬚   hexagon: ⬚   heptagon: ⬚

Theorem 6-16 If the diagonals of a parallelogram are perpendicular, then the parallelogram is a rhombus.

Theorem 6-17 If one diagonal of a parallelogram bisects a pair of opposite angles, then the parallelogram is a rhombus.

7. Insert a right angle symbol in the parallelogram at the right to illustrate Theorem 6-16. Insert congruent marks to illustrate Theorem 6-17.

Use the diagram from Exercise 7 to complete Exercises 8 and 9.

8. If *ABCD* is a parallelogram and $\overline{AC} \perp$ ▢ , then *ABCD* is a rhombus.

9. If *ABCD* is a parallelogram, $\angle 1 \cong$ ▢ , and $\angle 3 \cong$ ▢ , then *ABCD* is a rhombus.

Theorem 6-18 If the diagonals of a parallelogram are congruent, then the parallelogram is a rectangle.

10. Insert congruent marks and right angle symbols in the parallelogram to the right to illustrate Theorem 6-18.

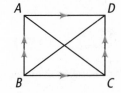

11. Use the diagram from Exercise 10 to complete the statement.

   If *ABCD* is a parallelogram, and $\overline{BD} \cong$ ▢ then *ABCD* is a rectangle.

12. Circle the parallelogram that has diagonals that are both perpendicular and congruent.

   parallelogram   rectangle   rhombus   square

 Problem 1 **Identifying Special Parallelograms**

Got It? A parallelogram has angle measures of 20, 160, 20, and 160. Can you conclude that it is a rhombus, a rectangle, or a square? Explain.

13. Draw a parallelogram in the box below. Label the angles with their measures. Use a protractor to help you make accurate angle measurements.

Underline the correct word or words to complete each sentence.

14. You do / do not know the lengths of the sides of the parallelogram.

15. You do / do not know the lengths of the diagonals.

16. The angles of a rectangle are all acute / obtuse / right angles.

17. The angles of a square are all acute / obtuse / right angles.

18. Can you conclude that the parallelogram is a rhombus, a rectangle, or a square? Explain.

_____

_____

_____

 Problem 2 **Using Properties of Special Parallelograms**

Got It? For what value of y is $\square DEFG$ a rectangle?

19. For $\square DEFG$ to be a parallelogram, the diagonals must __?__ each other.

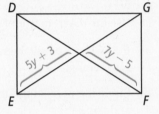

20. $EG = 2\ ($ _____ $)$ **21.** $DF = 2\ ($ _____ $)$

$=$ _____ $=$ _____

22. For $\square DEFG$ to be a rectangle, the diagonals must be __?__ .

23. Now write an equation and solve for y.

24. $\square DEFG$ is a rectangle for $y =$ _____ .

 Problem 3 **Using Properties of Parallelograms**

Got It? Suppose you are on the volunteer building team at the right. You are helping to lay out a square play area. How can you use properties of diagonals to locate the four corners?

25. You can cut two pieces of rope that will be the diagonals of the square play area. Cut them the same length because a parallelogram is a __?__ if the diagonals are congruent.

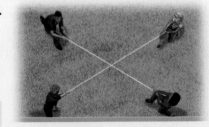

26. You join the two pieces of rope at their midpoints because a quadrilateral is a __?__ if the diagonals bisect each other.

27. You move so the diagonals are perpendicular because a parallelogram is a __?__ if the diagonals are perpendicular.

28. Explain why the polygon is a square when you pull the ropes taut.

Lesson Check • Do you UNDERSTAND?

Name all of the special parallelograms that have each property.

    A. Diagonals are perpendicular.   **B.** Diagonals are congruent.   **C.** Diagonals are angle bisectors.

    D. Diagonals bisect each other.   **E.** Diagonals are perpendicular bisectors of each other.

29. Place a ✓ in the box if the parallelogram has the property. Place an ✗ if it does not.

Property	Rectangle	Rhombus	Square
A			
B			
C			
D			
E			

Math Success

Check off the vocabulary words that you understand.

☐ rhombus   ☐ rectangle   ☐ square   ☐ diagonal

Rate how well you can *use properties of parallelograms*.

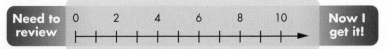

Vocabulary

● Review

Underline the correct word to complete each sentence.

1. An *isosceles* triangle always has two / three congruent sides.

2. An equilateral triangle is also a(n) *isosceles* / *right* triangle.

3. Cross out the length(s) that can NOT be side lengths of an *isosceles* triangle.

     3, 4, 5   8, 8, 10   3.6, 5, 3.6   7, 11, 11

● Vocabulary Builder

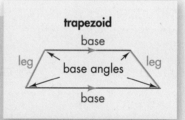

trapezoid (noun) TRAP **ih zoyd**

Related Words: base, leg

Definition: A **trapezoid** is a quadrilateral with exactly one pair of parallel sides.

Main Idea: The parallel sides of a **trapezoid** are called *bases*. The nonparallel sides are called *legs*. The two angles that share a base of a **trapezoid** are called *base angles*.

● Use Your Vocabulary

4. Cross out the figure that is NOT a *trapezoid*.

5. Circle the figure(s) than can be divided into two *trapezoids*. Then divide each figure that you circled into two *trapezoids*.

Theorems 6-19, 6-20, and 6-21

Theorem 6-19 If a quadrilateral is an isosceles trapezoid, then each pair of base angles is congruent.

Theorem 6-20 If a quadrilateral is an isosceles trapezoid, then its diagonals are congruent.

6. If *TRAP* is an isosceles trapezoid with bases $\overline{RA}$ and $\overline{TP}$, then $\angle T \cong \angle$ [ ] and $\angle R \cong \angle$ [ ].

7. Use Theorem 6-19 and your answers to Exercise 6 to draw congruence marks on the trapezoid at the right.

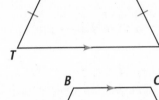

8. If *ABCD* is an isosceles trapezoid, then $\overline{AC} \cong$ [ ].

9. If *ABCD* is an isosceles trapezoid and $AB = 5$ cm, then $CD =$ [ ] cm.

10. Use Theorem 6-20 and your answer to Exercises 8 and 9 to label the diagram at the right.

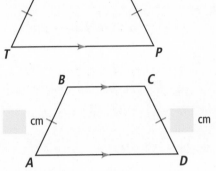

Theorem 6-21 Trapezoid Midsegment Theorem If a quadrilateral is a trapezoid, then

(1) the midsegment is parallel to the bases, and

(2) the length of the midsegment is half the sum of the lengths of the bases.

11. If *TRAP* is a trapezoid with midsegment $\overline{MN}$, then

(1) $\overline{MN} \parallel$ [ ] $\parallel$ [ ]   (2) $MN = \frac{1}{2} \left(\boxed{} + \boxed{} \right)$

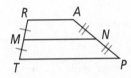

✓ **Problem 2** **Finding Angle Measures in Isosceles Trapezoids**

Got It? A fan has 15 angles meeting at the center. What are the measures of the base angles of the congruent isosceles trapezoids in its second ring?

Use the diagram at the right for Exercises 12–16.

12. Circle the number of isosceles triangles in each wedge. Underline the number of isosceles trapezoids in each wedge.

one	two	three	four

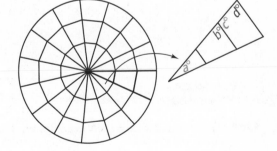

13. $a = 360 \div$ [ ] = [ ]

14. $b = \dfrac{180 - \boxed{}}{2} =$ [ ]

15. $c = 180 -$ [ ] = [ ]

16. $d = 180 -$ [ ] = [ ]

17. The measures of the base angles of the isosceles trapezoids are [ ] and [ ].

Lesson 6-6

Problem 3 Using the Midsegment Theorem

Got It? **Algebra** $\overline{MN}$ is the midsegment of trapezoid *PQRS*. What is *x*? What is *MN*?

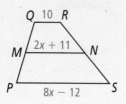

18. The value of *x* is found below. Write a reason for each step.

$MN = \frac{1}{2}(QR + PS)$

$2x + 11 = \frac{1}{2}[10 + (8x - 12)]$

$2x + 11 = \frac{1}{2}(8x - 2)$

$2x + 11 = 4x - 1$

$2x + 12 = 4x$

$12 = 2x$

$6 = x$

19. Use the value of *x* to find *MN*.

A *kite* is a quadrilateral with two pairs of consecutive sides congruent and no opposite sides congruent.

Theorem 6-22

Theorem 6-22 If a quadrilateral is a kite, then its diagonals are perpendicular.

20. If *ABCD* is a kite, then $\overline{AC} \perp$ ▢.

21. Use Theorem 6-22 and Exercise 20 to draw congruence marks and right angle symbol(s) on the kite at the right.

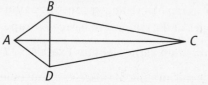

Problem 4 Finding Angle Measures in Kites

Got It? Quadrilateral *KLMN* is a kite. What are $m\angle 1$, $m\angle 2$, and $m\angle 3$?

22. Diagonals of a kite are perpendicular, so $m\angle 1 = $ ▢.

23. $\triangle KNM \cong \triangle KLM$ by SSS, so $m\angle 3 = m\angle NKM = $ ▢.

24. $m\angle 2 = m\angle 1 - m\angle$ ▢ by the Triangle Exterior Angle Theorem.

25. Solve for $m\angle 2$.

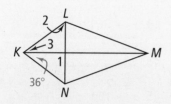

Lesson Check • Do you UNDERSTAND?

Compare and Contrast How is a kite similar to a rhombus? How is it different? Explain.

26. Place a ✓ in the box if the description fits the figure. Place an ✗ if it does not.

Kite	Description	Rhombus
☐	Quadrilateral	☐
☐	Perpendicular diagonals	☐
☐	Each diagonal bisects a pair of opposite angles.	☐
☐	Congruent opposite sides	☐
☐	Two pairs of congruent consecutive sides	☐
☐	Two pairs of congruent opposite angles	☐
☐	Supplementary consecutive angles	☐

27. How is a kite similar to a rhombus? How is it different? Explain.

_____

_____

_____

_____

_____

Math Success

Check off the vocabulary words that you understand.

☐ trapezoid   ☐ kite   ☐ base   ☐ leg   ☐ midsegment

Rate how well you can use *properties of trapezoids and kites*.

Need to review   0   2   4   6   8   10   Now I get it!

Polygons in the Coordinate Plane

Vocabulary

● Review

1. Draw a line from each item in Column A to the corresponding part of the *coordinate plane* in Column B.

Column A

origin

Quadrant I

Quadrant II

Quadrant III

Quadrant IV

x-axis

y-axis

Column B

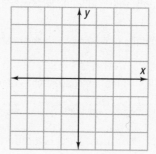

● Vocabulary Builder

classify (verb) **KLAS uh fy**

Definition: To **classify** is to organize by category or type.

Math Usage: You can **classify** figures by their properties.

Related Words: classification (noun), classified (adjective)

Example: Rectangles, squares, and rhombuses are **classified** as parallelograms.

● Use Your Vocabulary

Complete each statement with the correct word from the list. Use each word only once.

classification   classified   classify

2. Trapezoids are __?__ as quadrilaterals.

3. Taxonomy is a system of __?__ in biology.

4. Schools __?__ children by age.

Key Concept Formulas on the Coordinate Plane

	Distance Formula	Midpoint Formula	Slope Formula
Formula	$d = \sqrt{(x_2 - x_1)^2 + (y_2 - y_1)^2}$	$M = \left(\dfrac{x_1 + x_2}{2}, \dfrac{y_1 + y_2}{2}\right)$	$m = \dfrac{y_2 - y_1}{x_2 - x_1}$
When to Use It	To determine whether • sides are congruent • diagonals are congruent	To determine • the coordinates of the midpoint of a side • whether diagonals bisect each other	To determine whether • opposite sides are parallel • diagonals are perpendicular • sides are perpendicular

Decide when to use each formula. Write D for *Distance Formula*, M for *Midpoint Formula*, or S for *Slope Formula*.

5. You want to know whether diagonals bisect each other.

6. You want to find whether opposite sides of a quadrilateral are parallel.

7. You want to know whether sides of a polygon are congruent.

Problem 1 Classifying a Triangle

Got It? $\triangle DEF$ has vertices $D(0, 0)$, $E(1, 4)$, and $F(5, 2)$. Is $\triangle DEF$ *scalene, isosceles,* or *equilateral*?

8. Graph $\triangle DEF$ on the coordinate plane at the right.

Use the Distance Formula to find the length of each side.

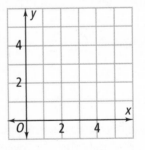

9. $EF = \sqrt{\left(5 - \boxed{}\right)^2 + \left(2 - \boxed{}\right)^2}$

$= \sqrt{\boxed{} + \boxed{}}$

$= \sqrt{\boxed{}}$

10. $DE = \sqrt{\left(1 - \boxed{}\right)^2 + \left(4 - \boxed{}\right)^2}$

$= \sqrt{\boxed{} + \boxed{}}$

$= \sqrt{\boxed{}}$

11. $DF = \sqrt{\left(5 - \boxed{}\right)^2 + \left(2 - \boxed{}\right)^2}$

$= \sqrt{\boxed{} + \boxed{}}$

$= \sqrt{\boxed{}}$

12. What type of triangle is $\triangle DEF$? Explain.

Lesson 6-7

Problem 2 Classifying a Parallelogram

Got It? ▱*MNPQ* has vertices *M*(0, 1), *N*(−1, 4), *P*(2, 5), and *Q*(3, 2). Is ▱*MNPQ* a rectangle? Explain.

13. Find *MP* and *NQ* to determine whether the diagonals $\overline{MP}$ and $\overline{NQ}$ are congruent.

$$MP = \sqrt{\left(2 - \boxed{}\right)^2 + \left(5 - \boxed{}\right)^2} \qquad NQ = \sqrt{\left(3 - \boxed{}\right)^2 + \left(2 - \boxed{}\right)^2}$$

$$= \sqrt{\boxed{} + \boxed{}} \qquad\qquad = \sqrt{\boxed{} + \boxed{}}$$

$$= \sqrt{\boxed{}} \qquad\qquad\qquad = \sqrt{\boxed{}}$$

14. Is ▱*MNPQ* a rectangle? Explain.

_____

_____

Problem 3 Classifying a Quadrilateral

Got It? An isosceles trapezoid has vertices *A*(0, 0), *B*(2, 4), *C*(6, 4), and *D*(8, 0). What special quadrilateral is formed by connecting the midpoints of the sides of *ABCD*?

15. Draw the trapezoid on the coordinate plane at the right.

16. Find the coordinates of the midpoints of each side.

$\overline{AB}$

$$\left(\frac{0 + \boxed{}}{2}, \frac{0 + \boxed{}}{2}\right) = \left(\boxed{}, \boxed{}\right)$$

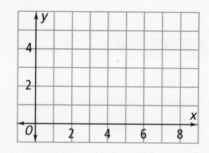

$\overline{CD}$ $\overline{BC}$ $\overline{AD}$

17. Draw the midpoints on the trapezoid and connect them. Judging by appearance, what type of special quadrilateral did you draw? Circle the most precise answer.

kite   parallelogram   rhombus   trapezoid

18. To verify your answer to Exercise 17, find the slopes of the segments.

connecting midpoints of $\overline{AB}$ and $\overline{BC}$:   connecting midpoints of $\overline{BC}$ and $\overline{CD}$:

connecting midpoints of $\overline{CD}$ and $\overline{AD}$:   connecting midpoints of $\overline{AD}$ and $\overline{AB}$:

19. Are the slopes of opposite segments equal?   Yes / No

20. Are consecutive segments perpendicular?   Yes / No

21. The special quadrilateral is a ___?___ .

Error Analysis A student says that the quadrilateral with vertices $D(1, 2)$, $E(0, 7)$, $F(5, 6)$, and $G(7, 0)$ is a rhombus because its diagonals are perpendicular. What is the student's error?

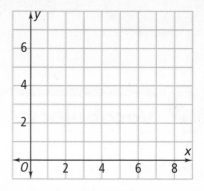

22. Draw *DEFG* on the coordinate plane at the right.

23. Underline the correct words to complete Theorem 6-16.

If the diagonals of a   parallelogram / polygon   are perpendicular,

then the   parallelogram / polygon   is a rhombus.

24. Check whether *DEFG* is a parallelogram.

slope of $\overline{DE}$: $\dfrac{7 - \boxed{}}{0 - \boxed{}} = \boxed{}$ slope of $\overline{FG}$: $\dfrac{0 - \boxed{}}{7 - \boxed{}} = \boxed{}$

slope of $\overline{DG}$: $\dfrac{0 - \boxed{}}{7 - \boxed{}} = \boxed{}$ slope of $\overline{EF}$: $\dfrac{6 - \boxed{}}{5 - \boxed{}} = \boxed{}$

25. Are both pairs of opposite sides parallel?   Yes / No

26. Find the slope of diagonal $\overline{DF}$.   **27.** Find the slope of diagonal $\overline{EG}$.

28. Are the diagonals perpendicular?   Yes / No

29. Explain the student's error.

_____

_____

Math Success

Check off the vocabulary words that you understand.

☐ distance   ☐ midpoint   ☐ slope

Rate how well you can *classify quadrilaterals in the coordinate plane*.

Need to review   0   2   4   6   8   10   Now I get it!

6-8 Applying Coordinate Geometry

Vocabulary

● Review

Write T for *true* or F for *false*.

_____ **1.** The *vertex* of an angle is the endpoint of two rays.

_____ **2.** When you name angles using three points, the *vertex* gets named first.

_____ **3.** A polygon has the same number of sides and *vertices*.

4. Circle the *vertex* of the largest angle in △ABC at the right.

5. Circle the figure that has the greatest number of *vertices*.

| hexagon | kite | rectangle | trapezoid |

● Vocabulary Builder

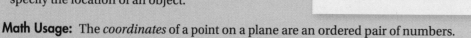

coordinates (noun) **koh AWR din its**

Definition: *Coordinates* are numbers or letters that specify the location of an object.

Math Usage: The *coordinates* of a point on a plane are an ordered pair of numbers.

Main Idea: The first *coordinate* of an ordered pair is the *x-coordinate*. The second is the *y-coordinate*.

coordinates

(−1, 3)

x-coordinate   y-coordinate

● Use Your Vocabulary

Draw a line from each point in Column A to its *coordinates* in Column B.

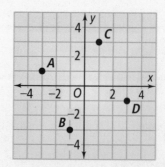

Column A		Column B
6. A		(−1, −3)
7. B		(1, 3)
8. C		(3, −1)
9. D		(−3, 1)

 **Problem 1** **Naming Coordinates**

Got It? *RECT* is a rectangle with height *a* and length 2*b*.
The *y*-axis bisects $\overline{EC}$ and $\overline{RT}$. What are the coordinates
of the vertices of *RECT*?

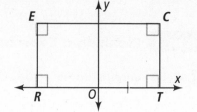

10. Use the information in the problem to mark
all segments that are congruent to $\overline{OT}$.

11. Rectangle *RECT* has length [ ] ,

so *RT* = [ ] and *RO* = *OT* = [ ] .

12. The coordinates of *O* are ([ ] , 0), so the coordinates of *T* are ([ ] , 0), and the

coordinates of *R* are (− [ ] , 0).

13. Rectangle *RECT* has height *a*, so *TC* = *RE* = [ ] .

14. The coordinates of *C* are ([ ] , [ ]), so the coordinates of *E* are ([ ] , [ ]).

15. Why is it helpful that one side of rectangle *RECT* is on the *x*-axis and the figure is
centered on the *y*-axis.

_____

_____

 Problem 2 **Using Variable Coordinates**

Got It? Reasoning The diagram at the right shows
a general parallelogram with a vertex at the origin and
one side along the *x*-axis. Explain why the *x*-coordinate
of *B* is the sum of 2*a* and 2*b*.

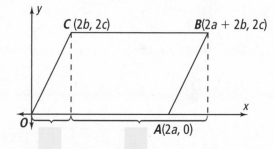

16. Complete the diagram.

17. Complete the reasoning model below.

Think	Write
Opposite sides of a parallelogram are congruent.	*OA* = [ ] = [ ]
The *x*-coordinate is the sum of the lengths in the brackets.	The *x*-coordinate of *B* is [ ] + [ ] = [ ] .

18. Explain why the *x*-coordinate of *B* is the sum of 2*a* + 2*b*.

_____

_____

_____

Lesson 6-8

You can use coordinate geometry and algebra to prove theorems in geometry. This kind of proof is called a *coordinate proof*.

Problem 3 **Planning a Coordinate Proof**

Got It? Plan a coordinate proof of the Triangle Midsegment Theorem (Theorem 5-1).

19. Underline the correct words to complete Theorem 5-1.

If a segment joins the vertices / midpoints of two sides of a triangle, then the

segment is perpendicular / parallel to the third side, and is half its length.

20. Write the coordinates of the vertices of △ABC on the grid below. Use multiples of 2 to name the coordinates.

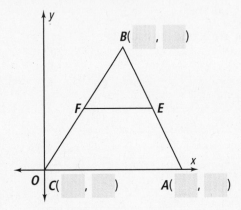

21. **Reasoning** Why should you make the coordinates of A and B multiples of 2?

22. Complete the *Given* and *Prove*.

Given: E is the _?_ of $\overline{AB}$ and F is the _?_ of $\overline{BC}$.

Prove: $\overline{EF} \parallel \overline{AC}$, and $EF = \frac{1}{2} AC$

23. Circle the formula you need to use to prove $\overline{EF} \parallel \overline{AC}$. Underline the formula you need to use to prove $EF = \frac{1}{2} AC$.

Distance Formula	Midpoint Formula	Slope Formula

Underline the correct word to complete each sentence.

24. If the slopes of $\overline{EF}$ and $\overline{AC}$ are equal, then $\overline{EF}$ and $\overline{AC}$ are congruent / parallel .

25. If you know the lengths of $\overline{EF}$ and $\overline{AC}$, then you can add / compare them.

26. Write three steps you must do before writing the plan for a coordinate proof.

Lesson Check • Do you UNDERSTAND?

Error Analysis A classmate says the endpoints of the midsegment of the trapezoid at the right are $\left(\frac{b}{2}, \frac{c}{2}\right)$ and $\left(\frac{d+a}{2}, \frac{c}{2}\right)$. What is your classmate's error? Explain.

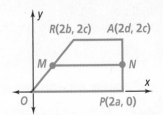

27. What is the Midpoint Formula?

$$M = \left(\frac{x_1 + x_2}{\boxed{}}, \frac{y_1 + y_2}{\boxed{}}\right)$$

28. Find the midpoint of each segment to find the endpoints of $\overline{MN}$.

$\overline{OR}$

$\overline{AP}$

29. The endpoints of the midsegment are (___ , ___) and (___ , ___).

30. How are the endpoints that your classmate found different from the endpoints that you found in Exercise 28?

_____

_____

31. What is your classmate's error? Explain.

_____

_____

_____

Math Success

Check off the vocabulary words that you understand.

☐ coordinate geometry   ☐ coordinate proof   ☐ variable coordinates

Rate how well you can *use properties of special figures.*

Lesson 6-8

Proofs Using Coordinate Geometry

Vocabulary

● Review

1. Circle the *Midpoint Formula* for a segment in the coordinate plane. Underline the *Distance Formula* for a segment in the coordinate plane.

$$M = \left(\frac{x_1 + x_2}{2}, \frac{y_1 + y_2}{2}\right) \qquad d = \sqrt{(x_2 - x_1)^2 + (y_2 - y_1)^2} \qquad m = \frac{y_2 - y_1}{x_2 - x_1}$$

2. Circle the *Midpoint Formula* for a segment on a number line. Underline the *Distance Formula* for a segment on a number line.

$$M = \frac{x_1 + x_2}{2} \qquad d = |x_1 - x_2| \qquad m = \frac{x_1 - x_2}{2}$$

● Vocabulary Builder

variable (noun) VEHR **ee uh bul**

> *x* and *y* are often used as **variables**.

Related Words: vary (verb), variable (adjective)

Definition: A **variable** is a symbol (usually a letter) that represents one or more numbers.

Math Usage: A **variable** represents an unknown number in equations and inequalities.

● Use Your Vocabulary

Underline the correct word to complete each sentence.

3. An interest rate that can change is a *variable* / vary interest rate.

4. You can *variable* / vary your appearance by changing your hair color.

5. The amount of daylight *variables* / varies from summer to winter.

6. Circle the *variable(s)* in each expression below.

$3n$ $\qquad\qquad$ $4 + x$ $\qquad\qquad$ $p^2 - 2p$ $\qquad\qquad$ $\frac{4}{y}$

7. Cross out the expressions that do NOT contain a *variable*.

$2 + m$ $\qquad\qquad$ $36 \div (2 \cdot 3)$ $\qquad\qquad$ $9a^2 - 4a$ $\qquad\qquad$ $8 - (15 \div 3)$

Problem 1 Writing a Coordinate Proof

Got It? Reasoning You want to prove that the midpoint of the hypotenuse of a right triangle is equidistant from the three vertices. What is the advantage of using coordinates $O(0, 0)$, $E(0, 2b)$, and $F(2a, 0)$ rather than $O(0, 0)$, $E(0, b)$, and $F(a, 0)$?

8. Label each triangle.

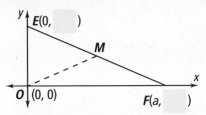 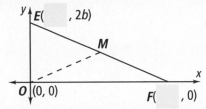

9. Use the Midpoint Formula $M = \left(\dfrac{x_1 + x_2}{2}, \dfrac{y_1 + y_2}{2} \right)$ to find the coordinates of M in each triangle.

Fisrt Triangle

$$\left(\frac{a + 0}{2}, \frac{\boxed{} + \boxed{}}{2} \right) = \left(\frac{a}{2}, \frac{\boxed{}}{2} \right)$$

Second Triangle

$$\left(\frac{\boxed{} + \boxed{}}{2}, \frac{0 + 2b}{2} \right) = \left(\boxed{}, b \right)$$

10. Use the Distance Formula, $d = \sqrt{(x_2 - x_1)^2 + (y_2 - y_1)^2}$ and your answers to Exercise 9 to verify that $EM = FM = OM$ for the first triangle.

EM	FM	OM

11. Use the Distance Formula, $d = \sqrt{(x_2 - x_1)^2 + (y_2 - y_1)^2}$ and your answers to Exercise 9 to verify that $EM = FM = OM$ for the second triangle.

EM	FM	OM

12. Which set of coordinates is easier to use? Explain.

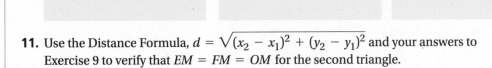

Lesson 6-9

Got It? Write a coordinate proof of the Triangle Midsegment Theorem (Theorem 5-1).

Given: E is the midpoint of $\overline{AB}$ and

F is the midpoint of $\overline{BC}$

Prove: $\overline{EF} \parallel \overline{AC}$, $EF = \frac{1}{2}AC$

Use the diagram at the right.

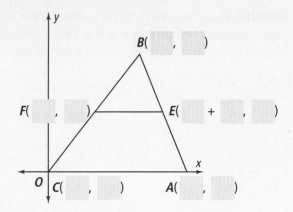

13. Label the coordinates of point C.

14. **Reasoning** Why should you make the coordinates of A and B multiples of 2?

15. Label the coordinates of A and B in the diagram.

16. Use the Midpoint Formula to find the coordinates of E and F. Label the coordinates in the diagram.

coordinates of E

$$\left(\frac{\boxed{} + \boxed{}}{2}, \frac{\boxed{} + \boxed{}}{2} \right) = \left(\boxed{}, \boxed{} \right)$$

coordinates of F

$$\left(\frac{\boxed{} + \boxed{}}{2}, \frac{\boxed{} + \boxed{}}{2} \right) = \left(\boxed{}, \boxed{} \right)$$

17. Use the Slope Formula to determine whether $\overline{EF} \parallel \overline{AC}$.

$$\text{slope of } \overline{EF} = \frac{\boxed{} - \boxed{}}{\boxed{} - \boxed{}} = \boxed{}$$

$$\text{slope of } \overline{AC} = \frac{\boxed{} - \boxed{}}{\boxed{} - \boxed{}} = \boxed{}$$

18. Is $\overline{EF} \parallel \overline{AC}$? Explain.

19. Use the Distance Formula to determine whether $EF = \frac{1}{2}AC$.

$$EF = \sqrt{(\boxed{} - \boxed{})^2 + (\boxed{} - \boxed{})^2} = \sqrt{(a)^2 + (0)^2} = \boxed{}$$

$$AC = \sqrt{(\boxed{} - \boxed{})^2 + (\boxed{} - \boxed{})^2} = \sqrt{(2a)^2 + (0)^2} = \boxed{}$$

20. $\frac{1}{2}AC = \frac{1}{2} \cdot \boxed{} = \boxed{} = EF$

Lesson Check • Do you know HOW?

Use coordinate geometry to prove that the diagonals of a rectangle are congruent.

21. Draw rectangle $PQRS$ with P at $(0, 0)$.

22. Label $Q(a,)$, $R(, b)$, and $S(,)$.

23. Complete the *Given* and *Prove* statements.

Given: $PQRS$ is a [   ].   Prove: $\overline{PR} \cong$ [   ]

24. Use the Distance Formula to find the length of each diagonal.

$$PR = \sqrt{(\quad - \quad)^2 + (\quad - \quad)^2} = \boxed{}$$

$$QS = \sqrt{(\quad - \quad)^2 + (\quad - \quad)^2} = \boxed{}$$

25. $PR = \boxed{}$, so $\overline{PR} \cong \boxed{}$.

Lesson Check • Do you UNDERSTAND?

Error Analysis Your classmate places a trapezoid on the coordinate plane. What is the error?

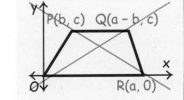

26. Check whether the coordinates are for an isosceles trapezoid.

$$OP = \sqrt{(b - \quad)^2 + (c - \quad)^2} = \boxed{}$$

$$QR = \sqrt{(a - \quad)^2 + (0 - \quad)^2} = \boxed{}$$

27. Does the trapezoid look like an isosceles triangle?   Yes / No

28. Describe your classmate's error.

_____

Math Success

Check off the vocabulary words that you understand.

☐ proof   ☐ theorem   ☐ coordinate plane   ☐ coordinate geometry

Rate how well you can *prove theorems using coordinate geometry.*

Vocabulary

● Review

1. Write a *ratio* to compare 9 red marbles to 16 blue marbles in three ways.

9 to ▢ $\dfrac{}{16}$ ▢ : ▢

In simplest form, write the *ratio* of vowels to consonants in each word below.

2. comparison

$\dfrac{}{}$

3. geometry

▢ to ▢

4. ratio

▢ : ▢

5. Cross out the *ratio* that is NOT equivalent to 12 to 8.

6 : 2   9 to 6 $\dfrac{24}{16}$ 48 : 32

● Vocabulary Builder

> A **proportion** always includes an **equal** sign, =.

proportion (noun) **pruh PAWR shun**

Other Word Form: proportional (adjective)

Definition: A **proportion** is an equation stating that two ratios are equal.

Examples: $\dfrac{2}{3} = \dfrac{8}{12}$ and $\dfrac{1}{2} = \dfrac{5}{10}$ are **proportions.**

● Use Your Vocabulary

6. Write 3 or 6 to make each *proportion* true.

$\dfrac{2}{3} = \dfrac{}{9}$ $\dfrac{}{4} = \dfrac{6}{8}$ $\dfrac{1}{3} = \dfrac{2}{}$ $\dfrac{5}{} = \dfrac{10}{6}$

Underline the correct word to complete each sentence.

7. Distance on a map is proportion / proportional to the actual distance.

8. The number of ounces in 3 lb is in proportion / proportional to the number of ounces in 1 lb.

Key Concept Properties of Proportions

Cross Products Property In a proportion $\frac{a}{b} = \frac{c}{d}$, where $b \neq 0$ and $d \neq 0$, the product of the extremes a and d equals the product of the means b and c.

$$\frac{a}{b} = \frac{c}{d}$$

$$a \cdot d = b \cdot \boxed{}$$

$$\boxed{} = \boxed{}$$

Equivalent Forms of Proportions

Property 1	Property 2	Property 3
$\frac{a}{b} = \frac{c}{d}$ is equivalent to	$\frac{a}{b} = \frac{c}{d}$ is equivalent to	$\frac{a}{b} = \frac{c}{d}$ is equivalent to
$\frac{b}{a} = \frac{d}{c}$.	$\frac{a}{c} = \frac{b}{d}$.	$\frac{a+b}{b} = \frac{c+d}{d}$.

9. Identify the *means* and *extremes* in the proportion $\frac{2}{3} = \frac{4}{x}$.

Means $\boxed{}$ and $\boxed{}$ **Extremes** $\boxed{}$ and $\boxed{}$

Identify the *Property of Proportions* each statement illustrates.

10. If $\frac{3}{12} = \frac{1}{4}$, then $\frac{3}{1} = \frac{12}{4}$.

11. If $\frac{4}{5} = \frac{8}{10}$, then $4(10) = 5(8)$.

12. If $\frac{1}{3} = \frac{3}{9}$, then $\frac{3}{1} = \frac{9}{3}$.

13. If $\frac{3}{4} = \frac{x}{y}$, then $\frac{7}{4} = \frac{x+y}{y}$.

Problem 1 Writing a Ratio

Got It? A bonsai tree is 18 in. wide and stands 2 ft tall. What is the ratio of the width of the bonsai to its height?

14. The bonsai is $\boxed{}$ in. wide and $\boxed{}$ in. tall.

15. Write the same ratio three different ways.

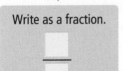

width of bonsai to height of bonsai

Write using the word "to."	Write as a fraction.	Write using a colon.
$\boxed{}$ to $\boxed{}$	$\dfrac{\boxed{}}{\boxed{}}$	$\boxed{}$: $\boxed{}$

Problem 3 **Using an Extended Ratio**

Got It? The lengths of the sides of a triangle are in the extended ratio $4:7:9$.
The perimeter is 60 cm. What are the lengths of the sides?

16. Label the triangle at the right. Use the extended ratio to write
an expression for each side length.

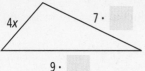

17. Complete the model to write an equation.

| Relate | the sum of the side lengths | is | the perimeter |

perimeter = [ ]

| Write | $4x +$ [ ] $+$ [ ] $=$ | 60 |

18. Use the justifications below to find the value of x.

$4x +$ [ ] $+$ [ ] $= 60$ Write the equation.

[ ] $\cdot x = 60$ Combine like terms.

$\dfrac{[\ ] \cdot x}{[\ ]} = \dfrac{60}{[\ ]}$ Divide each side by [ ].

$x = $ [ ]   Simplify.

19. Use the value of x to find each side length.

$4x = 4 \cdot$ [ ] 7[ ] $= 7 \cdot$ [ ]   [ ] $=$ [ ] $\cdot$ [ ]

$ = $ [ ] $ = $ [ ] $ = $ [ ]

20. The lengths of the sides of the triangle are [ ] cm, [ ] cm, and [ ] cm.

 Problem 4 **Solving a Proportion**

Got It? Algebra What is the solution of the proportion $\frac{9}{2} = \frac{a}{14}$?

21. Write a justification for each statement below.

$\dfrac{9}{2} = \dfrac{a}{14}$ _____

$9(14) = 2a$ _____

$126 = 2a$ _____

$\dfrac{126}{2} = \dfrac{2a}{2}$ _____

$a = 63$ _____

Problem 5 | **Writing Equivalent Proportions**

Got It? Use the proportion $\frac{x}{6} = \frac{y}{7}$. What ratio completes the equivalent proportion $\frac{6}{x} = \frac{\blacksquare}{\blacksquare}$? Justify your answer.

22. Use the diagram at the right. Draw arrows from the x and the 6 in the original proportion to the x and the 6 in the new proportion.

$$\frac{x}{6} = \frac{y}{7} \qquad\qquad \frac{6}{x} = \frac{\blacksquare}{\blacksquare}$$

23. Circle the proportion equivalent to $\frac{a}{b} = \frac{c}{d}$ that you can use.

$$\frac{b}{a} = \frac{d}{c} \qquad\qquad \frac{a}{c} = \frac{b}{d} \qquad\qquad \frac{a+b}{b} = \frac{c+d}{d}$$

24. Complete: $\frac{x}{6} = \frac{y}{7}$ is equivalent to $\frac{6}{x} = $ _____ .

Lesson Check • Do you UNDERSTAND?

Error Analysis What is the error in the solution of the proportion at the right?

25. Circle the means of the proportion. Then underline the extremes.

3	4	7	x

26. Write each product.

Means ☐ · ☐ = ☐   **Extremes** ☐ · ☐ = ☐

$$\frac{7}{3} = \frac{4}{x}$$
$$28 = 3x$$
$$\frac{28}{3} = x$$

27. What is the error in the solution of the proportion?

_____

28. Now solve the proportion correctly.

Math Success

Check off the vocabulary words that you understand.

☐ proportion   ☐ means   ☐ extremes   ☐ Cross Products Property

Rate how well you can *solve proportions*.

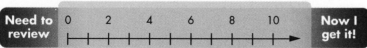

Vocabulary

● **Review**

1. What does it mean when two segments are *congruent*?

_____

2. What does it mean when two angles are *congruent*?

_____

3. Measure each segment. Then circle the congruent segments.

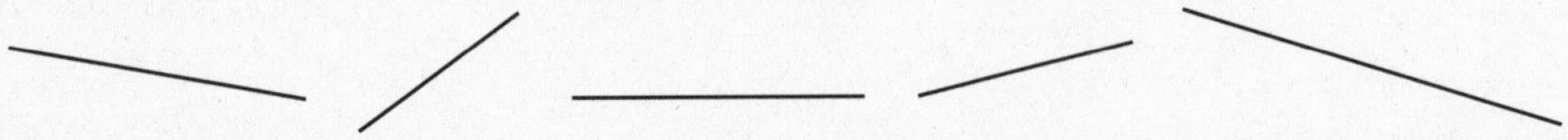

● **Vocabulary Builder**

| similar | (adjective) | SIM uh lur |

Other Word Forms: similarity (noun), similarly (adverb)

Definition: Things that are **similar** are alike, but not identical.

Math Usage: Figures that have the same shape but not necessarily the same size are **similar.**

> The symbol for similar is ~.

● **Use Your Vocabulary**

4. How are the two squares at the right *similar*?

_____

5. How are the two squares NOT *similar*?

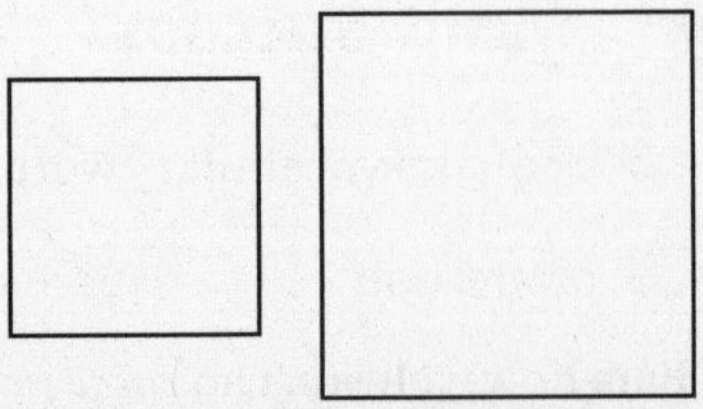

_____

Key Concept   Similar Polygons

Two polygons are **similar polygons** if corresponding angles are congruent and if the lengths of corresponding sides are proportional.

ABCD ~ GHIJ. Draw a line from each angle in Column A to its corresponding angle in Column B.

Column A	Column B
6. ∠A	∠H
7. ∠B	∠J
8. ∠C	∠G
9. ∠D	∠I

10. Complete the extended proportion to show that corresponding sides of *ABCD* and *GHIJ* are proportional.

$$\frac{AB}{GH} = \frac{BC}{\boxed{}} = \frac{\boxed{}}{IJ} = \frac{AD}{\boxed{}}$$

✓ Problem 1   Understanding Similarity

Got It? *DEFG ~ HJKL*. What are the pairs of congruent angles? What is the extended proportion for the ratios of the lengths of corresponding sides?

11. Complete each congruence statement.

∠D ≅ ∠ □

∠E ≅ ∠ □

∠K ≅ ∠ □

∠L ≅ ∠ □

12. Complete the extended proportion.

$$\frac{DE}{HJ} = \frac{EF}{\boxed{}} = \frac{\boxed{}}{KL} = \frac{\boxed{}}{\boxed{}}$$

A *scale factor* is the ratio of the lengths of corresponding sides of similar triangles.

✓ Problem 2   Determining Similarity

Got It? Are the polygons similar? If they are, write a similarity statement and give the scale factor.

13. Circle the short sides of each rectangle. Underline the long sides.

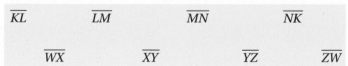

$\overline{KL}$	$\overline{LM}$	$\overline{MN}$	$\overline{NK}$
$\overline{WX}$	$\overline{XY}$	$\overline{YZ}$	$\overline{ZW}$

14. Write the ratios of corresponding sides in simplest form.

$$\frac{KL}{XY} = \frac{10}{15} = \frac{}{\boxed{}} \qquad \frac{LM}{YZ} = \frac{15}{\boxed{}} = \frac{}{\boxed{}} \qquad \frac{MN}{ZW} = \frac{\boxed{}}{15} = \frac{}{\boxed{}} \qquad \frac{NK}{WX} = \frac{\boxed{}}{\boxed{}} = \frac{}{\boxed{}}$$

Lesson 7-2

15. Place a ✓ in the box if the statement is correct. Place an ✗ if it is incorrect.

☐ $KLMN \sim XYZW$ and the scale factor is $\frac{2}{3}$.

☐ $KLMN \sim XYZW$ and the scale factor is $\frac{3}{4}$.

☐ The polygons are not similar.

 Problem 3 **Using Similar Polygons**

Got It? $ABCD \sim EFGD$. What is the value of y?

16. Circle the side of $ABCD$ that corresponds to $\overline{EF}$.

$\overline{AB}$ $\qquad$ $\overline{BC}$ $\qquad$ $\overline{CD}$ $\qquad$ $\overline{AD}$

17. Use the justifications at the right to find the value of y.

$\dfrac{EF}{\boxed{}} = \dfrac{ED}{AD}$ $\qquad$ Corresponding sides of similar polygons are proportional.

$\dfrac{y}{\boxed{}} = \dfrac{6}{9}$ $\qquad$ Substitute.

$9y = \boxed{}$ $\qquad$ Cross Products Property

$y = \boxed{}$ $\qquad$ Divide each side by 9.

 Problem 4 **Using Similarity**

Got It? A rectangular poster's design is 6 in. high by 10 in. wide. What are the dimensions of the largest complete poster that will fit in a space 3 ft high by 4 ft wide?

18. Determine how many times the design can be enlarged.

Height: 3 ft = ▨ in. $\qquad\qquad$ **Width:** 4 ft = ▨ in.

▨ in. ÷ 6 in. = 6 $\qquad\qquad\qquad$ ▨ in. ÷ 10 in. = 4.8

The design can be enlarged at most ▨ times.

19. Let x represent the height of the poster. Write a proportion and solve for x.

20. The largest complete poster that will fit is ▨ in. by ▨ in.

Got It? Use the scale drawing of the bridge. What is the actual height of the towers above the roadway?

21. Use a centimeter ruler to measure the height of the towers above the roadway in the scale drawing. Label the drawing with the height.

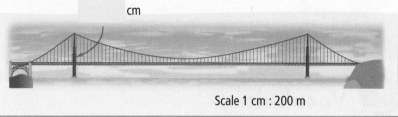
cm

Scale 1 cm : 200 m

22. Identify the variable.

Let $h =$ the __?__ of the towers.

23. Use the information on the scale drawing to write a proportion. Then solve to find the value of the variable.

$$\left(Hint: \frac{1}{200} = \frac{\text{tower height in drawing (cm)}}{\text{actual height (m)}} \right)$$

24. The actual height of the towers above the roadway is ____ m.

Lesson Check • Do you UNDERSTAND?

The triangles at the right are similar. What are three similarity statements for the triangles?

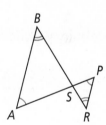

25. The triangles are △ _____ and △ _____.

26. $\angle A \cong \angle$ _____ $\angle B \cong \angle$ _____ $\angle S \cong \angle$ _____

27. $\triangle ABS \sim$ _____ $\triangle BSA \sim$ _____ $\triangle SAB \sim$ _____

Math Success

Check off the vocabulary words that you understand.

☐ similar   ☐ extended proportion   ☐ scale factor   ☐ scale drawing

Rate how well you can *identify and apply similar polygons.*

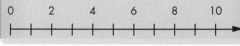

Need to review 0 2 4 6 8 10 Now I get it!

7-3 Proving Triangles Similar

Vocabulary

● Review

Write the converse of each *theorem*.

1. If the diagonals of a parallelogram are perpendicular, then the parallelogram is a rhombus.

If _____,

then _____.

2. If a point is on the perpendicular bisector of a segment, then it is equidistant from the endpoints of the segment.

If _____,

then _____.

● Vocabulary Builder

verify (verb) VEHR **uh fy**

Related Word: proof (noun)

Definition: To **verify** something means to find the truth or accuracy of it.

Math Usage: A proof is a way to **verify** a conjecture or statement.

● Use Your Vocabulary

Write T for *true* or F for *false*.

_____ **3.** You can *verify* that two triangles are similar by showing that corresponding angles are proportional.

_____ **4.** You can use properties, postulates, and previously proven *theorems* to *verify* steps in a proof.

Key Concept Postulate 7–1, Theorem 7–1, Theorem 7–2

Postulate 7-1 Angle-Angle Similarity (AA ~) Postulate If two angles of one triangle are congruent to two angles of another triangle, then the triangles are similar.

Theorem 7-1 Side-Angle-Side Similarity (SAS ~) Theorem If an angle of one triangle is congruent to an angle of a second triangle, and the sides that include the two angles are proportional, then the triangles are similar.

Theorem 7-2 Side-Side-Side Similarity (SSS ~) Theorem If the corresponding sides of two triangles are proportional, then the triangles are similar.

5. Write the postulate or theorem that proves the triangles similar.

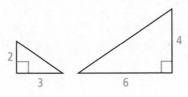

Problem 1 **Using the AA~Postulate**

Got It? Are the two triangles similar? How do you know?

6. Complete the diagram.

7. Are the triangles similar? Explain.

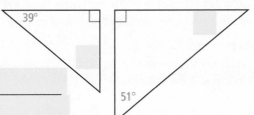

Problem 2 **Verifying Triangle Similarity**

Got It? Are the triangles similar? If so, write a similarity statement for the triangles and explain how you know the triangles are similar.

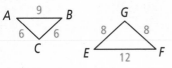

8. Write ratios for each pair of corresponding sides.

9. Circle the postulate or theorem you can use to verify that the triangles are similar.

    AA ~ Postulate   SAS ~ Theorem   SSS ~ Theorem

10. Complete the similarity statement.

    $\triangle ABC \sim \triangle$

Problem 3 Proving Triangles Similar

Got It? Given: $\overline{AC} \parallel \overline{MP}$ Prove: $\triangle ABC \sim \triangle PBM$

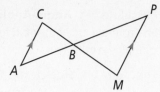

11. The proof is shown below. Write a reason from the box for each statement.

> AA ~ Postulate
>
> Given
>
> Vertical angles are congruent.

Statements	Reasons
1) $\overline{AC} \parallel \overline{MP}$	1) _____
2) $\angle A \cong \angle P$	2) If parallel lines are cut by a transversal, alternate interior angles are congruent.
3) $\angle ABC \cong \angle PBM$	3) _____
4) $\triangle ABC \sim \triangle PBM$	4) _____

Problem 4 Finding Lengths in Similar Triangles

Got It? **Reasoning** Why is it important that the ground be flat to use the method of indirect measurement illustrated in the problem below? Explain.

Before rock climbing, Darius wants to know how high he will climb. He places a mirror on the ground and walks backward until he can see the top of the cliff in the mirror.

12. If the ground is NOT flat, will $\angle HTV$ and $\angle JSV$ be right angles?   Yes / No

13. If the ground is NOT flat, will you be able to find congruent angles?   Yes / No

14. Why is it important that the ground be flat? Explain.

_____

_____

Lesson Check • Do you UNDERSTAND?

Error Analysis Which solution for the value of *x* in the figure at the right is *not* correct? Explain.

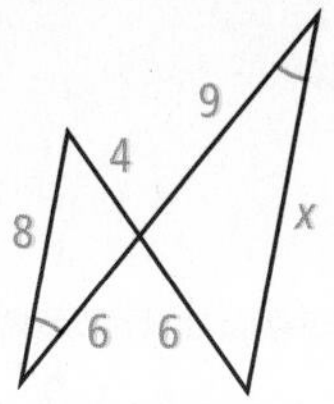

A.

$$\frac{4}{8} = \frac{8}{x}$$
$$4x = 72$$
$$x = 18$$

B.

$$\frac{8}{x} = \frac{4}{6}$$
$$48 = 4x$$
$$12 = x$$

15. Write the side lengths of the triangles.

Triangle	Shortest Side	Longest Side	Third Side
Larger	6		
Smaller			

16. Write ratios to compare the lengths of the corresponding sides.

shortest sides: longest sides: third sides:

17. Cross out the proportion that does NOT show ratios of corresponding sides.

$$\frac{9}{6} = \frac{6}{4} \qquad \frac{9}{4} = \frac{x}{8} \qquad \frac{x}{8} = \frac{6}{4} \qquad \frac{x}{8} = \frac{9}{6}$$

18. Cross out the solution that does NOT show ratios of corresponding sides.

Solution A   Solution B

19. Explain why the solution you crossed out does NOT show the correct value of *x*.

_____

Math Success

Check off the vocabulary words that you understand.

☐ indirect measurement   ☐ similar triangles

Rate how well you can *prove triangles similar*.

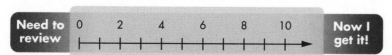

Lesson 7-3

7-4 Similarity in Right Triangles

Vocabulary

● Review

Underline the correct word to complete the sentence.

1. The *altitude* of a triangle is a segment from a vertex to the opposite side that is parallel / perpendicular to the opposite side.

2. In an isosceles triangle, the *altitude* to the base divides the triangle into two congruent / isosceles triangles.

3. Circle the *altitude* of $\triangle ABC$.

   $\overline{AB}$ $\overline{AC}$ $\overline{BC}$ $\overline{CD}$

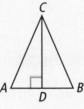

● Vocabulary Builder

> **geometric mean** (noun) **jee uh MEH trik meen**
>
> **Definition:** For any two positive numbers a and b, the **geometric mean** of a and b is the positive number x such that $\frac{a}{x} = \frac{x}{b}$.
>
> **Example:** The **geometric mean** of 4 and 10 is the value of x in $\frac{4}{x} = \frac{x}{10}$, or $x = 2\sqrt{10}$.

● Use Your Vocabulary

4. **Multiple Choice** Which proportion can you use to find the *geometric mean* of 5 and 15?

   Ⓐ $\frac{x}{5} = \frac{x}{15}$ Ⓑ $\frac{5}{x} = \frac{15}{x}$ Ⓒ $\frac{5}{x} = \frac{x}{15}$ Ⓓ $\frac{5}{15} = \frac{x}{x}$

Underline the correct equation to complete each sentence.

5. The *geometric mean* x of a and b is $x = \sqrt{ab}$ / $x = ab$.

6. The *geometric mean* x of 3 and 7 is $x = \sqrt{21}$ / $x = 21$.

7. Circle the geometric mean of $\sqrt{3}$ and $\sqrt{3}$.

   $\sqrt{3}$ 3 $3\sqrt{3}$ $\sqrt{33}$

Theorem 7-3 The altitude to the hypotenuse of a right triangle divides the triangle into two triangles that are similar to the original triangle and to each other.

If . . .

$\triangle ABC$ is a right triangle with right $\angle ACB$, and $\overline{CD}$ is the altitude to the hypotenuse

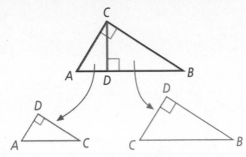

Then . . .

$\triangle ABC \sim \triangle ACD$

$\triangle ABC \sim \triangle CBD$

$\triangle ACD \sim \triangle CBD$

Corollary 1 to Theorem 7-3

The length of the altitude to the hypotenuse of a right triangle is the geometric mean of the lengths of the segments of the hypotenuse.

If . . .

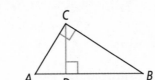

Then . . .

$\dfrac{AD}{CD} = \dfrac{CD}{DB}$

Corollary 2 to Theorem 7-3

The altitude to the hypotenuse of a right triangle separates the hypotenuse so that the length of each leg of the triangle is the geometric mean of the length of the hypotenuse and the length of the segment of the hypotenuse adjacent to the leg.

If . . .

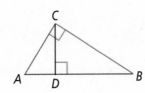

Then . . .

$\dfrac{AB}{AC} = \dfrac{AC}{AD}$

$\dfrac{AB}{CB} = \dfrac{CB}{DB}$

8. $\triangle LMN$ is a right triangle with right $\angle LMN$. $\overline{NP}$ is the altitude to the hypotenuse. Complete the similarity statements.

$\triangle LMN \sim \triangle$ ⬚

$\triangle LMN \sim \triangle$ ⬚

$\triangle LNP \sim \triangle$ ⬚

Use the triangle at the right. Write *Corollary 1* or *Corollary 2* for each proportion.

9. $\dfrac{c}{a} = \dfrac{a}{x}$ _____

10. $\dfrac{x}{m} = \dfrac{m}{y}$ _____

11. $\dfrac{c}{b} = \dfrac{b}{y}$ _____

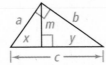

Problem 1   Identifying Similar Triangles

Got It? What similarity statement can you write relating the three triangles in the diagram?

12. Write the names of the triangles.

$\triangle RPQ$ $\triangle$ ▓▓▓▓ $\triangle$ ▓▓▓▓

13. Write the three right angles.

$\angle RPQ$ $\angle$ ▓▓▓ $\angle$ ▓▓▓

14. Write the three smallest angles.

$\angle QRP$ $\angle$ ▓▓▓ $\angle$ ▓▓▓

15. Use your answers to Exercises 13 and 14 to write three similarity statements beginning with the vertex of the smallest angle in each triangle and ending with the vertex of the right angle.

$\triangle RQP \sim \triangle$ ▓▓▓ $\triangle RQP \sim \triangle$ ▓▓▓ $\triangle$ ▓▓▓ $\sim \triangle$ ▓▓▓

Problem 2   Finding the Geometric Mean

Got It? What is the geometric mean of 4 and 18?

16. Use the justifications below to find the geometric mean.

$\dfrac{4}{x} = \dfrac{x}{\boxed{}}$ Definition of geometric mean

$x^2 = \boxed{}$ Cross Products Property

$x = \sqrt{\boxed{}}$ Take the positive square root of each side.

$x = \boxed{}\sqrt{\boxed{}}$ Write in simplest radical form.

Problem 3   Using the Corollaries

Got It? What are the values of x and y?

Underline the correct word to complete each sentence.

17. x is the length of a leg of the largest triangle, so use Corollary 1 / Corollary 2 to find the value of x.

18. y is the length of the altitude of the largest triangle, so use Corollary 1 / Corollary 2 to find the value of y.

19. The values of x and y are found below. Write a justification for each step.

$\dfrac{4}{x} = \dfrac{x}{4 + 5}$ _____ $\dfrac{4}{y} = \dfrac{y}{5}$

$x^2 = 36$ _____ $y^2 = 20$

$x = \sqrt{36}$ _____ $y = \sqrt{20}$

$x = 6$ _____ $y = 2\sqrt{5}$

Got It? Points *A*, *B*, and *C* are located so that *AB* = 20 in., and $\overline{AB} \perp \overline{BC}$. Point *D* is located on $\overline{AC}$ so that $\overline{BD} \perp \overline{AC}$ and *DC* = 9 in. You program a robot to move from *A* to *D* and to pick up a plastic bottle at *D*. From point *D*, the robot must turn right and move to point *B* to put the bottle in a recycling bin. How far does the robot travel from *D* to *B*?

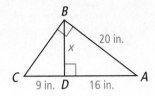

20. Place a ✓ in the box if the statement is correct. Place an ✗ if it is incorrect.

☐ I know the length of the hypotenuse of △*ABC*.

☐ I know the lengths of the segments of the hypotenuse of △*ABC*.

☐ I know the length of the altitude of △*ABC*.

☐ I can use Corollary 1 to solve the problem.

21. Find the length of $\overline{BD}$.

22. The robot travels ☐ in. from *D* to *B*.

Lesson Check • Do you UNDERSTAND?

Vocabulary Identify the following in △*RST*.

23. The hypotenuse is ☐ .

24. The segments of the hypotenuse are ☐ and ☐ .

25. The segment of the hypotenuse adjacent to leg $\overline{ST}$ is ☐ .

Math Success

Check off the vocabulary words that you understand.

☐ geometric mean   ☐ altitude   ☐ similarity

Rate how well you understand *similar right triangles*.

Need to review   0   2   4   6   8   10   Now I get it!

Vocabulary

● Review

1. Circle the model that can form a *proportion* with $\frac{10}{15}$.

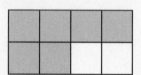 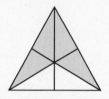 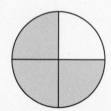

2. Circle the ratios that you can use to form a *proportion*.

$$\frac{1}{2} \qquad\qquad \frac{3}{4} \qquad\qquad \frac{25}{100} \qquad\qquad \frac{75}{100}$$

3. Cross out the *proportion* that does NOT have the same solution as the others.

$$\frac{12}{17} = \frac{n}{20} \qquad\qquad \frac{12}{n} = \frac{17}{20} \qquad\qquad \frac{n}{17} = \frac{20}{12} \qquad\qquad \frac{20}{n} = \frac{17}{12}$$

● Vocabulary Builder

bisector (noun) BY **sek tur**

Other Word Form: bisect (verb)

Definition: A **bisector** divides a whole into two equal parts.

Math Usage: A **bisector** is a point, segment, ray, or line that divides an angle or a segment into two congruent angles or segments.

● Use Your Vocabulary

Use the diagram at the right. Complete each statement with the correct word from the list below. Use each word only once.

bisects   bisector   bisected

4. $\overrightarrow{BD}$ is the __?__ of $\angle ABC$.

5. $\angle ABC$ is __?__ by $\overrightarrow{BD}$.

6. $\overrightarrow{BD}$ __?__ $\angle ABC$.

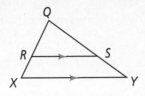

Theorem 7-4 Side-Splitter Theorem and Its Corollary

Side-Splitter Theorem

If a line is parallel to one side of a triangle and intersects the other two sides, then it divides those sides proportionally.

If $\overleftrightarrow{RS} \parallel \overleftrightarrow{XY}$, then $\dfrac{XR}{RQ} = \dfrac{\boxed{}}{SQ}$.

7. If $XR = 4$, $RQ = 4$, and $YS = 5$, then $SQ = \boxed{}$.

8. If $XR = 3$, $RQ = 6$, and $YS = 4$, then $SQ = \boxed{}$.

Corollary to the Side-Splitter Theorem

If three parallel lines intersect two transversals, then the segments intercepted on the transversals are proportional.

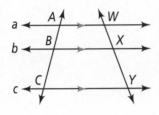

If $a \parallel b \parallel c$, then $\dfrac{AB}{BC} = \dfrac{WX}{XY}$.

Complete each proportion.

9. $\dfrac{BC}{AB} = \dfrac{XY}{\boxed{}}$

10. $\dfrac{\boxed{}}{BA} = \dfrac{YX}{XW}$

11. $\dfrac{AC}{AB} = \dfrac{\boxed{}}{WX}$

Problem 1 **Using the Side-Splitter Theorem**

Got It? What is the value of a in the diagram at the right?

12. The value of a is found below. Use one of the reasons in the box to justify each step.

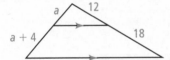

Cross Products Property	Divide each side by 6.
Side-Splitter Theorem	Simplify.
Subtract 12a from each side.	

$$\frac{a}{a+4} = \frac{12}{18}$$

$$18a = 12a + 48$$

$$18a - 12a = 12a - 12a + 48$$

$$6a = 48$$

$$\frac{6a}{6} = \frac{48}{6}$$

$$a = 8$$

Lesson 7-5

Problem 2 Finding a Length

Got It? Camping Three campsites are shown in the diagram. What is the length of Site C along the road?

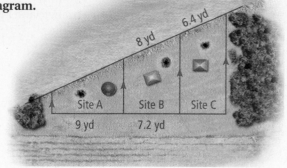

13. Let y be the length of Site C along the road. Use the justifications at the right to find the value of y.

$$\frac{y}{7.2} = \frac{6.4}{\boxed{}}$$ Corollary to Side-Splitter Theorem

$$\boxed{} \cdot y = 46.08$$ Cross Products Property

$$\frac{\boxed{} \cdot y}{\boxed{}} = \frac{46.08}{\boxed{}}$$ Divide each side by the coefficient of y.

$$y = \boxed{}$$ Simplify.

14. The length of Site C along the road is $\boxed{}$ yd.

---

take note

Theorem 7-5 Triangle-Angle-Bisector Theorem

Triangle-Angle-Bisector Theorem

If a ray bisects an angle of a triangle, then it divides the opposite side into two segments that are proportional to the other two sides of the triangle.

If $\overrightarrow{AD}$ bisects $\angle CAB$, then $\dfrac{CD}{DB} = \dfrac{CA}{BA}$.

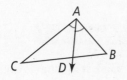

Problem 3 Using the Triangle-Angle-Bisector Theorem

Got It? What is the value of y in the diagram at the right?

15. Complete the reasoning model below.

Think	Write
I can use the Triangle-Angle-Bisector Theorem to write a proportion.	$\dfrac{9.6}{16} = \dfrac{y}{\boxed{}}$
Then I can use the Cross-Products Property.	$\boxed{} = 16y$
Now I divide each side by $\boxed{}$ and simplify.	$\dfrac{\boxed{}}{16} = \dfrac{16}{16}y$ $y = \boxed{}$

16. The value of y is $\boxed{}$.

Lesson Check • Do you know HOW?

What is the value of *x* in the figure at the right?

17. Circle the proportion you can use to solve the problem.

$$\frac{10}{30} = \frac{x}{45} \qquad \frac{x}{10} = \frac{30}{45} \qquad \frac{x}{x+10} = \frac{30}{45} \qquad \frac{10}{x+10} = \frac{30}{45}$$

18. Solve the proportion.

Lesson Check • Do you UNDERSTAND?

Error Analysis A classmate says you can use the Side-Splitter Theorem to find both *x* and *y* in the diagram. **Explain what is wrong with your classmate's statement.**

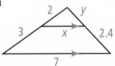

19. Cross out the lengths that are NOT parts of the sides intersected by the parallel line.

| 2 | 2.4 | 3 | 7 | *x* | *y* |

20. Can you use the Side-Splitter Theorem to find *x*?　　　Yes / No

21. Can you use the Side-Splitter Theorem to find *y*?　　　Yes / No

22. Explain what is wrong with your classmate's statement.

_____

_____

Math Success

Check off the vocabulary words that you understand.

☐ bisector　　　☐ proportion　　　☐ Side-Splitter Theorem

Rate how well you understand *side and angle bisectors*.

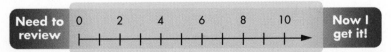

Lesson 7-5

Vocabulary

● **Review**

1. Write the *square* and the positive *square root* of each number.

Number	Square	Positive Square Root
9		
$\frac{1}{4}$	$\frac{1}{16}$	

● **Vocabulary Builder**

leg (noun) **leg**

Related Word: hypotenuse

Definition: In a right triangle, the sides that form the right angle are the **legs**.

Main Idea: The **legs** of a right triangle are perpendicular. The hypotenuse is the side opposite the right angle.

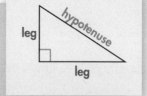

● **Use Your Vocabulary**

2. Underline the correct word to complete the sentence.

The *hypotenuse* is the longest / shortest side in a right triangle.

Write T for *true* or F for *false*.

_____ **3.** The *hypotenuse* of a right triangle can be any one of the three sides.

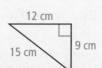

_____ **4.** One *leg* of the triangle at the right has length 9 cm.

_____ **5.** The *hypotenuse* of the triangle at the right has length 15 cm.

Theorems 8-1 and 8-2 Pythagorean Theorem and Its Converse

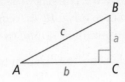

Pythagorean Theorem If a triangle is a right triangle, then the sum of the squares of the lengths of the legs is equal to the square of the length of the hypotenuse.

If $\triangle ABC$ is a right triangle, then $a^2 + b^2 = c^2$.

Converse of the Pythagorean Theorem If the sum of the squares of the lengths of two sides of a triangle is equal to the square of the length of the third side, then the triangle is a right triangle.

If $a^2 + b^2 = c^2$, then $\triangle ABC$ is a right triangle.

6. Circle the equation that shows the correct relationship among the lengths of the legs and the hypotenuse of a right triangle.

$13^2 + 5^2 = 12^2$ $\qquad$ $5^2 + 12^2 = 13^2$ $\qquad$ $12^2 + 13^2 = 5^2$

Underline the correct words to complete each sentence.

7. A triangle with side lengths 3, 4, and 5 is / is not a right triangle because $3^2 + 4^2$ is equal / not equal to 5^2.

8. A triangle with side lengths 4, 5, and 6 is / is not a right triangle because $4^2 + 5^2$ is equal / not equal to 6^2.

 Problem 1 **Finding the Length of the Hypotenuse**

Got It? The legs of a right triangle have lengths 10 and 24. What is the length of the hypotenuse?

9. Label the triangle at the right.

10. Use the justifications below to find the length of the hypotenuse.

$a^2 + b^2 = c^2$	Pythagorean Theorem
$\boxed{}^2 + \boxed{}^2 = c^2$	Substitute for a and b.
$\boxed{} + \boxed{} = c^2$	Simplify.
$\boxed{} = c^2$	Add.
$\boxed{} = c$	Take the positive square root.

11. The length of the hypotenuse is $\boxed{}$.

12. One Pythagorean triple is 5, 12, and 13. If you multiply each number by 2, what numbers result? How do the numbers that result compare to the lengths of the sides of the triangle in Exercises 9–11?

_____

_____

Lesson 8-1

Got It? The size of a computer monitor is the length of its diagonal. You want to buy a 19-in. monitor that has a height of 11 in. What is the width of the monitor? Round to the nearest tenth of an inch.

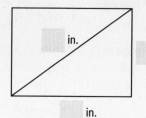

13. Label the diagram of the computer monitor at the right.

14. The equation is solved below. Write a justification for each step.

$$a^2 + b^2 = c^2$$

_____

$$11^2 + b^2 = 19^2$$

_____

$$121 + b^2 = 361$$

_____

$$121 - 121 + b^2 = 361 - 121$$

_____

$$b^2 = 240$$

_____

$$b = \sqrt{240}$$

_____

$$b \approx 15.49193338$$

_____

15. To the nearest tenth of an inch, the width of the monitor is [   ] in.

Got It? A triangle has side lengths 16, 48, and 50. Is the triangle a right triangle? Explain.

16. Circle the equation you will use to determine whether the triangle is a right triangle.

$$16^2 + 48^2 \stackrel{?}{=} 50^2 \qquad\qquad 16^2 + 50^2 \stackrel{?}{=} 48^2 \qquad\qquad 48^2 + 50^2 \stackrel{?}{=} 16^2$$

17. Simplify your equation from Exercise 16.

18. Underline the correct words to complete the sentence.

The equation is true / false , so the triangle is / is not a right triangle.

A *Pythagorean triple* is a set of nonzero whole numbers a, b, and c that satisfy the equation $a^2 + b^2 = c^2$. If you multiply each number in a Pythagorean triple by the same whole number, the three numbers that result also form a Pythagorean triple.

Theorems 8-3 and 8-4 Pythagorean Inequality Theorems

Theorem 8-3 If the square of the length of the longest side of a triangle is greater than the sum of the squares of the lengths of the other two sides, then the triangle is obtuse.

Theorem 8-4 If the square of the length of the longest side of a triangle is less than the sum of the squares of the lengths of the other two sides, then the triangle is acute.

Use the figures at the right. Complete each sentence with *acute* or *obtuse*.

19. In $\triangle ABC$, $c^2 > a^2 + b^2$, so $\triangle ABC$ is __?__.

20. In $\triangle RST$, $s^2 < r^2 + t^2$, so $\triangle RST$ is __?__.

Lesson Check • Do you UNDERSTAND?

Error Analysis A triangle has side lengths 16, 34, and 30. Your friend says it is not a right triangle. Look at your friend's work and describe the error.

$$16^2 + 34^2 \overset{?}{=} 30^2$$
$$256 + 1156 \overset{?}{=} 900$$
$$1412 \neq 900$$

21. Underline the length that your friend used as the longest side. Circle the length of the longest side of the triangle.

| 16 | 30 | 34 |

22. Write the comparison that your friend should have used to determine whether the triangle is a right triangle.

23. Describe the error in your friend's work.

_____

_____

Math Success

Check off the vocabulary words that you understand.

☐ hypotenuse   ☐ leg   ☐ Pythagorean Theorem   ☐ Pythagorean triple

Rate how well you can *use the Pythagorean Theorem and its converse*.

Need to review   0   2   4   6   8   10   Now I get it!

Special Right Triangles

Vocabulary

● Review

1. Circle the segment that is a *diagonal* of square *ABCD*.

$\overline{AB}$ $\qquad$ $\overline{AC}$ $\qquad$ $\overline{AD}$ $\qquad$ $\overline{BC}$ $\qquad$ $\overline{CD}$

2. Underline the correct word to complete the sentence.

A *diagonal* is a line segment that joins two sides / vertices of a polygon.

● Vocabulary Builder

complement (noun) ᴋᴀʜᴍ **pluh munt**

Other Word Form: complementary (adjective)

Math Usage: When the measures of two angles have a sum of 90, each angle is a **complement** of the other.

Nonexample: Two angles whose measures sum to 180 are supplementary.

● Use Your Vocabulary

Complete each statement with the word *complement* or *complementary*.

3. If $m\angle A = 40$ and $m\angle B = 50$, the angles are __?__ .

4. If $m\angle A = 30$ and $m\angle B = 60$, $\angle B$ is the __?__ of $\angle A$.

5. $\angle P$ and $\angle Q$ are __?__ because the sum of their measures is 90.

Complete.

6. If $\angle R$ has a measure of 35, then the *complement* of $\angle R$ has a measure of ____ .

7. If $\angle X$ has a measure of 22, then the *complement* of $\angle X$ has a measure of ____ .

8. If $\angle C$ has a measure of 65, then the *complement* of $\angle C$ has a measure of ____ .

9. Circle the *complementary* angles.

60°　　　40°　　　50°　　　120°

Theorem 8-5 45°-45°-90° Triangle Theorem

In a 45°-45°-90° triangle, both legs are congruent and the length of the hypotenuse is $\sqrt{2}$ times the length of a leg.

Complete each statement for a 45° −45° −90° triangle.

10. hypotenuse = [ ] · leg

11. If leg = 10, then hypotenuse = [ ] · [ ] .

Problem 1 Finding the Length of the Hypotenuse

Got It? What is the length of the hypotenuse of a 45°-45°-90° triangle with leg length $5\sqrt{3}$?

12. Use the justifications to find the length of the hypotenuse.

hypotenuse = [ ] · leg   45°-45°-90° Triangle Theorem

$= \sqrt{2} \cdot$ [ ]   Substitute.

$=$ [ ] $\cdot$ [ ]   Commutative Property of Multiplication.

$=$ [ ]   Simplify.

Problem 2 Finding the Length of a Leg

Got It? The length of the hypotenuse of a 45°-45°-90° triangle is 10. What is the length of one leg?

13. Will the length of the leg be *greater than* or *less than* 10? Explain.

_____

14. Use the justifications to find the length of one leg.

hypotenuse = $\sqrt{2} \cdot$ leg   45°-45°-90° Triangle Theorem

[ ] $= \sqrt{2} \cdot$ leg   Substitute.

$\dfrac{[\ ]}{\sqrt{2}} = \dfrac{\sqrt{2}}{\sqrt{2}} \cdot$ leg   Divide each side by $\sqrt{2}$.

leg $= \dfrac{[\ ]}{\sqrt{2}}$ Simplify.

leg $= \dfrac{[\ ]}{\sqrt{2}} \cdot \dfrac{[\ ]}{\sqrt{2}}$ Multiply by a form of 1 to rationalize the denominator.

leg $= \dfrac{[\ ]}{2}$ Simplify.

leg $=$ [ ]   Divide by 2.

207

Problem 3 Finding Distance

Got It? You plan to build a path along one diagonal of a 100 ft-by-100 ft square garden. To the nearest foot, how long will the path be?

15. Use the words *path, height,* and *width* to complete the diagram.

16. Write L for *leg* or H for *hypotenuse* to identify each part of the right triangle in the diagram.

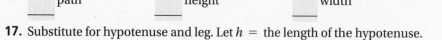

_____ path   _____ height   _____ width

17. Substitute for hypotenuse and leg. Let h = the length of the hypotenuse.

$$\text{hypotenuse} = \sqrt{2} \cdot \text{leg}$$
$$\boxed{} = \sqrt{2} \cdot \boxed{}$$

18. Solve the equation. Use a calculator to find the length of the path.

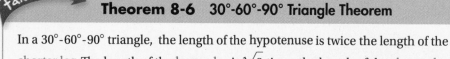

19. To the nearest foot, the length of the path will be _____ feet.

---

take note

Theorem 8-6 30°-60°-90° Triangle Theorem

In a 30°-60°-90° triangle, the length of the hypotenuse is twice the length of the shorter leg. The length of the longer leg is $\sqrt{3}$ times the length of the shorter leg.

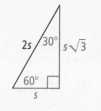

Complete each statement for a 30°-60°-90° triangle.

20. hypotenuse = $\boxed{}$ · shorter leg

21. longer leg = $\boxed{}$ · shorter leg

Problem 4 Using the Length of One Side

Got It? What is the value of f in simplest radical form?

22. Complete the reasoning model below.

Think	Write
f is the length of the hypotenuse. I can write an equation relating the hypotenuse and the shorter leg $\dfrac{5\sqrt{3}}{3}$ of the 30°-60°-90° triangle.	hypotenuse = $\boxed{}$ · shorter leg $f = \boxed{} \cdot \dfrac{\boxed{}}{\boxed{}}$
Now I can solve for f.	$f = \dfrac{\boxed{}}{\boxed{}}$

Got It? Jewelry Making An artisan makes pendants in the shape of equilateral triangles. Suppose the sides of a pendant are 18 mm long. What is the height of the pendant to the nearest tenth of a millimeter?

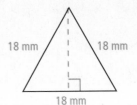

23. Circle the formula you can use to find the height of the pendant.

hypotenuse $= 2 \cdot$ shorter leg   longer leg $= \sqrt{3} \cdot$ shorter leg

24. Find the height of the pendant.

25. To the nearest tenth of a millimeter, the height of the pendant is _____ mm.

Lesson Check • Do you UNDERSTAND?

Reasoning A test question asks you to find two side lengths of a 45°-45°-90° triangle. You know that the length of one leg is 6, but you forgot the special formula for 45°-45°-90° triangles. Explain how you can still determine the other side lengths. What are the other side lengths?

26. Underline the correct word(s) to complete the sentence. In a 45°-45°-90° triangle,

the lengths of the legs are different / the same .

27. Use the Pythagorean Theorem to find the length of the longest side.

28. The other two side lengths are _____ and _____ .

Math Success

Check off the vocabulary words that you understand.

☐ leg   ☐ hypotenuse   ☐ right triangle   ☐ Pythagorean Theorem

Rate how well you can *use the properties of special right triangles.*

| Need to review | 0 | 2 | 4 | 6 | 8 | 10 | Now I get it! |

8-3 Trigonometry

Vocabulary

● Review

The Venn diagram at the right shows the relationship between *similar* and congruent figures. Write T for *true* or F for *false*.

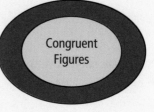

Similar Figures

Congruent Figures

_____ **1.** All *similar* figures are congruent figures.

_____ **2.** All congruent figures are *similar* figures.

_____ **3.** Some *similar* figures are congruent figures.

4. Circle the postulate or theorem you can use to verify that the triangles at the right are *similar*.

AA ~ Postulate   SAS ~ Theorem   SSS ~ Theorem

● Vocabulary Builder

ratio (noun) RAY shee oh

Related Words: rate, rational

Definition: A **ratio** is the comparison of two quantities by division.

Example: If there are 6 triangles and 5 squares, the **ratio** of triangles to squares is $\frac{6}{5}$ and the **ratio** of squares to triangles is $\frac{5}{6}$.

● Use Your Vocabulary

Use the triangle at the right for Exercises 5–7.

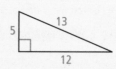

5. Circle the *ratio* of the length of the longer leg to the length of the shorter leg.

$\frac{5}{13}$ $\frac{5}{12}$ $\frac{12}{13}$ $\frac{13}{12}$ $\frac{12}{5}$ $\frac{13}{5}$

6. Circle the *ratio* of the length of the shorter leg to the length of the hypotenuse.

$\frac{5}{13}$ $\frac{5}{12}$ $\frac{12}{13}$ $\frac{13}{12}$ $\frac{12}{5}$ $\frac{13}{5}$

7. Circle the *ratio* of the length of the longer leg to the length of the hypotenuse.

$\frac{5}{13}$ $\frac{5}{12}$ $\frac{12}{13}$ $\frac{13}{12}$ $\frac{12}{5}$ $\frac{13}{5}$

Key Concept The Trigonometric Ratios

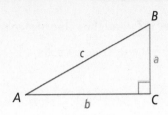

$\text{sine of } \angle A = \dfrac{\text{length of leg opposite} \angle A}{\text{length of hypotenuse}} = \dfrac{a}{c}$

$\text{cosine of } \angle A = \dfrac{\text{length of leg adjacent to} \angle A}{\text{length of hypotenuse}} = \dfrac{}{c}$

$\text{tangent of } \angle A = \dfrac{\text{length of leg opposite} \angle A}{\text{length of leg adjacent to} \angle A} = \dfrac{}{}$

Draw a line from each trigonometric ratio in Column A to its corresponding ratio in Column B.

Column A

8. sin *B*

9. cos *B*

10. tan *B*

Column B

$\dfrac{a}{c}$

$\dfrac{b}{a}$

$\dfrac{b}{c}$

11. Reasoning Suppose $\triangle ABC$ is a right isosceles triangle. What would the tangent of $\angle B$ equal? Explain.

_____

 Problem 1 **Writing Trigonometric Ratios**

Got It? What are the sine, cosine, and tangent ratios for $\angle G$?

12. Circle the measure of the leg opposite $\angle G$.

| 8 | 15 | 17 |

13. Circle the measure of the hypotenuse.

| 8 | 15 | 17 |

14. Circle the measure of the leg adjacent to $\angle G$.

| 8 | 15 | 17 |

15. Write each trigonometric ratio.

$\sin G = \dfrac{\text{opposite}}{\text{hypotenuse}} = \underline{}$

$\cos G = \dfrac{\text{adjacent}}{\text{hypotenuse}} = \underline{}$

$\tan G = \dfrac{\text{opposite}}{\text{adjacent}} = \underline{}$

Lesson 8-3

Got It? Find the value of w to the nearest tenth.

Below is one student's solution.

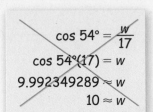

$$\cos 54° = \frac{w}{17}$$
$$\cos 54°(17) = w$$
$$9.992349289 \approx w$$
$$10 \approx w$$

16. Circle the trigonometric ratio that uses sides w and 17.

    sin 54°   cos 54°   tan 54°

17. What error did the student make?

_____

_____

18. Find the value of w correctly.

19. The value of w to the nearest tenth is _____ .

 Problem 3 **Using Inverses**

Got It? Use the figure below. What is $m\angle Y$ to the nearest degree?

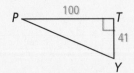

20. Circle the lengths that you know.

    hypotenuse   side adjacent to $\angle Y$ side opposite $\angle Y$

21. Cross out the ratios that you will NOT use to find $m\angle Y$.

    sine   cosine   tangent

22. Underline the correct word to complete the statement.

If you know the sine, cosine, or tangent ratio of an angle, you can use the

inverse / ratio to find the measure of the angle.

23. Follow the steps to find $m\angle Y$.

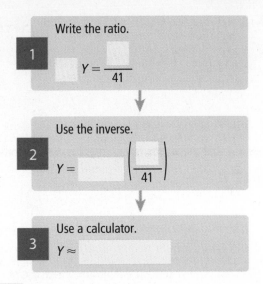

1. Write the ratio.

$\boxed{}\, Y = \dfrac{\boxed{}}{41}$

2. Use the inverse.

$Y = \boxed{}\left(\dfrac{\boxed{}}{41}\right)$

3. Use a calculator.

$Y \approx \boxed{}$

24. To the nearest degree, $m\angle Y \approx \boxed{}$.

Lesson Check • Do you UNDERSTAND?

Error Analysis A student states that $\sin A > \sin X$ because the lengths of the sides of $\triangle ABC$ are greater than the lengths of the sides of $\triangle XYZ$. What is the student's error? Explain.

Underline the correct word(s) to complete each sentence.

25. $\triangle ABC$ and $\triangle XYZ$ are / are not similar.

26. $\angle A$ and $\angle X$ are / are not congruent, so $\sin 35°$ is / is not equal to $\sin 35°$.

27. What is the student's error? Explain.

_____

_____

_____

Math Success

Check off the vocabulary words that you understand.

☐ trigonometric ratios   ☐ sine   ☐ cosine   ☐ tangent

Rate how well you can *use trigonometric ratios*.

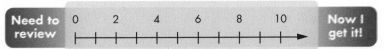

Need to review   0   2   4   6   8   10   Now I get it!

Lesson 8-3

Vocabulary

● Review

Underline the correct word(s) or number to complete each sentence.

1. The measure of a *right angle* is greater / less than the measure of an acute angle and greater / less than the measure of an obtuse angle.

2. A *right angle* has a measure of 45 / 90 / 180 .

3. Lines that intersect to form four *right angles* are parallel / perpendicular lines.

4. Circle the *right angle*(s) in the figure.

∠ACB	∠ADB	∠BAC
∠BAD	∠CBA	∠DBA

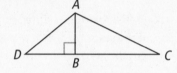

● Vocabulary Builder

elevation (noun) **el uh VAY shun**

Related Word: depression

Definition: The **elevation** of an object is its height above a given level, such as eye level or sea level.

Math Usage: Angles of **elevation** and **depression** are acute angles of right triangles formed by a horizontal distance and a vertical height.

● Use Your Vocabulary

Complete each statement with the correct word from the list below. Use each word only once.

elevate   elevated   elevation

5. John __?__ his feet on a footstool.

6. The __?__ of Mt McKinley is 20,320 ft.

7. You __?__ an object by raising it to a higher position.

Problem 1 Identifying Angles of Elevation and Depression

Got It? What is a description of ∠2 as it relates to the situation shown?

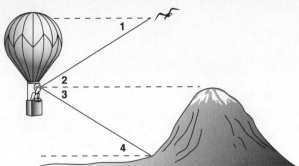

Write T for *true* or F for *false*.

_____ **8.** ∠2 is above the horizontal line.

_____ **9.** ∠2 is the *angle of elevation* from the person in the hot-air balloon to the bird.

_____ **10.** ∠2 is the *angle of depression* from the person in the hot-air balloon to the bird.

_____ **11.** ∠2 is the *angle of elevation* from the top of the mountain to the person in the hot-air balloon.

12. Describe ∠2 as it relates to the situation shown.

_____

_____

Problem 2 Using the Angle of Elevation

Got It? You sight a rock climber on a cliff at a 32° angle of elevation. Your eye level is 6 ft above the ground and you are 1000 feet from the base of the cliff. What is the approximate height of the rock climber from the ground?

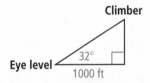

13. Use the information in the problem to complete the problem-solving model below.

Know	**Need**	**Plan**
Angle of elevation is ☐°.	Height of climber from the ground	Find the length of the leg opposite 32° by using tan ☐°.
Distance to the cliff is ☐ ft.		Then add ☐ ft.
Eye level is ☐ ft above the ground.		

215

Lesson 8-4

14. Explain why you use tan 32° and not sin 32° or cos 32°.

_____

_____

_____

15. The problem is solved below. Use one of the reasons from the list at the right to justify each step.

$$\tan 32° = \frac{d}{1000}$$

_____

$$(\tan 32°)\,1000 = d$$

_____

$$d \approx 624.8693519$$

_____

> Solve for _d_.
> Use a calculator.
> Write the equation.

16. The height from your eye level to the climber is about ____ ft.

17. The height of the rock climber from the ground is about ____ ft.

✓ **Problem 3** **Using the Angle of Depression**

Got It? An airplane pilot sights a life raft at a 26° angle of depression. The airplane's altitude is 3 km. What is the airplane's horizontal distance _d_ from the raft?

18. Label the diagram below.

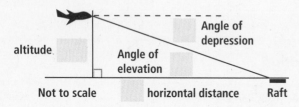

altitude

Angle of
depression

Angle of
elevation

Not to scale   horizontal distance   Raft

19. Circle the equation you could use to find the horizontal distance _d_.

$$\sin 26° = \frac{3}{d}\qquad\qquad \cos 26° = \frac{3}{d}\qquad\qquad \tan 26° = \frac{3}{d}$$

20. Solve your equation from Exercise 19.

21. To the nearest tenth, the airplane's horizontal distance from the raft is ____ km.

Lesson Check • Do you UNDERSTAND?

Vocabulary How is an angle of elevation formed?

Underline the correct word(s) to complete each sentence.

22. The angle of elevation is formed above / below a horizontal line.

23. The angle of depression is formed above / below a horizontal line.

24. The measure of an angle of elevation is equal to / greater than / less than the measure of the angle of depression.

Lesson Check • Do you UNDERSTAND?

Error Analysis A homework question says that the angle of depression from the bottom of a house window to a ball on the ground is 20°. At the right is your friend's sketch of the situation. Describe your friend's error.

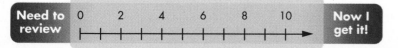

25. Is the angle that your friend identified as the angle of depression formed by the horizontal and the line of sight?   Yes / No

26. Is the correct angle of depression *adjacent to* or *opposite* the angle identified by your friend?

adjacent to / opposite

27. Describe your friend's error.

_____

_____

_____

Math Success

Check off the vocabulary words that you understand.

☐ angle of elevation   ☐ angle of depression   ☐ trigonometric ratios

Rate how well you can *use angles of elevation and depression*.

Need to review   0   2   4   6   8   10   Now I get it!

8-5   Vectors

Vocabulary

● Review

1. Circle the drawing that shows only *segment AB*.

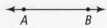 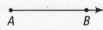 

Use the number line below to find the length of each *segment*.

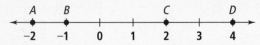

2. $AB =$ ☐   **3.** $AC =$ ☐   **4.** $BC =$ ☐   **5.** $BD =$ ☐

6. Explain how a line *segment* is different from a line.

_____

_____

_____

● Vocabulary Builder

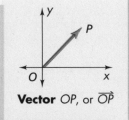

Vector *OP*, or $\overrightarrow{OP}$

vector (noun) VEK **tur**

Related Words: magnitude, direction

Definition: A **vector** is any quantity with magnitude (size) and direction.

Main Idea: You can use **vectors** to model motion and direction.

Example: A car's speed and direction together represent a **vector**.

● Use Your Vocabulary

Write T for *true* or F for *false*.

_____ **7.** A *vector* has an initial point and a terminal point.

_____ **8.** The terminal point of the *vector* at the right is point *O*.

_____ **9.** In symbols, *vector OB* is written as $\overrightarrow{OB}$.

Problem 1 Describing a Vector

Got It? What is the vector at the right as an ordered pair? Round the coordinates to the nearest tenth.

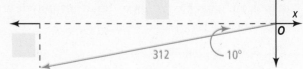

10. Label the diagram with the lengths *x* and *y*.

11. Circle the part of the triangle that has a length of 312.

leg opposite 10°-angle	leg adjacent to 10°-angle	hypotenuse

12. Circle the part of the triangle that has length *x*.

leg opposite 10°-angle	leg adjacent to 10°-angle	hypotenuse

13. Circle the part of the triangle that has length *y*.

leg opposite 10°-angle	leg adjacent to 10°-angle	hypotenuse

14. Use the justifications below to find the values of *x* and *y*.

$$\cos 10° = \dfrac{x}{}$$ Write the ratios. $$\sin 10° = \dfrac{y}{}$$

$$ \cdot \cos 10° = x$$ Solve for *x* and *y*. $$ \cdot \sin 10° = y$$

$$ \approx x$$ Use a calculator. $$ \approx y$$

$$ \approx x$$ Round to the nearest tenth. $$ \approx y$$

15. Decide whether each coordinate is *positive* or *negative*.

x-coordinate: __?__   _____

y-coordinate: __?__   _____

16. The coordinates of the vector are ⟨ _____ , _____ ⟩.

Problem 2 Describing a Vector Direction

Got It? What is the direction of the vector at the right?

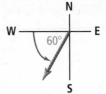

17. Is the angle above (north) or below (south) the west-east line?   above / below

18. Is the angle to the left (west) or to the right (east) of the north-south line?   left / right

19. Circle the direction of the vector.

60° south of east	60° north of east	60° south of west	60° north of west

Lesson 8-5

Problem 3 Finding the Magnitude and Direction of a Vector

Got It? An airplane lands 246 mi east and 76 mi north from where it took off. What are the approximate magnitude and direction of its flight vector?

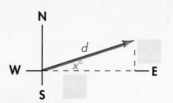

20. Label the diagram with the lengths 246 and 76.

21. The vector ⟨ ___ , ___ ⟩ describes the result of the trip.

22. Complete the reasoning model below.

Think	Write
The magnitude is the distance from the initial point to the terminal point. I can use the Distance Formula to find the distance between (0, 0) and (246, 76)	$d = \sqrt{(246-0)^2 + (76-0)^2}$ = ____ = ____ = ____
The vector is $x°$ north of east. I can use the tangent ratio to find this angle formed by the vector. Then I can use a calculator to find the inverse tangent.	$\tan x° = \dfrac{}{}$ $x = \tan^{-1} \dfrac{}{}$ $x \approx$ ____

23. The magnitude is about ____ mi and the direction is about ____ north of east.

Property Adding Vectors

For $\vec{a} = \langle x_1, y_1 \rangle$ and $\vec{c} = \langle x_2, y_2 \rangle$, $\vec{a} + \vec{c} = \langle x_1 + x_2, y_1 + y_2 \rangle$

Problem 4 Adding Vectors

Got It? What is the resultant of ⟨2, 3⟩ and ⟨−4, −2⟩ as an ordered pair?

24. The sum is found below. Use one of the reasons in the list to justify each step.

$\vec{e} = \vec{a} + \vec{c}$ _____

$\vec{e} = \langle 2, 3 \rangle + \langle -4, -2 \rangle$ _____

$\vec{e} = \langle 2 + (-4), 3 + (-2) \rangle$ _____

$\vec{e} = \langle -2, 1 \rangle$ _____

Substitute.
Write the sum.
Simplify.
Add the coordinates.

Got It? **Reasoning** The speed of a powerboat in still water is 35 mi/h. The river flows directly south at 8 mi/h. At what angle should the powerboat head up river in order to travel directly west?

25. Label the sides of the triangle in the diagram.

26. Use trigonometry to find x.

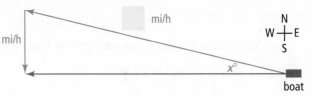

27. The angle at which the powerboat should head up river is about _____ .

Lesson Check • Do you UNDERSTAND?

Error Analysis Your friend says that the magnitude of vector $\langle 10, 7 \rangle$ is greater than that of vector $\langle -10, -7 \rangle$ because the coordinates of $\langle 10, 7 \rangle$ are positive and the coordinates of $\langle -10, -7 \rangle$ are negative. Explain why your friend's statement is incorrect.

28. Complete to find the magnitude of each vector.

$$d_1 = \sqrt{(10-0)^2 + (7-0)^2}$$

$$= \sqrt{\boxed{}^2 + 7^2}$$

$$= \sqrt{\boxed{} + \boxed{}}$$

$$= \sqrt{\boxed{}}$$

$$d_2 = \sqrt{(-10-0)^2 + (-7-0)^2}$$

$$= \sqrt{(-10)^2 + (\boxed{})^2}$$

$$= \sqrt{\boxed{} + \boxed{}}$$

$$= \sqrt{\boxed{}}$$

29. Explain why your friend's statement is incorrect.

_____

_____

Math Success

Check off the vocabulary words that you understand.

☐ vector ☐ magnitude ☐ initial point ☐ terminal point ☐ resultant

Rate how well you can use and *describe vectors*.

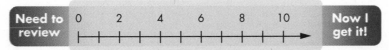

Lesson 8-5

9-1 Translations

Vocabulary

● Review

1. Underline the correct word to complete the sentence.

A *transformation* of a geometric figure is a change in the position, shape, or color / size of the figure.

2. Cross out the word that does NOT describe a *transformation*.

erase   flip   rotate   slide   turn

● Vocabulary Builder

isometry (noun) **eye SAHM uh tree**

Definition: An **isometry** is a transformation in which the preimage and the image of a geometric figure are congruent.

Example:

Preimage

Image

Non-Example:

Preimage

Image

● Use Your Vocabulary

Complete each statement with *congruent, image* or *preimage.*

3. In an *isometry* of a triangle, each side of the __?__ is congruent to each side of the preimage.

_____

4. In an *isometry* of a trapezoid, each angle of the image is congruent to each angle of the __?__ .

_____

5. An *isometry* maps a preimage onto a(n) __?__ image.

_____

Problem 1 Identifying an Isometry

Got It? Does the transformation below appear to be an isometry? Explain.

Preimage   Image

6. Name the polygon that is the preimage.

7. Name the polygon that is the image.

8. Do the preimage and image appear congruent?   Yes / No

9. Does the transformation appear to be an isometry? Explain.

_____

_____

Problem 2 Naming Images and Corresponding Parts

Got It? In the diagram, $\triangle NID \rightarrow \triangle SUP$. What are the images of $\angle I$ and point D?

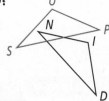

10. The arrow ($\rightarrow$) shows that $\triangle$ _____ is the image of $\triangle NID$,

so $\triangle NID \cong \triangle$ _____ .

11. Describe how to list corresponding parts of the preimage and image.

_____

_____

12. Circle the image of $\angle I$.

$\angle I$ $\angle S$ $\angle P$ $\angle U$

13. Circle the image of point D.

I S P U

take note

Key Concept Translation

A **translation** is a transformation that maps all points of a figure the same distance in the same direction.

A translation is an isometry. Prime notation ($'$) identifies image points.

14. If $\square PQRS$ is translated right 2 units, then every point on

$\square P'Q'R'S'$ is _____ units to the right of its preimage point.

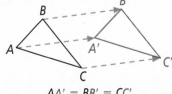

$AA' = BB' = CC'$

Lesson 9-1

Problem 3 **Finding the Image of a Translation**

Got It? What are the images of the vertices of $\triangle ABC$ for the translation $(x, y) \rightarrow (x + 1, y - 4)$? Graph the image of $\triangle ABC$.

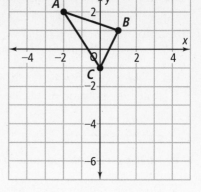

15. Identify the coordinates of each vertex.

$A(\quad , \quad)$

$B(\quad , \quad)$

$C(\quad , \quad)$

16. Use the translation rule $(x, y) \rightarrow (x + 1, y - 4)$ to find A', B', and C'.

$A'(\quad + 1, \quad - 4) = A'(\quad , \quad)$

$B'(\quad + 1, \quad - 4) = B'(\quad , \quad)$

$C'(\quad + 1, \quad - 4) = C'(\quad , \quad)$

17. Circle how each point is translated.

1 unit to the right and 4 units up	1 unit to the right and 4 units down
1 unit to the left and 4 units up	1 unit to the left and 4 units down

18. Graph the image of $\triangle ABC$ on the coordinate plane above.

 Problem 4 **Writing a Rule to Describe a Translation**

Got It? The translation image of $\triangle LMN$ is $\triangle L'M'N'$ with $L'(1, -2)$, $M'(3, -4)$, and $N'(6, -2)$. What is a rule that describes the translation?

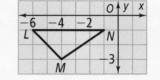

19. Circle the coordinates of point L.

$(6, -1)$ $(-1, -6)$ $(-6, -1)$ $(-1, 6)$

20. Circle the coordinates of point M.

$(-4, -3)$ $(-3, -4)$ $(-4, 3)$ $(-3, 4)$

21. Circle the coordinates of point N.

$(-1, 1)$ $(1, -1)$ $(-1, 0)$ $(-1, -1)$

22. Find the horizontal change from L to L'.   **23.** Find the vertical change from L to L'.

$1 - \quad = \quad$ $-2 - \quad = \quad$

Underline the correct word to complete each sentence.

24. From $\triangle LMN$ to $\triangle L'M'N'$, each value of x increases / decreases .

25. From $\triangle LMN$ to $\triangle L'M'N'$, each value of y increases / decreases .

26. A rule that describes the translation is? $(x, y) \rightarrow (\quad , \quad)$.

Got It? The diagram at the right shows a chess game with the black bishop 6 squares right and 2 squares down from its original position after two moves. The bishop next moves 3 squares left and 3 squares down. Where is the bishop in relation to its original position?

27. If (0, 0) represents the bishop's original position, the bishop is now at the point (____ , ____).

28. Write the translation rule that represents the bishop's next move.

$(x, y) \rightarrow (x -$ ____ $, y -$ ____ $)$

29. Substitute the point you found in Exercise 27 into the rule you wrote in Exercise 28.

(____ , ____) → (____ − ____ , ____ − ____)

30. In relation to (0, 0), the bishop is at (____ , ____).

Lesson Check • Do you UNDERSTAND?

Error Analysis Your friend says the transformation $\triangle ABC \rightarrow \triangle PQR$ is a translation. Explain and correct her error.

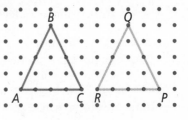

31. Find the distance between the preimage and image of each vertex.

$BQ =$ ____ $AP =$ ____ $CR =$ ____

32. Does this transformation map all points the same distance?   Yes / No

33. Is $\triangle ABC \rightarrow \triangle PQR$ a translation? Explain.

_____

34. Correct your friend's error.

_____

Math Success

Check off the vocabulary words that you understand.

☐ transformation   ☐ preimage   ☐ image   ☐ isometry   ☐ translation

Rate how well you can *find transformation images.*

| Need to review | 0 | 2 | 4 | 6 | 8 | 10 | Now I get it! |

Vocabulary

● **Review**

1. Circle the *translation* rule that shows a mapping 2 units left and 1 unit up.
Underline the translation rule that shows a mapping 2 units right and 1 unit down.

$$(x, y) \rightarrow (x - 2, y + 1) \qquad (x, y) \rightarrow (x + 2, y - 1) \qquad (x, y) \rightarrow (x - 2, y - 1)$$

● **Vocabulary Builder**

reflection (noun) rih FLEK shun

Related Words: line of **reflection**

Definition: A **reflection** is a mirror image of an object that has the same size and shape but an opposite orientation.

Math Usage: A **reflection** is a transformation where each point on the preimage is the same distance from the line of reflection as its **reflection** image.

● **Use Your Vocabulary**

Write T for *true* or F for *false*.

_____ **2.** A *reflection* is the same shape as the original figure.

_____ **3.** A *reflection* makes a figure larger.

---

take note

Key Concept Reflection Across a Line

Reflection across a line r, called the line of reflection, is a transformation with these two properties:

- If a point A is on line r, then the image of A is itself (that is, $A' = A$).

- If a point B is not on line r, then r is the perpendicular bisector of $\overline{BB'}$.

A reflection across a line is an isometry.

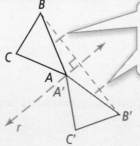

The preimage B and its image B' are equidistant from the line of reflection.

4. Line ____ is the perpendicular bisector of $\overline{CC'}$.

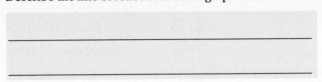 **Problem 1** **Reflecting a Point Across a Line**

Got It? What is the image of $P(3, 4)$ reflected across the line $x = -1$?

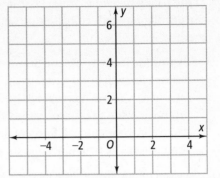

5. Graph P on the coordinate plane at the right.

6. Describe the line of reflection. Then graph the line of reflection.

_____

_____

7. The distance from point P to the line of reflection is ⬚ units.

Underline the correct word(s) to complete each sentence.

8. The x-coordinates of P and P' are different / the same .

9. The y-coordinates of P and P' are different / the same .

10. Point P is reflected to the left / right across the line of reflection.

11. Graph the image of $P(3, 4)$ and label it P'.

12. The coordinates of P' are (⬚ , ⬚).

 Problem 2 **Graphing a Reflection Image**

Got It? Graph points $A(-3, 4)$, $B(0, 1)$, and $C(4, 2)$. What is the image of $\triangle ABC$ reflected across the x-axis?

13. The x-axis is the line $y =$ ⬚ .

14. Circle the distance in units from point A to the x-axis. Underline the distance from point B to the x-axis. Put a square around the distance from point C to the x-axis.

    0   1   2   3   4

15. Point B' is ⬚ unit(s) below the x-axis.

16. Point C' is ⬚ unit(s) below the x-axis.

17. The arrow shows how to find vertex A'. Graph the image of $\triangle ABC$ and label vertices B' and C' on the coordinate plane below.

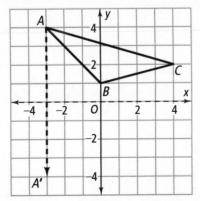

Lesson 9-2

Problem 3 Minimizing a Distance

Got It? **Reasoning** The diagram shows one solution of the problem below. Your classmate began to solve the problem by reflecting point *R* across line *t*. Will her method work? Explain.

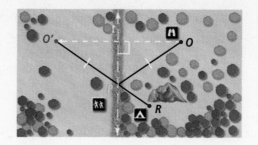

Beginning from a point on Summit Trail (line *t*), a hiking club will build a trail to the Overlook (point *O*) and a trail to Balance Rock (point *R*). The club members want to minimize the total length of the two trails. How can you find the point on Summit Trail where the two new trails should start?

You need to find the point *P* on line *t* such that the distance $OP + PR$ is as small as possible. In the diagram, the problem was solved by locating *O′*, the reflection image of *O* across *t*. Because *t* is the perpendicular bisector of $\overline{OO'}$, $PO = PO'$, and $OP + PR = O'P + PR$. By the Triangle Inequality Theorem, the sum $O'P + PR$ is least when *R*, *P*, and *O′* are collinear. So, the trails should start at the point *P* where $\overline{RO'}$ intersects line *t*.

Place a ✓ in the box if the response is correct. Place an ✗ if it is incorrect.

18. When point *R* is reflected across line *t*, *t* is the perpendicular bisector of $\overline{RR'}$.

19. $PR \neq PR'$

20. $RP + PO = R'P + PO$

21. Points *O*, *P*, and *R′* are NOT collinear.

22. The trails should start at the point *P* where $\overline{OR'}$ intersects *t*.

23. Reflect *R* across line *t* in the diagram at the right. Label the reflection *R′*.

24. Draw $\overline{RR'}$.

25. Draw $\overline{R'O}$.

26. Label the point where $\overline{R'O}$ intersects line *t* as point *P*. Draw $\overline{PR}$.

27. What do you notice about point *P* after reflecting *R* across line *t*?

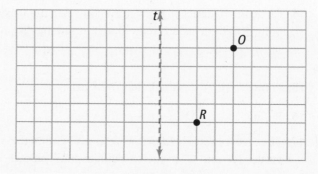

28. Will your classmate's method work? Explain.

Lesson Check • Do you UNDERSTAND?

What are the coordinates of a point $P(x, y)$ reflected across the y-axis? Across the x-axis?

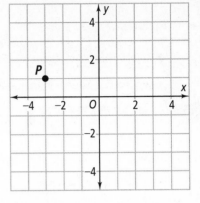

29. Reflect point P across the y-axis. Label the image P'.

30. Circle the coordinates of point P.

$(3, 1)$	$(-3, -1)$	$(-3, 1)$	$(3, -1)$

31. Circle the coordinates of point P'.

$(3, 1)$	$(-3, -1)$	$(-3, 1)$	$(3, -1)$

32. Describe how the coordinates of P' are different from the coordinates of P.

_____

_____

33. Reflect point P across the x-axis. Label the image P''. The coordinates of P''

are (___ , ___).

34. Describe how the coordinates of P'' are different from the coordinates of P.

_____

35. Complete the model below to find the coordinates of $P(x, y)$ reflected across the y-axis and across the x-axis.

Math Success

Check off the vocabulary words that you understand.

☐ reflection   ☐ line of reflection

Rate how well you can *find reflection images of figures.*

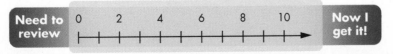

Lesson 9-2

9-3 Rotations

Vocabulary

● Review

1. The diagram at the right shows the reflection of point *A* across a *line of reflection*. Draw the *line of reflection*.

2. Circle the equation of the *line of reflection* in the diagram above.

   $x = 1$ $y = 1$ $x = 2$ $y = 2$

● Vocabulary Builder

rotation

rotation (noun) **roh TAY shun**

Definition: A **rotation** is a spinning motion that turns a figure about a point or a line.

Related Words: center of **rotation**, axis of **rotation**

Math Usage: A **rotation** about a point is a transformation that turns a figure clockwise or counterclockwise a given number of degrees.

● Use Your Vocabulary

Complete each statement with *always*, *sometimes*, or *never*.

3. The *rotation* of the moon about Earth __?__ takes a year.

4. A *rotation* image __?__ has the same orientation as the preimage.

5. A transformation is __?__ a *rotation*.

6. A *rotation* is __?__ a transformation.

7. A 110° counterclockwise *rotation* is the same as a 250° clockwise *rotation* about the same point.

Key Concept   Rotation About a Point

A **rotation** of $x°$ about a point R, called the **center of rotation,** is a transformation with these two properties:

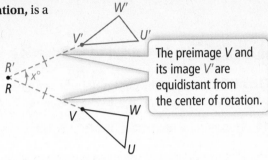

The preimage V and its image V' are equidistant from the center of rotation.

- The image of R is itself (that is, $R' = \boxed{}$).

- For any other point V, $RV' = RV$ and $m\angle VRV' = x$.

The positive number of degrees a figure rotates is the **angle of rotation.**

A **rotation** about a point is an isometry.

Use the diagram above for Exercises 8–10.

8. The preimage is △ $\boxed{}$ and the image is △ $\boxed{}$.

9. $RW' = \boxed{}$ and $m\angle WRW' = \boxed{}$.

10. $RU' = \boxed{}$ and $m\angle URU' = \boxed{}$.

Problem 1 Drawing a Rotation Image

Got It? What is the image of △LOB for a 50° rotation about B?

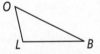

11. Describe the image of B.

_____

_____

12. Follow the steps below to draw a rotation image.

   Step 1 Use a protractor to draw a 50° counterclockwise angle with vertex B and side $\overline{BO}$.

   Step 2 Use a compass to construct $\overline{BO'} \cong \overline{BO}$.

   Step 3 Use a protractor to draw a 50° angle with vertex B and side $\overline{BL}$.

   Step 4 Use a compass to construct $\overline{BL'} \cong \overline{BL}$.

   Step 5 Draw △$L'O'B'$.

Lesson 9-3

The **center of a regular polygon** is the point that is equidistant from its vertices. The center and the vertices of a regular *n*-gon determine *n* congruent triangles.

13. The center and the vertices of a square determine [ ] congruent triangles.

Problem 2 Identifying a Rotation Image

Got It? Point *X* is the center of regular pentagon *PENTA*.
What is the image of *E* for a 144° rotation about *X*?

14. The center and vertices divide *PENTA* into [ ] congruent triangles.

15. Divide 360° by [ ] to find the measure of each central angle.

16. Each central angle measures [ ]°.

Underline the correct word to complete each sentence.

17. A 144° rotation is one / two / three times the rotation of the measure in Exercise 16.

18. A 144° rotation moves each vertex counterclockwise two / three vertices.

19. Circle the image of *E* for a 144° rotation about *X*.

> *P*   *E*   *N*   *T*   *A*

Problem 3 Finding an Angle of Rotation

Got It? Hubcaps of car wheels often have interesting designs that involve rotations.
What is the angle of rotation about *C* that maps *M* to *Q*?

20. The hubcap design has [ ] spokes that divide the circle into [ ] congruent parts.

21. The angle at the center of each part is 360° ÷ [ ] = [ ]°.

22. As *M* rotates counterclockwise about *C* to *Q*, *M* touches [ ] spokes.

23. As *M* rotates counterclockwise about *C* to *Q*, *M* rotates through
[ ] · [ ]°, or [ ]°.

24. The angle of rotation about *C* that maps *M* to *Q* is [ ]°.

Problem 4 **Finding a Composition of Rotations**

Got It? What are the coordinates of the image of point $A(-2, 3)$ for a composition of two 90° rotations about the origin?

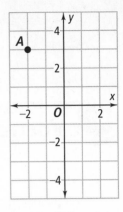

25. The composition of two 90° rotations is one ▢° + ▢° , or ▢° rotation.

26. Complete each step to locate point A' on the diagram at the right.

    Step 1 Draw $\overline{AO}$.

    Step 2 Use a protractor to draw a 180° angle with the vertex at O and side $\overline{OA}$.

    Step 3 Use a compass to construct $\overline{OA'} \cong \overline{OA}$. Graph point A'.

27. The coordinates of A' are (▢ , ▢).

 Lesson Check • **Do you UNDERSTAND?**

Compare and Contrast Compare rotating a figure about a point to reflecting the figure across a line. How are the transformations alike? How are they different?

28. Rotate $\triangle RST$ 90° about the origin.

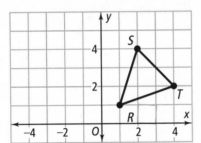

29. Reflect $\triangle RST$ across the y-axis.

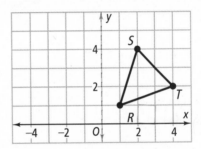

30. Circle the transformation(s) that preserve the size and shape of the preimage. Underline the transformation(s) that preserve the orientation of the preimage.

    reflection across a line   rotation about a point

31. How are rotating and reflecting a figure alike? How are they different?

_____

 Math Success

Check off the vocabulary words that you understand.

☐ rotation   ☐ center of rotation   ☐ angle of rotation   ☐ center of a regular polygon

Rate how well you can *draw and identify rotation images*.

Need to review   0   2   4   6   8   10   Now I get it!

Lesson 9-3

Symmetry

Vocabulary

● Review

1. Circle the *center of rotation* for the transformation at the right.

A		B		C	
	D		E		F

2. If S is the *center of rotation* of a figure that contains point Y, then $SY' = $ ☐ .

3. Cross out the figure(s) for which point A is NOT the *center of rotation*.

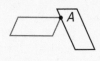

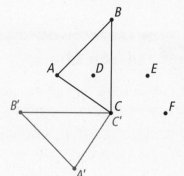

● Vocabulary Builder

symmetry (noun) SIM **uh tree**

Related Word: symmetrical (adjective)

Math Usage: A figure has **symmetry** if there is an isometry that maps the figure onto itself. Figures having **symmetry** are symmetrical.

● Use Your Vocabulary

4. Complete each statement with the appropriate form of the word *symmetry*.

NOUN   Some figures have rotational __?__ .

ADJECTIVE   A figure that maps onto itself is __?__ .

Underline the correct word to complete each sentence.

5. A figure that is its own image is symmetrical / *symmetry* .

6. A line of reflection is a line of symmetrical / *symmetry* .

7. A butterfly's wings are symmetrical / *symmetry* .

Key Concept   Types of Symmetry

A figure has **line symmetry** or **reflectional symmetry** if there is a reflection for which the figure is its own image. The line of reflection is called a *line of symmetry*. It divides the figure into congruent halves.

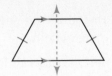

8. Does the trapezoid at the right have a horizontal line of symmetry?

Yes / No

A figure has **rotational symmetry** if there is a rotation of 180° or less for which the figure is its own image. The angle of rotation for rotational symmetry is the smallest angle needed for the figure to rotate onto itself.

9. Is the measure of the angle of rotation for an equilateral triangle 60°?

Yes / No

A figure with 180° rotational symmetry also has **point symmetry**. Each segment joining a point and its 180° rotation image passes through the center of rotation.

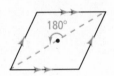

A square, which has both 90° and 180° rotational symmetry, also has point symmetry.

10. Is the center of rotation of the parallelogram at the right equidistant from all vertices?

Yes / No

Problem 1   Identifying Lines of Symmetry

Got It? Draw a rectangle that is not a square. How many lines of symmetry does your rectangle have?

11. Circle the figure that is a rectangle but not a square.

12. Draw a rectangle that is not a square on the grid at the right.

13. Lines of symmetry divide a figure into [ ] congruent parts.

14. Draw the line(s) of symmetry on your rectangle.

15. Does your rectangle have a vertical line of symmetry?

Yes / No

16. Does your rectangle have a horizontal line of symmetry?

Yes / No

17. Does your rectangle have a diagonal line of symmetry?

Yes / No

18. A rectangle that is not a square has [ ] line(s) of symmetry.

Problem 2 Identifying a Rotational Symmetry

Got It? Does the figure at the right have rotational symmetry? If so, what is the angle of rotation?

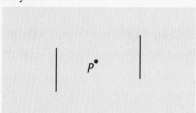

19. Underline the correct word to complete the sentence.

    Each / No side is horizontal or vertical.

20. To keep the same orientation of the sides, the angle of rotation must be

    a multiple of ⬚° .

21. Draw the image after a 90° rotation about point *P*. Two sides are drawn for you.

22. Draw the figure after a 180° rotation about point *P*. Two sides are drawn for you.

23. Does the figure have rotational symmetry? If so, what is the angle of rotation?

Problem 3 Identifying Symmetry in a Three-Dimensional Object

Got It? Does the lampshade have *reflectional symmetry in a plane*, *rotational symmetry about a line*, or *both*?

Write T for *true* or F for *false*.

24. A plane that is parallel to the top of the lampshade and passes through its middle divides the lampshade into two congruent parts.

25. A plane that is perpendicular to the top of the lampshade and passes through its middle divides the lampshade into two congruent parts.

26. The lampshade can be rotated about a horizontal line so that it matches perfectly.

27. The lampshade can be rotated about a vertical line so that it matches perfectly.

28. Does the lampshade have *reflectional symmetry in a plane, rotational symmetry about a line*, or *both*? Explain.

Lesson Check • Do you UNDERSTAND?

Error Analysis Your friend thinks that the regular pentagon in the diagram at the right has 10 lines of symmetry. Explain and correct your friend's error.

29. Place a ✓ in the box if the response is correct. Place an ✗ if it is incorrect.

☐ Each line of symmetry bisects an angle of the pentagon.

☐ Each line of symmetry bisects a side of the pentagon.

☐ Each line of symmetry is parallel to another line of symmetry.

☐ The pentagon has 10 congruent angles.

☐ The pentagon has 10 congruent sides.

☐ The pentagon has 5 congruent angles.

☐ The pentagon has 5 lines of symmetry.

30. Explain your friend's error.

_____

_____

31. Use the regular pentagon below. Draw each line of symmetry in a different color.

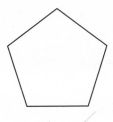

Math Success

Check off the vocabulary words that you understand.

☐ symmetry   ☐ line of symmetry

Rate how well you can *identify symmetry in a figure.*

Need to review   0   2   4   6   8   10   Now I get it!

Lesson 9-4

9-5 Dilations

Vocabulary

● Review

Complete each statement with *ratio* or *similar*.

1. The ? of corresponding parts of similar figures is the *scale factor*.

2. You can use a *scale factor* to make a larger or smaller copy that is ? to the original figure.

3. Circle the *scale factor* that makes an image larger than the preimage.

   $\frac{2}{3}$ $\frac{4}{3}$ $\frac{7}{8}$ $\frac{1}{10}$

4. Circle the *scale factor* that makes an image smaller than the preimage.

   $\frac{5}{2}$ $\frac{9}{2}$ $\frac{1}{4}$ 3

● Vocabulary Builder

dilation (noun) **dy LAY shun**

Definition: A **dilation** is the widening of an object such as the pupil of an eye or a blood vessel.

Math Usage: A **dilation** is a transformation that reduces or enlarges a figure so that the image is similar to the preimage.

Related Words: reduction, enlargement, scale factor, center of dilation

Examples: an enlargement of a photograph, a model of the solar system

● Use Your Vocabulary

5. Underline the correct word to complete the sentence.

   A *dilation* is an enlargement if the figure decreases / increases in size.

6. Cross out the transformation that does NOT have a center.

   | reflection | rotation | dilation |

7. Circle the transformations that are isometries.

   | reflection | rotation | dilation |

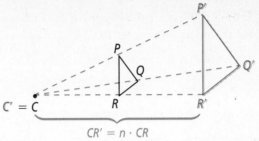

Key Concept   Dilation

A **dilation** with center C and **scale factor** n, $n > 0$, is a transformation with these two properties:

• The image of C is itself (that is, $C' = C$).

• For any other point R, R' is on $\overrightarrow{CR}$ and
$CR' = n \cdot CR$, or $n = \dfrac{CR'}{CR}$.

The image of a dilation is similar to its preimage.

8. For a dilation of $\triangle PQR$ with scale factor 2, $CR' = \boxed{} \cdot CR$.

Problem 1   Finding a Scale Factor

Got It? $J'K'L'M'$ is a dilation image of $JKLM$. The center of dilation is O. Is the dilation an *enlargement* or a *reduction*? What is the scale factor of the dilation?

Underline the correct word to complete each sentence.

9. The image is larger / smaller than preimage.

10. The dilation is a(n) enlargement / reduction .

11. How can you tell which segments are corresponding sides of $JKLM$ and $J'K'L'M'$?

_____

_____

_____

12. Circle the side that corresponds to $\overline{JK}$.

$\overline{J'K'}$ $\qquad\qquad\qquad$ $\overline{J'M'}$ $\qquad\qquad\qquad$ $\overline{L'K'}$

13. Find the length of each side.

$$JK = \sqrt{(\boxed{} - \boxed{})^2 + (\boxed{} - \boxed{})^2} = \sqrt{\boxed{}}$$

$$J'K' = \sqrt{(\boxed{} - \boxed{})^2 + (\boxed{} - \boxed{})^2} = \sqrt{\boxed{}}$$

14. Find the scale factor.

$$\frac{J'K'}{JK} = \frac{\boxed{}}{\boxed{}} = \sqrt{\frac{\boxed{}}{\boxed{}}} = \frac{\boxed{}}{\boxed{}}$$

15. The scale factor is $\boxed{}$.

Lesson 9-5

Problem 2 Finding a Dilation Image

Got It? What are the images of the vertices of $\triangle PZG$ for a dilation with center $(0, 0)$ and scale factor $\frac{1}{2}$?

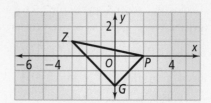

16. Complete the problem-solving model below.

Know
Coordinates of vertices:

$P(2, 0)$, $Z(\boxed{}, \boxed{})$,

and $G(\boxed{}, \boxed{})$

Center of dilation:

$(\boxed{}, \boxed{})$

Scale factor: $\boxed{}$

Need
Coordinates of the images of the vertices

Plan
Substitute the coordinates of the vertices into the dilation rule: $(x, y) \rightarrow$

$(\boxed{} \cdot x, \boxed{} \cdot y)$

17. Use the dilation rule to find the coordinates of the images of the vertices.

$P(\boxed{}, \boxed{}) \rightarrow P'(\boxed{}, \boxed{})$

$Z(\boxed{}, \boxed{}) \rightarrow Z'(\boxed{}, \boxed{})$

$G(\boxed{}, \boxed{}) \rightarrow G'(\boxed{}, \boxed{})$

18. Graph the images of the vertices of $\triangle PZG$ on the coordinate plane. Graph $\triangle P'Z'G'$.

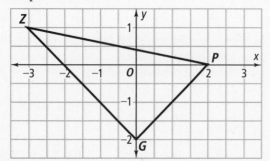

Problem 3 Using a Scale Factor to Find a Length

Got It? The height of a document on your computer screen is 20.4 cm. When you change the zoom setting on your screen from 100% to 25%, the new image of your document is a dilation of the previous image with scale factor 0.25. What is the height of the new image?

19. Underline the correct word to complete the sentence.

The scale factor 0.25 is less than 1, so the dilation is a(n) enlargement / reduction .

20. Image length = scale factor · original length, so image height = $\boxed{}$ · $\boxed{}$,

or $\boxed{}$ cm.

Lesson Check • Do you UNDERSTAND?

Error Analysis The blue figure is a dilation image of the black figure for a dilation with center A.

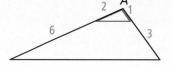

Two students made errors when asked to find the scale factor. Explain and correct their answers.

A.

$n = \dfrac{2}{6} = \dfrac{1}{3}$

B.

$n = \dfrac{4}{1} = 4$

Write T for *true* or F for *false*.

_____ **21.** The dilation is an enlargement.

_____ **22.** The side lengths of the black triangle are 6 and 3.

_____ **23.** The side lengths of the blue triangle are 2 and 1.

_____ **24.** The scale factor is between 0 and 1.

25. Explain the error the student made in solution A.

_____

_____

26. Explain the error the student made in solution B.

_____

_____

27. The correct scale factor is _____ .

Math Success

Check off the vocabulary words that you understand.

☐ dilation   ☐ center of dilation   ☐ scale factor of a dilation

☐ enlargement   ☐ reduction

Rate how well you *understand dilation images of figures*.

Need to review   0   2   4   6   8   10   Now I get it!

Lesson 9-5

9-6 Compositions of Reflections

Vocabulary

● **Review**

Write T for *true* or F for *false*.

_____ **1.** A *reflection* flips a figure across a line of *reflection*.

_____ **2.** A *reflection* turns a figure about a point.

_____ **3.** A *reflection* preimage and image are congruent.

_____ **4.** The orientation of a figure reverses after a *reflection*.

_____ **5.** A line of *reflection* is either horizontal or vertical.

● **Vocabulary Builder**

composition (noun) kahm puh ZISH un

Other Word Forms: compose (verb), composite (adjective), composite (noun)

Definition: A **composition** combines parts.

Math Usage: A **composition** of transformations combines two or more transformations in a given order.

● **Use Your Vocabulary**

Complete each statement with the appropriate word from the list. Use each word only once.

reflections   rotation   symmetry

6. A *composition* of reflections has at least one line of __?__ . _____

7. You can map any congruent figure onto another using a *composition* of __?__ . _____

8. A *composition* of rotations is always a __?__ . _____

Theorem 9-1 and Theorem 9-2

Theorem 9-1 A translation or rotation is a composition of two reflections.

Theorem 9-2

A composition of reflections across parallel lines is a translation.

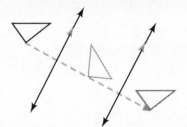

A composition of reflections across two intersecting lines is a rotation.

Problem 1 Composing Reflections Across Parallel Lines

Got It? Lines ℓ and m are parallel. R is between ℓ and m. What is the image of R reflected first across line ℓ and then across line m? What are the direction and distance of the resulting translation?

9. The diagram shows a dashed line perpendicular to ℓ and m that intersects ℓ at point A, m at point B, and R only at point P. Complete each step to show the composition of the reflections.

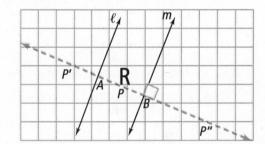

   Step 1 Reflect R across line ℓ. Point P' should correspond to point P.

   Step 2 Reflect the image across line m. Point P'' should correspond to point P'.

10. Underline the correct word to complete each sentence.

    The translation is to the right / left along the dashed line.

    The direction of the translation is parallel / perpendicular to lines ℓ and m.

11. Use the justifications at the right to find the distance PP'' of the resulting translation.

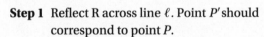

$PP'' = \boxed{} + BP''$ Segment Addition Postulate

$= \boxed{} + BP'$ Definition of reflection across line m

$= \boxed{} + (BP + PA + AP')$ Segment Addition Postulate

$= \boxed{} + BP + 2PA$ Definition of reflection across line ℓ

$= \boxed{} \cdot BP + 2PA$ Simplify.

$= \boxed{} \cdot (BP + PA)$ Use the Distributive Property.

$= \boxed{} \cdot \boxed{}$ Segment Addition Postulate

12. The resulting translation moved R a distance of $\boxed{}$.

Lesson 9-6

take note Theorem 9-3 Fundamental Theorem of Isometries

In a plane, one of two congruent figures can be mapped onto the other by a composition of at most three reflections.

13. Underline the correct word to complete the sentence.

If two congruent figures in a plane have opposite orientations, an **even / odd** number of reflections maps one figure onto the other.

Problem 3 Finding a Glide Reflection Image

Got It? What is the image of $\triangle TEX$ for a glide reflection where the translation is $(x, y) \rightarrow (x + 1, y)$ and the line of reflection is $y = -2$?

Use the coordinate plane at the right for Exercises 14–17.

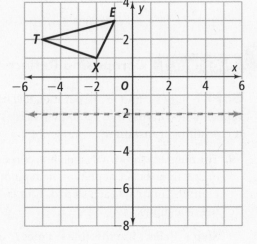

14. Find the vertices of the translation image. Then graph the translation image.

$T(-5, 2) \rightarrow (-5 + \quad, \quad) = (\quad, \quad)$

$E(-1, 3) \rightarrow (-1 + \quad, \quad) = (\quad, \quad)$

$X(-2, 1) \rightarrow (-2 + \quad, \quad) = (\quad, \quad)$

15. In a reflection across a horizontal line,

only the [ ]-coordinate changes.

16. Find the vertices of the triangle you graphed in Exercise 14 after reflection across

the line $y = -2$.

$(\quad, \quad) \rightarrow T'(\quad, \quad)$

$(\quad, \quad) \rightarrow E'(\quad, \quad)$

$(\quad, \quad) \rightarrow X'(\quad, \quad)$

17. The image of $\triangle TEX$ for the given glide reflection is the triangle with vertices

$T'(\quad, \quad)$, $E'(\quad, \quad)$, and $X'(\quad, \quad)$. Graph $\triangle T'E'X'$.

take note Theorem 9-4 Isometry Classification Theorem

There are only four isometries.

Translation	Rotation	Reflection	Glide Reflection

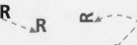

Orientations are the same.   Orientations are opposite.

Got It? Each figure is an isometry image of the figure at the right. Are the orientations of the preimage and image the *same* or *opposite*? What type of isometry maps the preimage to the image?

A.   B.   C. Ь

Choose the correct words from the list to complete each sentence.

18. Image A has the __?__ orientation and is a __?__ .

19. Image B has the __?__ orientation and is a __?__ .

20. Image C has the __?__ orientation and is a __?__ .

opposite
same
translation
rotation
reflection
glide reflection

Lesson Check • **Do you UNDERSTAND?**

Error Analysis You reflect △*DEF* first across line *m* and then across line *n*. Your friend says you can get the same result by reflecting △*DEF* first across line *n* and then across line *m*. Explain your friend's error.

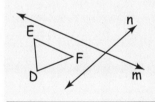

21. Place a ✓ in the box if the response is correct. Place an ✗ if it is incorrect.

☐ Lines *m* and *n* are perpendicular.

☐ A clockwise or counterclockwise rotation has the same image.

22. Explain your friend's error.

Math Success

Check off the vocabulary words that you understand.

☐ composition of reflections   ☐ glide reflection   ☐ isometry

Rate how well you can *find compositions of reflections*.

Need to review 0 2 4 6 8 10 Now I get it!

Vocabulary

Review

1. Underline the correct word to complete the sentence.

   A square has two / four lines of *symmetry*.

2. Circle the figure that has exactly two lines of *symmetry*.

   circle equilateral triangle isosceles triangle rectangle square

Vocabulary Builder

tessellation (noun) **tes uh LAY shun**

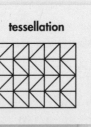

tessellation

Related Words: tessellate (verb), tiling (noun)

Definition: A **tessellation** is a repeated pattern of figures that completely covers a plane, without gaps or overlaps.

Main Idea: You can identify the transformations and symmetries in tessellations.

Example: Squares make a **tessellation** because laying them side by side completely covers the plane without gaps or overlaps.

Non-Example: Circles cannot make a **tessellation** because they leave gaps when placed so they touch but do not overlap.

Use Your Vocabulary

Write T for *true* or F for *false*.

_____ **3.** A *tessellation* of two figures may overlap.

_____ **4.** You can make a *tessellation* with translations.

_____ **5.** You cannot make a *tessellation* with reflections.

_____ **6.** You can use any two figures to make a *tessellation*.

_____ **7.** A tiled floor is an example of a *tessellation*.

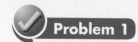
Got It? What is the repeating figure in the tessellation? What transformation does the tessellation use?

8. Underline the correct word to complete the sentence.

   The repeating figure in the tessellation is a lizard / bird / turtle .

9. Describe the orientation of repeating figures in the tessellation.

   _____

   _____

10. Circle the transformation used in the tessellation.

   glide reflection   reflection   rotation   translation

 Problem 2 **Determining Whether a Figure Tessellates**

Got It? Does a regular hexagon tessellate? Explain.

11. Place a ✓ in the box if the statement is correct. Place an ✗ if it is incorrect.

   ☐ If the measure of one angle of a regular polygon is a factor of 360°, the polygon tessellates.

   ☐ If the sum of the measures of n angles of a regular polygon is less than 360°, there are gaps when n copies of the polygon are placed around a vertex.

   ☐ If the sum of the measures of n angles of a regular polygon is greater than 360°, there are gaps when n copies of the polygon are placed around a vertex.

12. The sum of the measures of the angles of a regular hexagon is [　]°.

13. The measure of each angle of a regular hexagon is [　]°.

14. Does a regular hexagon tessellate? Explain.

   _____

   _____

   _____

Problem 3 Identifying Symmetries in a Tessellation

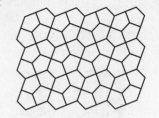

Got It? What types of symmetry does the tessellation at the right have?

Draw a line from the type of symmetry in Column A to its description in Column B.

Column A

15. glide reflectional symmetry

16. reflectional symmetry

17. rotational symmetry

18. translational symmetry

Column B

A figure maps onto itself after a turn.

A figure is its own image after moving a given distance.

A line of symmetry divides the figure into two congruent halves.

A figure maps onto itself after a translation and a reflection.

Use the diagrams below for Exercises 19–23.

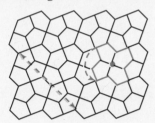

Tessellation A

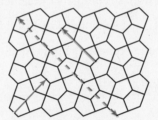

Tessellation B

19. Circle the type of symmetry shown by the red point and arc in Tessellation A.

| glide reflectional | reflectional | rotational | translational |

20. Circle the type of symmetry shown by the blue line in Tessellation A.

| glide reflectional | reflectional | rotational | translational |

21. Circle the type of symmetry shown by the red arrow in Tessellation B.

| glide reflectional | reflectional | rotational | translational |

22. Circle the type of symmetry shown by the blue arrow and dashed line in tessellation B.

| glide reflectional | reflectional | rotational | translational |

23. What types of symmetry does the tessellation have?

Lesson Check • Do you UNDERSTAND?

Reasoning If you arrange three regular octagons so that they meet at one vertex, will they leave a gap or will they overlap? Explain.

24. Complete the reasoning model below.

Think	Write
I know that all angles of a regular polygon have the same measure.	Let a = the measure of one angle.
I can use the Polygon Angle-Sum Theorem to find a.	$a = \dfrac{180(\boxed{} - 2)}{\boxed{}}$
I know that a regular octagon has $\boxed{}$ sides. I can substitute $\boxed{}$ for n.	$a = \dfrac{\boxed{}}{\boxed{}}$
Now I can simplify.	$a = \boxed{}$
Finally, I should find the total measure of $\boxed{}$ angles.	$\boxed{} \cdot \boxed{} = \boxed{}$

25. If you arrange three regular octagons so that they meet at one vertex, will they leave a gap or will they overlap? Explain.

_____

_____

_____

Math Success

Check off the vocabulary words that you understand.

☐ tessellation   ☐ tiling

Rate how well you can *identify figures that tessellate.*

Lesson 9-7

Vocabulary

● Review

The diagram below shows the different types of *parallelograms*.

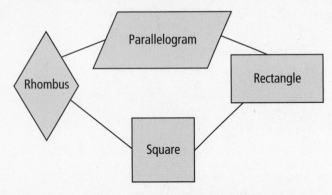

Underline the correct word to complete each sentence.

1. All *parallelograms* are quadrilaterals / rectangles .

2. All *parallelograms* have opposite sides parallel / perpendicular .

3. Some *parallelograms* are trapezoids / rectangles .

● Vocabulary Builder

area (noun) EHR **ee uh**

Definition: **Area** is the number of square units needed to cover a given surface.

Main Idea: You can find the **area** of a parallelogram or a triangle when you know the length of its base and its height.

● Use Your Vocabulary

Find the area of each figure.

4.

5.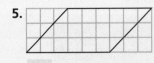

6.

_____ square units   _____ square units   _____ square units

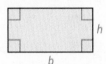

Theorems 10-1 and 10-2 Area of a Rectangle and a Parallelogram

Theorem 10-1 Area of a Rectangle
The area of a rectangle is the product of its base and height.

$$A = bh$$

Theorem 10-2 Area of a Parallelogram
The area of a parallelogram is the product of a base and the corresponding height.

$$A = bh$$

7. Explain how finding the area of a parallelogram and finding the area of a rectangle are alike.

_____

_____

_____

Problem 1 Finding the Area of a Parallelogram

Got It? What is the area of a parallelogram with base length 12 m and height 9 m?

8. Label the parallelogram at the right.

9. Find the area.

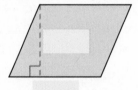

$A = bh$ Write the formula.

$= 12\,(\quad)$ Substitute.

$=$ Simplify.

10. The area of the parallelogram is m^2.

Problem 2 Finding a Missing Dimension

Got It? A parallelogram has sides 15 cm and 18 cm. The height corresponding to a 15-cm base is 9 cm. What is the height corresponding to an 18-cm base?

11. Label the parallelogram at the right.
Let h represent the height corresponding to the 18-cm base.

12. Find the area.

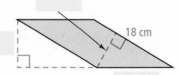

18 cm

13. The area of the parallelogram is cm^2.

Lesson 10-1

14. Use the area of the parallelogram to find the height corresponding to an 18-cm base.

$A = bh$ Write the formula.

$\boxed{} = (\boxed{})h$ Substitute.

$\dfrac{135}{\boxed{}} = \dfrac{(\boxed{})h}{\boxed{}}$ Divide each side by the length of the base.

$\boxed{} = h$ Simplify.

15. The height corresponding to an 18-cm base is $\boxed{}$ cm.

---

take note

Theorem 10-3   Area of a Triangle

The area of a triangle is half the product of a base and the corresponding height.

$A = \frac{1}{2}bh$

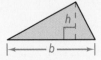

16. Explain how finding the area of a triangle is different from finding the area of a rectangle.

_____

_____

✓ **Problem 3**   **Finding the Area of a Triangle**

Got It? What is the area of the triangle?

17. Circle the formula you can use to find the area of the triangle.

$A = bh$ $A = \frac{1}{2}bh$

5 in.   1 ft 1 in.   1 ft

18. Convert the lengths of the base and the hypotenuse to inches.

     base   hypotenuse

1 ft = $\boxed{}$ in.   1 ft 1 in. = $\boxed{}$ in.

19. Find the area of the triangle.

20. The area of the triangle is $\boxed{}$ in.^{2}.

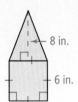

Problem 4 **Finding the Area of an Irregular Figure**

Got It? **Reasoning** Suppose the base lengths of the square and triangle in the figure are doubled to 12 in., but the height of each polygon remains the same. How is the area of the figure affected?

8 in.

6 in.

21. Complete to find the area of each irregular figure.

Area of Original Irregular Figure

$A = 6(6) + \frac{1}{2}(6)(8)$

$= \boxed{} + 24$

$= \boxed{}$

Area of New Irregular Figure

$A = (2)(6)(6) + \frac{1}{2}(2)(6)(8)$

$= (2)(36) + (2)(\boxed{})$

$= (2)(\boxed{} + \boxed{}) = (2)(\boxed{}) = \boxed{}$

22. How is the area affected?

_____

Lesson Check • Do you UNDERSTAND?

▱*ABCD* is divided into two triangles along diagonal $\overline{AC}$. If you know the area of the parallelogram, how do you find the area of △*ABC*?

Write T for *true* or F for *false*.

_____ 23. Since $\overline{AC}$ is a diagonal of ▱*ABCD*, △*ABC* is congruent to △*CDA*.

_____ 24. The area of △*ABC* is greater than the area △*CDA*.

_____ 25. The area of △*ABC* is half the area of ▱*ABCD*.

26. If you know the area of the parallelogram, how do you find the area of △*ABC*?

_____

Math Success

Check off the vocabulary words that you understand.

☐ base of a parallelogram   ☐ height of a parallelogram

☐ base of a triangle   ☐ height of a triangle

Rate how well you can *find the area of parallelograms and triangles*.

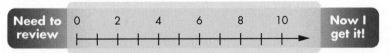

Lesson 10-1

Vocabulary

● Review

1. Is a *rhombus* a parallelogram?   Yes / No

2. Are all *rhombuses* squares?   Yes / No

3. Are all squares *rhombuses*?   Yes / No

4. Cross out the figure that is NOT a *rhombus*.

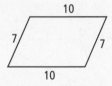 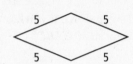

● Vocabulary Builder

kite (noun) <u>kyt</u>

Definition: A **kite** is a quadrilateral with two pairs of congruent adjacent sides.

Main Idea: You can find the area of a **kite** when you know the lengths of its diagonals.

Word Origin: The name for this quadrilateral is taken from the name of the flying toy that it looks like.

● Use Your Vocabulary

5. Circle the *kite*.

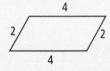 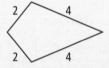 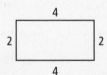

6. The figure at the right is a *kite*. What is the value of x? Explain.

_____

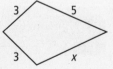

Theorem 10-4   Area of a Trapezoid

The area of a trapezoid is half the product of the height and the sum of the bases.

$$A = \frac{1}{2}h(b_1 + b_2)$$

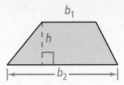

Underline the correct word to complete each sentence.

7. The bases of a trapezoid are parallel / perpendicular .

8. The height / width of a trapezoid is the perpendicular distance between the bases.

 Problem 1 **Area of a Trapezoid**

Got It? What is the area of a trapezoid with height 7 cm and bases 12 cm and 15 cm?

9. Use the justifications below to find the area of the trapezoid.

$A = \frac{1}{2}h(b_1 + b_2)$ Use the formula for area of a trapezoid.

$= \frac{1}{2}(\ \ \ )(\ \ \ + 15)$ Substitute.

$= \frac{1}{2}(\ \ \ )(\ \ \ )$ Add.

$= \boxed{}$ Simplify.

10. The area of the trapezoid is $\boxed{}$ cm^2.

 Problem 2 **Finding Area Using a Right Triangle**

Got It? Suppose h decreases in trapezoid $PQRS$ so that $m\angle P = 45$ while angles R and Q and the bases stay the same. What is the area of trapezoid $PQRS$?

11. If $m\angle P = 45$, is the triangle still a 30°-60°-90° triangle?   Yes / No

12. Is the triangle a 45°-45°-90° triangle?   Yes / No

13. Are the legs of a 45°-45°-90° triangle congruent?   Yes / No

14. The height of the triangle is $\boxed{\ }$ m.

15. The area is found below. Write a justification for each step.

$A = \frac{1}{2}h(b_1 + b_2)$

$= \frac{1}{2}(2)(5 + 7)$

$= \frac{1}{2}(2)(12)$

$= 12$

16. The area of trapezoid $PQRS$ is $\boxed{\ }$ m^2.

Lesson 10-2

Theorem 10-5 Area of a Rhombus or a Kite

The area of a rhombus or a kite is half the product of the
lengths of its diagonals.

$$A = \frac{1}{2}(d_1 d_2)$$

Rhombus   Kite

17. Describe one way that finding the area of rhombus or a kite is different from
finding the area of a trapezoid.

_____

_____

18. Find the lengths of the diagonals of the kite and the rhombus below.

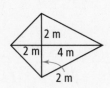

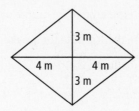

lengths of the diagonals of the kite: lengths of the diagonals of the rhombus:

[   ] m and [   ] m   [   ] m and [   ] m

 Problem 3 Finding the Area of a Kite

Got It? What is the area of a kite with diagonals that are 12 in. and 9 in. long?

19. Error Analysis Below is one student's solution. What error did the student make?

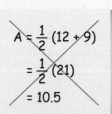

_____

_____

20. Find the area of the kite.

21. The area of the kite is [   ] in.^{2}.

256

Problem 4 Finding the Area of a Rhombus

Got It? A rhombus has sides 10 cm long. If the longer diagonal is 16 cm, what is the area of the rhombus?

Underline the correct words to complete the sentence.

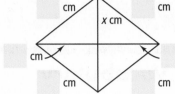

22. The diagonals of a rhombus bisect each <u>other</u> / side and are parallel / <u>perpendicular</u> .

23. Label the rhombus at the right.

24. The shorter diagonal is [   ] + [   ] , or [   ] .

25. Use the Pythagorean Theorem to find the value of *x*.

26. Find the area of the rhombus.

27. The area of the rhombus is [   ] cm².

Lesson Check • Do you UNDERSTAND?

Reasoning Do you need to know the lengths of the sides to find the area of a kite? Explain.

28. Cross out the length you do NOT need to find the area of each triangle in a kite.

each leg   hypotenuse

29. Now answer the question.

_____

_____

_____

Math Success

Check off the vocabulary words that you understand.

☐ kite   ☐ height of a trapezoid

Rate how well you can *find the area of a trapezoid, rhombus, or kite.*

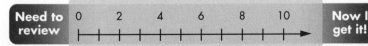

Lesson 10-2

10-3 Areas of Regular Polygons

Vocabulary

● **Review**

Write T for *true* or F for *false*.

_____ **1.** In a *regular polygon*, all sides are congruent.

_____ **2.** In a *regular polygon*, all angles are acute.

3. Cross out the figure that is NOT a *regular polygon*.

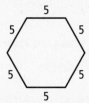

● **Vocabulary Builder**

apothem (noun) AP **uh them**

Related Words: center, regular polygon

Definition: The **apothem** is the perpendicular distance from the center of a regular polygon to one of its sides.

● **Use Your Vocabulary**

4. Underline the correct word to complete the statement.

In a regular polygon, the *apothem* is the perpendicular distance from the center to a(n) angle / side .

5. Label the regular polygon below using *apothem, center,* or *side.*

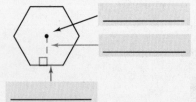

_____

_____

_____

Problem 1 Finding Angle Measures

Got It? At the right, a portion of a regular octagon has radii and an apothem drawn. What is the measure of each numbered angle?

6. A regular octagon has ☐ sides.

7. Circle the type of triangles formed by the radii of the regular octagon.

equilateral   isosceles   right

8. Use the justifications below to find the measure of each numbered angle.

$m\angle 1 = \dfrac{360}{\boxed{}} = \boxed{}$ Divide 360 by the number of sides.

$m\angle 2 = \boxed{} (m\angle 1)$ The apothem bisects the vertex angle of the triangle formed by the radii.

$\quad = \frac{1}{2}(\boxed{}) = \boxed{}$

$90 + m\angle 2 + m\angle 3 = \boxed{}$ Triangle Angle-Sum Theorem

$90 + \boxed{} + m\angle 3 = \boxed{}$ Substitute.

$\boxed{} + m\angle 3 = \boxed{}$ Simplify.

$m\angle 3 = \boxed{}$ Subtraction Property of Equality

9. Write the measure of each numbered angle.

$m\angle 1 = \boxed{}$ $m\angle 2 = \boxed{}$ $m\angle 3 = \boxed{}$

take note

Postulate 10-1 and Theorem 10-6

Postulate 10-1 If two figures are congruent, then their areas are equal.

The isosceles triangles in the regular hexagon at the right are congruent. Complete each statement.

10. If the area of △AOB is 24 in.², then the area of △BOC is ☐ in.².

11. If the area of △BOC is 8 cm², then the area of △AOC is ☐ cm².

Theorem 10-6 Area of a Regular Polygon
The area of a regular polygon is half the product of the apothem and the perimeter.

$A = \frac{1}{2}ap$

Complete.

12. apothem: 10   perimeter: 80   area: $\frac{1}{2}(10) \cdot \boxed{}$

13. apothem: 5   perimeter: $30\sqrt{3}$ area: $\frac{1}{2} \cdot \boxed{} \cdot \boxed{}$

14. apothem: $5\sqrt{3}$ perimeter: 60   area: $\boxed{} \cdot \boxed{} \cdot \boxed{}$

Lesson 10-3

Problem 2 Finding the Area of a Regular Polygon

Got It? What is the area of a regular pentagon with an 8-cm apothem and 11.6-cm sides?

15. Label the regular pentagon with the lengths of the apothem and the sides.

16. Use the justifications below to find the perimeter.

$p = ns$ Use the formula for the perimeter of an n-gon.

= ☐ (11.6)   Substitute for n and for s.

= ☐   Simplify.

17. Use the justifications below to find the area.

$A = \frac{1}{2}ap$ Use the formula for the area of a regular polygon.

$= \frac{1}{2} \cdot$ ☐ $\cdot$ ☐   Substitute for a and for p.

= ☐   Simplify.

18. The regular pentagon has an area of ☐ cm^2.

Problem 3 Using Special Triangles to Find Area

Got It? The side of a regular hexagon is 16 ft. What is the area of the hexagon? Round your answer to the nearest square foot.

19. Use the information in the problem to complete the problem-solving model below.

Know	Need	Plan
I know that the length of each side of the regular hexagon is ☐ ft.		Draw a diagram to help find the length of the apothem. Then use the perimeter and area formulas.

Use the diagram at the right.

20. Label the diagram.

21. Circle the relationship you can use to find the length of the apothem.

    hypotenuse = 2 · shorter leg   longer leg = $\sqrt{3}$ · shorter leg

22. Complete.

    length of shorter leg = ☐ ft

    length of longer leg (apothem) = ☐ ft

23. Use the formula $p = ns$ to find the perimeter of the hexagon.

24. Now use the perimeter and the formula $A = \frac{1}{2}ap$ to find the area of the hexagon.

25. To the nearest square foot, the area of the hexagon is ⬜ ft².

Lesson Check • Do you UNDERSTAND?

What is the relationship between the side length and the apothem in each figure?

square

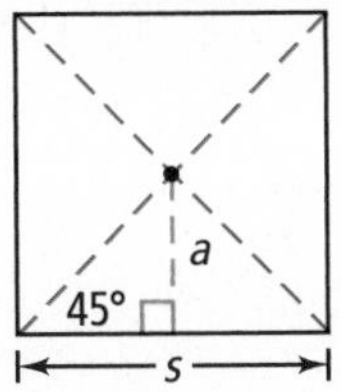

regular hexagon

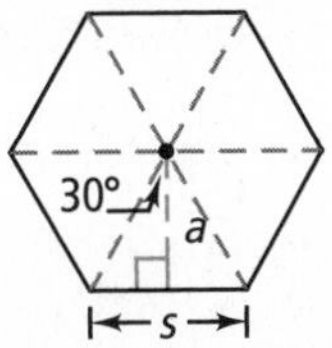

equilateral triangle

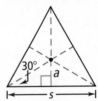

26. The radius and apothem form what type of triangle in each figure?

square

⬜°-⬜°-⬜° triangle

regular hexagon

⬜°-⬜°-⬜° triangle

equilateral triangle

⬜°-⬜°-⬜° triangle

27. Complete to show the relationship between the side length and the apothem.

square

leg = leg

$a = $ ⬜ s

regular hexagon

longer leg = $\sqrt{3}$ · shorter leg

$a = \sqrt{3} \cdot$ ⬜ s

$a = $ ⬜ s

equilateral triangle

longer leg = $\sqrt{3}$ · shorter leg

$\frac{1}{2}s = \sqrt{3} \cdot$ ⬜

$s = $ ⬜ a

Math Success

Check off the vocabulary words that you understand.

☐ radius of a regular polygon   ☐ apothem

Rate how well you can *find the area of a regular polygon*.

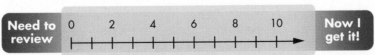

Vocabulary

● Review

1. What does it mean when two figures are *similar*?

_____

2. Are the corresponding angles of *similar* figures always congruent? | Yes / No

3. Are the corresponding sides of *similar* figures always proportional? | Yes / No

4. Circle the pairs of *similar* figures.

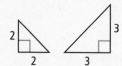 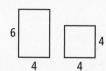

● Vocabulary Builder

> **radius** (noun) RAY **dee us** (plural radii)
>
> **Related Words:** apothem, center
>
> **Definition:** The **radius** of a regular polygon is the distance from the center to a vertex.
>
> **Main Idea:** The **radii** of a regular polygon divide the polygon into congruent triangles.

● Use Your Vocabulary

5. Cross out the segment that is NOT a *radius* of regular pentagon *ABCDE*.

$\overline{OA}$ $\overline{OD}$ $\overline{OB}$ $\overline{OE}$ $\overline{OC}$ $\overline{OF}$

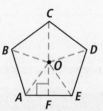

Underline the correct word(s) to complete each sentence.

6. The *radii* of a regular polygon are / are not congruent.

7. The triangles formed by the *radii* and sides of regular pentagon *ABCDE* are / are not congruent.

Theorem 10-7 Perimeters and Areas of Similar Figures

If the scale factor of two similar figures is $\frac{a}{b}$, then

(1) the ratio of their perimeters is $\frac{a}{b}$ and

(2) the ratio of their areas is $\frac{a^2}{b^2}$.

8. The name for the ratio of the length of one side of a figure to the length of the corresponding side of a similar figure is the __?__ .

_____

9. If the scale factor of two figures is $\frac{1}{2}$, then the ratio of their perimeters is ——.

10. If the scale factor of two figures is $\frac{3}{x}$, then the ratio of their perimeters is ——.

11. If the scale factor of two figures is $\frac{3}{5}$, then the ratio of their areas is $\dfrac{^2}{^2}$.

12. If the scale factor of two figures is $\frac{1}{x}$ then the ratio of their areas is $\dfrac{^2}{^2}$.

 Problem 1 Finding Ratios in Similar Figures

Got It? Two similar polygons have corresponding sides in the ratio 5 : 7. What is the ratio (larger to smaller) of their perimeters? What is the ratio (larger to smaller) of their areas?

13. Circle the similar polygons that have corresponding sides in the ratio 5 : 7.

Underline the correct word to complete each sentence.

14. In similar figures, the ratio of the areas / perimeters equals the ratio of corresponding sides.

15. In similar figures, the ratio of the areas / perimeters equals the ratio of the squares of corresponding sides.

16. Complete.

ratio (larger to smaller) of corresponding sides	ratio (larger to smaller) of perimeters	ratio (larger to smaller) of areas
——	——	$\dfrac{^2}{^2} = $ ——

Lesson 10-4

Problem 2 **Finding Areas Using Similar Figures**

Got It? The scale factor of two similar parallelograms is $\frac{3}{4}$. The area of the larger parallelogram is 96 in.^{2}. What is the area of the smaller parallelogram?

Write T for *true* or F for *false*.

_____ **17.** The ratio of the areas is $\frac{3}{4}$.

_____ **18.** The ratio of the areas is $\frac{9}{16}$.

19. Use the justifications below to find the area A of the smaller parallelogram.

$\dfrac{\boxed{}}{16} = \dfrac{A}{96}$ Write a proportion.

$16A = (96)\boxed{}$ Cross Products Property

$16A = \boxed{}$ Multiply.

$\dfrac{16A}{\boxed{}} = \dfrac{\boxed{}}{\boxed{}}$ Divide each side by $\boxed{}$.

$A = \boxed{}$ Simplify.

20. The area of the smaller parallelogram is $\boxed{}$ in.^{2}.

Problem 3 **Applying Area Ratios**

Got It? The scale factor of the dimensions of two similar pieces of window glass is 3 : 5. The smaller piece costs $2.50. How much should the larger piece cost?

21. Use the information in the problem to complete the reasoning model below.

Think	Write
The ratio of areas is the square of the scale factor.	Ratio of areas = $3^2 : 5^2$ = $\boxed{} : \boxed{}$
I can use a proportion to find the cost c of the larger piece to the nearest hundredth.	$\dfrac{\boxed{}}{\boxed{}} = \dfrac{2.50}{c}$ $\boxed{} \cdot c = 2.50 \cdot \boxed{}$ $\boxed{} \cdot c = \boxed{}$ $\dfrac{\boxed{} \, c}{\boxed{}} = \dfrac{\boxed{}}{\boxed{}}$ $c \approx \boxed{}$

22. The larger piece of glass should cost about $ $\boxed{}$.

Problem 4 **Finding Perimeter Ratios**

Got It? The areas of two similar rectangles are 1875 ft² and 135 ft².
What is the ratio of their perimeters?

23. The scale factor is found below. Use one of the reasons listed in the blue
box to justify each step.

$$\frac{a^2}{b^2} = \frac{135}{1875}$$ _____

$$\frac{a^2}{b^2} = \frac{9}{125}$$ _____

$$\frac{a}{b} = \frac{3}{5\sqrt{5}}$$ _____

$$\frac{a}{b} = \frac{3}{5\sqrt{5}} \cdot \frac{\sqrt{5}}{\sqrt{5}}$$ _____

$$\frac{a}{b} = \frac{3\sqrt{5}}{25}$$ _____

> Rationalize the denominator.
>
> Simplify.
>
> Simplify.
>
> Take the positive square root of each side.
>
> Write a proportion.

24. The ratio of the perimeters equals the scale factor ⬚ : ⬚ .

Lesson Check • **Do you UNDERSTAND?**

Reasoning The area of one rectangle is twice the area of another. What is the ratio of
their perimeters? How do you know?

25. Let x and y be the sides of the smaller rectangle. Complete.

area of smaller rectangle   area of larger rectangle   ratio of larger to smaller areas

     xy ⬚ xy ⬚ : ⬚

26. Find the square root of the ratio of larger to smaller areas to find the scale factor.

27. The ratio of perimeters is ⬚ : ⬚   because the scale factor is ⬚ : ⬚ .

Math Success

Check off the vocabulary words that you understand.

☐ similar polygons   ☐ radius   ☐ perimeter   ☐ area

Rate how well you can *find the perimeters and areas of similar polygons*.

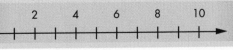

Lesson 10-4

10-5 Trigonometry and Area

Vocabulary

● Review

1. Underline the correct word to complete the sentence.

   Area is the number of cubic / square units needed to cover a given surface.

2. Circle the formula for the *area* of a triangle.

$$A = bh \qquad A = \frac{1}{2}bh \qquad A = \frac{1}{2}h(b_1 + b_2) \qquad A = \frac{1}{2}d_1d_2$$

● Vocabulary Builder

trigonometry (noun) **trig uh NAHM uh tree**

Other Word Form: trigonometric (adjective)

Related Words: cosine, sine, tangent

Definition: Trigonometry is the study of the relationships among two sides and an angle in a right triangle.

Main Idea: You can use **trigonometry** to find the area of a regular polygon.

● Use Your Vocabulary

Complete each sentence with the word *trigonometry* or *trigonometric*.

3. The sine, cosine, and tangent ratios are __?__ ratios.

4. This year I am studying __?__ in math.

Draw a line from each *trigonometric ratio* in Column A to its name in Column B.

Column A	Column B
5. $\dfrac{\text{length of opposite leg}}{\text{length of hypotenuse}}$	cosine
6. $\dfrac{\text{length of adjacent leg}}{\text{length of hypotenuse}}$	sine
7. $\dfrac{\text{length of opposite leg}}{\text{length of adjacent leg}}$	tangent

Got It? What is the area of a regular pentagon with 4-in. sides? Round your answer to the nearest square inch.

8. Underline the correct words to complete the sentence.

   To find the area using the formula $A = \frac{1}{2}ap$, you need to know the length of the

   apothem / radius and the perimeter / width of the pentagon.

9. In the regular pentagon at the right, label center C, apothem $\overline{CR}$, and radii $\overline{CD}$ and $\overline{CE}$.

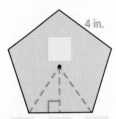

4 in.

10. The perimeter of the pentagon is 5 · ____ in., or ____ in.

11. The measure of central angle DCE is $\dfrac{360}{}$, or ____ .

Complete Exercises 12 and 13.

12. $m\angle DCR = \frac{1}{2}m\angle DCE$

    $= \frac{1}{2} \cdot$ ____

    $=$ ____

13. $DR = \frac{1}{2}DE$

    $= \frac{1}{2} \cdot$ ____

    $=$ ____

14. Use your results from Exercises 12 and 13 to label the diagram below.

C

a

D R

15. Circle the equation you can use to find the apothem a.

   $\tan 72° = \dfrac{36}{a}$ $\tan 36° = \dfrac{2a}{a}$ $\tan 36° = \dfrac{2}{a}$

   $\tan 36° = \dfrac{a}{2}$ $\tan 72° = \dfrac{2}{a}$

16. Use the justifications below to find the apothem and the area.

   $\tan 72° = \dfrac{\boxed{}}{a}$ Use the tangent ratio.

   $a \cdot \tan 36° =$ ____   Multiply each side by a.

   $a = \dfrac{\boxed{}}{\tan 36°}$ Divide each side by $\tan 36°$.

   $A = \frac{1}{2}ap$ Write the formula for the area of a regular polygon.

   $= \frac{1}{2} \cdot \dfrac{}{\tan 36°} \cdot \boxed{}$ Substitute for a and p.

   $\approx$ ____   Use a calculator.

17. To the nearest square inch, the area of the regular pentagon is ____ in.^{2}.

Lesson 10-5

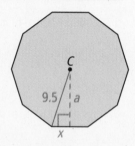

Problem 2 Finding Area

Got It? A tabletop has the shape of a regular decagon with a radius of 9.5 in. What is the area of the tabletop to the nearest square inch?

18. Complete the problem-solving model below.

Know	Need	Plan
		Use trigonometric ratios to find the apothem and the length of a side.

19. Look at the decagon at the right. Explain why the measure of each central angle of a decagon is 36 and $m\angle C$ is 18.

_____

_____

20. Use the cosine ratio to find the apothem a.

$$\cos 18° = \frac{a}{\rule{1.5cm}{0.4pt}}$$

$$\rule{1.5cm}{0.4pt} \cdot \cos 18° = a$$

21. Use the sine ratio to find x.

$$\sin 18° = \frac{x}{\rule{1.5cm}{0.4pt}}$$

$$\rule{1.5cm}{0.4pt} \cdot \sin 18° = x$$

22. Use the justifications below to find the perimeter.

$p = \boxed{} \cdot$ length of one side   perimeter = number of sides times length of one side

$= 10 \cdot \boxed{} \cdot x$ The length of each side is $2x$.

$= 10 \cdot \boxed{} \cdot \boxed{}$ Substitute for x.

$= \boxed{} \cdot \sin 18°$ Simplify.

23. Find the area. Use a calculator.

24. To the nearest square inch, the area of the tabletop is $\boxed{}$ in.^{2}.

Theorem 10-8 Area of a Triangle Given SAS

The area of a triangle is half the product of the lengths of two sides and the sine of the included angle.

25. Complete the formula below.

$$\text{Area of } \triangle ABC = \frac{1}{2}bc(\sin \boxed{})$$

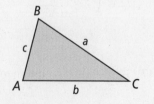

Got It? What is the area of the triangle? Round your answer to the nearest square inch.

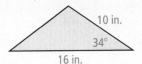

26. Complete the reasoning model below.

Think	Write
I know the lengths of two sides and the measure of the included angle.	Side lengths: ☐ in. and 16 in. Angle measure: ☐
I can use the formula for the area of a triangle given SAS.	$A = \frac{1}{2} \cdot$ ☐ $\cdot 16 \cdot \sin$ ☐ $\approx$ ☐

27. To the nearest square inch, the area of the triangle is ☐ in.²

Lesson Check • **Do you UNDERSTAND?**

Error Analysis Your classmate needs to find the area of a regular pentagon with 8-cm sides. To find the apothem, he sets up and solves a trigonometric ratio. What error did he make? Explain.

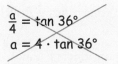

28. The lengths of the legs of the triangle in the regular pentagon are ☐ and ☐ cm.

29. The tangent of the 36° angle is $\dfrac{\text{length of opposite leg}}{\text{length of adjacent leg}}$, or _____ .

30. Explain the error your classmate made.

_____

Math Success

Check off the vocabulary words that you understand.

☐ area   ☐ trigonometry

Rate how well you can use *trigonometry to find area.*

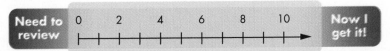

Lesson 10-5

Circles and Arcs

Vocabulary

Review

1. Is a *circle* a two-dimensional figure?   Yes / No

2. Is a *circle* a polygon?   Yes / No

3. Is every point on a circle the same distance from the center?   Yes / No

4. Circle the figure that is a *circle*.

Vocabulary Builder

arc (noun) **ahrk**

Definition: An **arc** is part of a circle.

Related Words: minor arc, major arc, semicircle

Example: Semicircle *AB* is an **arc** of the circle.

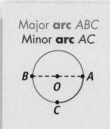

Major **arc** ABC
Minor **arc** AC

Use Your Vocabulary

Underline the correct word to complete each sentence.

5. A *minor arc* is larger / smaller than a semicircle.

6. A *major arc* is larger / smaller than a semicircle.

7. You use two / three points to name a *major arc*.

8. You use two / three points to name a *minor arc*.

9. Circle the name of the red *arc*.

   $\overset{\frown}{JK}$ $\overset{\frown}{KL}$ $\overset{\frown}{LJK}$ $\overset{\frown}{LKJ}$

10. Circle the name of the blue *arc*.

   $\overset{\frown}{JK}$ $\overset{\frown}{KL}$ $\overset{\frown}{LJK}$ $\overset{\frown}{LKJ}$

Problem 1 Naming Arcs

Got It? What are the minor arcs of ⊙A?

Draw a line from each central angle in Column A to its corresponding minor arc in Column B.

Column A	Column B
11. ∠PAQ	$\overset{\frown}{RS}$
12. ∠QAR	$\overset{\frown}{SP}$
13. ∠RAS	$\overset{\frown}{PQ}$
14. ∠SAP	$\overset{\frown}{QR}$
15. ∠SAQ	$\overset{\frown}{SQ}$

16. The minor arcs of ⊙A are ____ , ____ , ____ , ____ , and ____ .

Key Concepts Arc Measure and Postulate 10-2

Arc Measure

The measure of a minor arc is equal to the measure of its corresponding central angle.

The measure of a major arc is the measure of the related minor arc subtracted from 360.

The measure of a semicircle is 180.

Use ⊙S at the right for Exercises 17 and 18.

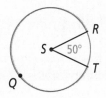

17. $m\overset{\frown}{RT} = m\angle RST = $ ____

18. $m\overset{\frown}{TQR} = 360 - m\overset{\frown}{RT} = 360 - $ ____ $ = $ ____

Postulate 10-2 Arc Addition Postulate

The measure of the arc formed by two adjacent arcs is the sum of the measures of the two arcs.

$$m\overset{\frown}{ABC} = m\overset{\frown}{AB} + m\overset{\frown}{BC}$$

Use the circle at the right for Exercises 19 and 20.

19. If $m\overset{\frown}{AB} = 40$ and $m\overset{\frown}{BC} = 100$, then $m\overset{\frown}{ABC} = $ ____ .

20. If $m\overset{\frown}{AB} = x$ and $m\overset{\frown}{BC} = y$, then $m\overset{\frown}{ABC} = $ ____ .

Problem 2 Finding the Measures of Arcs

Got It? What are the measures of $\overset{\frown}{PR}$, $\overset{\frown}{RS}$, $\overset{\frown}{PRQ}$, and $\overset{\frown}{PQR}$ in ⊙C?

Complete.

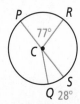

21. $m\angle PCR = $ ____ , so $m\overset{\frown}{PR} = $ ____ .

Lesson 10-6

22. $m\angle RCS = m\angle PCS - m\angle PCR$

   $= 180 - \boxed{} = \boxed{}$

23. $m\angle RCS = \boxed{}$, so $m\,\overset{\frown}{RS} = \boxed{}$.

24. $m\overset{\frown}{PRQ} = m\,\overset{\frown}{PR} + m\,\overset{\frown}{RS} + m\,\overset{\frown}{SQ}$

   $= \boxed{} + \boxed{} + \boxed{} = \boxed{}$

25. $m\overset{\frown}{PQR} = 360 - m\,\overset{\frown}{PR}$

   $= 360 - \boxed{} = \boxed{}$

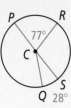

Theorem 10-9   Circumference of a Circle

The circumference of a circle is π times the diameter.

   $C = \pi d$ or $C = 2\pi r$

26. Explain why you can use either $C = \pi d$ or $C = 2\pi r$ to find the circumference of a circle.

_____

_____

_____

✓ **Problem 3 Finding a Distance**

Got It? A car has a circular turning radius of 16.1 ft. The distance between the two front tires is 4.7 ft. How much farther does a tire on the outside of the turn travel than a tire on the inside?

27. The two circles have the same center. To find the radius of the inner circle, do you *add* or *subtract*?   _____

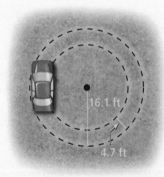

Complete.

28. radius of outer circle = $\boxed{}$

   radius of inner circle = $\boxed{} - 4.7 = \boxed{}$

29. circumference of outer circle $= 2\pi r = 2\pi \cdot \boxed{} = \boxed{} \cdot \pi$

   circumference of inner circle $= 2\pi r = 2\pi \cdot \boxed{} = \boxed{} \cdot \pi$

30. Find the differences in the two distances traveled. Use a calculator.

   $\boxed{} \cdot \pi - \boxed{} \cdot \pi = \boxed{} \cdot \pi$

   $\approx \boxed{}$

31. A tire on the outer circle travels about $\boxed{}$ ft farther.

Theorem 10-10 Arc Length

The length of an arc of a circle is the product of the ratio $\frac{\text{measure of the arc}}{360}$ and the circumference of the circle.

32. Complete the formula below.

length of _____ $= \dfrac{m\,\widehat{AB}}{360} \cdot 2\pi r = \dfrac{m\,\widehat{AB}}{360} \cdot \pi d$

Write T for *true* or F for *false*.

_____ **33.** The length of an arc is a fraction of the circumference of a circle.

_____ **34.** In $\odot O$, $m\,\widehat{AB} = m\angle AOB$.

Lesson Check • Do you UNDERSTAND?

Error Analysis Your class must find the length of $\widehat{AB}$. A classmate submits the following solution. What is the error?

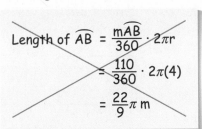

Length of $\widehat{AB} = \dfrac{m\widehat{AB}}{360} \cdot 2\pi r$

$\quad = \dfrac{110}{360} \cdot 2\pi(4)$

$\quad = \dfrac{22}{9}\pi$ m

35. Is $\widehat{AC}$ a semicircle?   Yes / No

36. Does $m\,\widehat{AB} = 180 - 70 = 110$?   Yes / No

37. Is the length of the radius 4?   Yes / No

38. What is the error?

_____

Math Success

Check off the vocabulary words that you understand.

☐ circle   ☐ minor arc   ☐ major arc   ☐ circumference

Rate how well you can *use central angles, arcs, and circumference.*

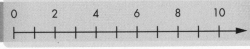

Lesson 10-6

Vocabulary

● Review

1. Explain how the *area* of a figure is different from the perimeter of the figure.

_____

_____

2. Circle the formula for the *area* of a parallelogram.

$A = bh$　　　　$A = \frac{1}{2}bh$　　　　$A = \frac{1}{2}h(b_1 + b_2)$　　　　$A = \frac{1}{2}d_1d_2$

3. Find the *area* of each figure.

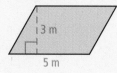　　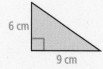　　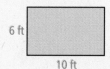

$A = \boxed{}\ m^2$　　　　$A = \boxed{}\ cm^2$　　　　$A = \boxed{}\ ft^2$

● Vocabulary Builder

sector *RST*

sector (noun) SEK **tur**

Definition: A **sector** of a circle is a region bounded by an arc of the circle and the two radii to the arc's endpoints.

Main Idea: The area of a **sector** is a fractional part of the area of a circle.

● Use Your Vocabulary

4. Name the arc and the radii that are the boundaries of the shaded *sector*.

arc $\boxed{}$　　　　　　　　radii $\boxed{}$ and $\boxed{}$

5. Circle the name of the shaded *sector*.

sector *ABC*　　　　　　sector *ACB*　　　　　　sector *BAC*

6. The shaded *sector* is what fractional part of the area of the circle? Explain.

_____

_____

take note

Theorem 10-11   Area of a Circle

The area of a circle is the product of π and the square of the radius.

$$A = \pi r^2$$

Complete each statement.

7. If the radius is 5 ft, then $A = \pi \cdot \boxed{} \cdot \boxed{}$.

8. If the diameter is 1.8 cm, then $A = \pi \cdot \boxed{} \cdot \boxed{}$.

✓ Problem 1   Finding the Area of a Circle

Got It? What is the area of a circular wrestling region with a 42-ft diameter?

9. The radius of the wrestling region is $\boxed{}$ ft.

10. Complete the reasoning model below.

Think	Write
I can use the formula for the area of a circle.	$A = \pi r^2$
I can subtitute the radius into the formula and then simplify.	$= \pi \cdot \boxed{}^2$ $= \boxed{} \cdot \pi$
I can use a calculator to find the approximate area.	$\approx \boxed{}$

11. The area of the wrestling region is about $\boxed{}$ ft^2 .

take note

Theorem 10-12   Area of a Sector of a Circle

The area of a sector of a circle is the product of the ratio $\dfrac{\text{measure of the arc}}{360}$ and the area of the circle.

$$\text{Area of sector } AOB = \frac{m\,\widehat{AB}}{360} \cdot \pi r^2$$

Complete.

measure of the arc	$\dfrac{\text{measure of the arc}}{360}$	area of the sector
12. 60	$\dfrac{60}{360} = \dfrac{1}{\boxed{}}$	$\dfrac{1}{\boxed{}} \cdot \boxed{} \cdot r^2$
13. 120	$\dfrac{\boxed{}}{360} = \dfrac{\boxed{}}{\boxed{}}$	$\dfrac{\boxed{}}{\boxed{}} \cdot \boxed{} \cdot r^2$

Lesson 10-7

✓ **Problem 2** **Finding the Area of a Sector of a Circle**

Got It? A circle has a radius of 4 in. What is the area of a sector bounded by a 45° minor arc? Leave your answer in terms of π.

14. At the right is one student's solution. What error did the student make?

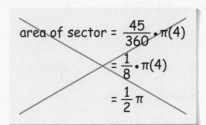

$$\text{area of sector} = \frac{45}{360} \cdot \pi(4)$$
$$= \frac{1}{8} \cdot \pi(4)$$
$$= \frac{1}{2}\pi$$

_____

_____

15. Find the area of the sector correctly.

16. The area of the sector is ⬜ in.^{2}.

---

take note

Key Concept **Area of a Segment**

The area of a segment is the difference of the area of the sector and the area of the triangle formed by the radii and the segment joining the endpoints.

 — =

Area of sector — Area of triangle = Area of segment

✓ **Problem 3** **Finding the Area of a Segment of a Circle**

Got It? What is the area of the shaded segment shown at the right? Round your answer to the nearest tenth.

17. Use the justifications below to find the area of sector PQR.

$$\text{area of sector } PQR = \frac{m\widehat{PR}}{⬜} \cdot \pi r^2 \qquad \text{Use the formula for the area of a sector.}$$

$$= \frac{90}{360} \cdot \pi(\quad)^2 \qquad \text{Substitute.}$$

$$= ⬜ \cdot \pi \qquad \text{Simplify.}$$

18. $\triangle PQR$ is a right triangle, so the base is ⬜ m and the height is ⬜ m.

19. Find the area of △PQR.

20. Complete to find the area of the shaded segment. Use a calculator.

area of shaded segment = area of sector PQR − area of △PQR

$$= \boxed{} \cdot \pi - \boxed{}$$

$$\approx \boxed{}$$

 21. To the nearest tenth, the area of the shaded segment is $\boxed{}$ m^2.

Lesson Check • Do you UNDERSTAND?

Reasoning Suppose a sector in ⊙P has the same area as a sector in ⊙O. Can you conclude that ⊙P and ⊙O have the same area? Explain.

Use the figures at the right for Exercises 22–24.

22. Find the area of sector AOC in ⊙O.

23. Find the area of sector RPT in ⊙P.

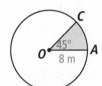

24. Do the sectors have the same area? Can you conclude that the circles have the same area? Explain.

_____

_____

Math Success

Check off the vocabulary words that you understand.

☐ sector of a circle   ☐ segment of a circle   ☐ area of a circle

Rate how well you can *find areas of circles, sectors, and segments.*

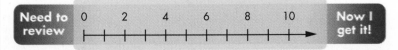

Lesson 10-7

Vocabulary

● Review

Write T for *true* or F for *false*.

_____ **1.** A *point* indicates a location and has no size.

_____ **2.** A line contains a finite number of *points*.

3. Use the diagram at the right. Circle the segment that includes *point S.*

$\overline{PR}$ $\overline{PT}$ $\overline{QR}$

P Q R S T

● Vocabulary Builder

probability (noun) **prah buh BIL uh tee**

theoretical **probability**

$$P(\text{event}) = \frac{\text{number of favorable outcomes}}{\text{number of possible outcomes}}$$

Related Term: geometric probability

Definition: The **probability** of an event is the likelihood that the event will occur.

Main Idea: In geometric **probability,** favorable outcomes and possible outcomes are geometric measures such as lengths of segments or areas of regions.

● Use Your Vocabulary

4. Underline the correct words to complete the sentence.

The *probability* of an event is the ratio of the number of favorable / possible

outcomes to the number of favorable / possible outcomes.

5. There are 7 red marbles and 3 green marbles in a bag. One marble is chosen at random. Write the *probability* that a green marble is chosen.

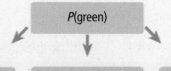

P(green)

Write as a fraction.	Write as a decimal.	Write as a percent.
		%

Key Concept   Probability and Length or Area

Probability and Length

Point S on $\overline{AD}$ is chosen at random. The probability that S is on $\overline{BC}$ is the ratio of the length of $\overline{BC}$ to the length of $\overline{AD}$.

$$P(S \text{ on } \overline{BC}) = \frac{BC}{AD}$$

Complete.

6. $P(S \text{ on } \overline{AC}) = \dfrac{\boxed{}}{AD}$

7. $P(S \text{ on } \overline{AB}) = \dfrac{\boxed{}}{\boxed{}}$

Probability and Area

Point S in region R is chosen at random. The probability that S is in region N is the ratio of the area of region N to the area of region R.

$$P(S \text{ in region } N) = \frac{\text{area of region } N}{\text{area of region } R}$$

8. Find the probability for the given areas.

area of region R = 11 cm^2 area of region N = 3 cm^2

$P(S \text{ in } N) = \dfrac{\boxed{}}{\boxed{}}$

Problem 1   Using Segments to Find Probability

Got It? Point H on $\overline{ST}$ is selected at random. What is the probability that H lies on $\overline{SR}$?

9. Find the length of each segment.

length of $\overline{SR} = \left| 2 - \boxed{} \right| = \boxed{}$ length of $\overline{ST} = \left| \boxed{} - \boxed{} \right| = \boxed{}$

10. Find the probability.

$$P(H \text{ on } \overline{SR}) = \frac{\text{length of } \overline{SR}}{\text{length of } \boxed{}} = \frac{\boxed{}}{\boxed{}} = \boxed{}$$

11. The probability that H is on $\overline{SR}$ is $\boxed{}$, or $\boxed{}$%.

Problem 2   Using Segments to Find Probability

Got It? Transportation A commuter train runs every 25 min. If a commuter arrives at the station at a random time, what is the probability that the commuter will have to wait no more than 5 min for the train?

12. Circle the time t (in minutes) before the train arrives that the commuter will need to arrive in order to wait *no more than* 5 minutes.

$0 \le t \le 5$	$5 < t \le 10$	$10 < t \le 15$
$15 < t \le 20$	$20 < t \le 25$	

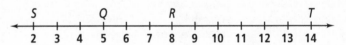

279

Lesson 10-8

Copyright © by Pearson Education, Inc. or its affiliates. All Rights Reserved.

13. Circle the diagram that models the situation.

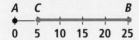 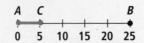 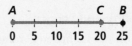

14. Complete.

length of favorable segment = [　]   length of entire segment = [　]

15. Find the probability.

$P(\text{waiting no more than 5 min}) = \dfrac{\text{length of favorable segment}}{\text{length of entire segment}}$

$= \dfrac{}{}$, or $\dfrac{}{}$

16. The probability of waiting no more than 5 min for the train is [　], or [　]%.

Problem 3 **Using Area to Find Probability**

Got It? A triangle is inscribed in a square. Point *T* in the square is selected at random. What is the probability that *T* lies in the shaded region?

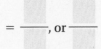

5 in.

17. Complete the model below to write an equation.

Define   Let s = the area of the shaded region.

Relate | area of the shaded region | is | area of the square | minus | area of the triangle |

Write $s \quad = \quad \boxed{}^{2} \quad - \quad \dfrac{1}{2} \cdot \boxed{} \cdot \boxed{}$

18. Now solve the equation to find the area of the shaded region.

19. Find the probability.

$P(\text{point } T \text{ is in shaded region}) = \dfrac{\text{area of shaded region}}{\text{area of square}}$

$= \dfrac{}{}$, or $\dfrac{}{2}$

20. The probability that *T* lies in the shaded region is [　], or [　]%.

Problem 4 Using Area to Find Probability

Got It? **Archery** An archery target has 5 colored scoring zones formed by concentric circles. The target's diameter is 122 cm. The radius of the yellow zone is 12.2 cm. The width of each of the other zones is also 12.2 cm. If an arrow hits the target at a random point, what is the probability that it hits the yellow zone?

21. The radius of the target is $\dfrac{\boxed{}}{2}$, or $\boxed{}$ cm.

22. Find the probability. Write the probability as a decimal.

$$P(\text{arrow hits yellow zone}) = \frac{\text{area of yellow zone}}{\text{area of entire target}}$$

$$= \frac{\pi(12.2)^2}{\pi(\boxed{})^2} = \frac{\boxed{}}{\boxed{}} = \boxed{}$$

23. Explain why the calculation with π is not an estimate.

_____
_____

24. The probability that the arrow hits the yellow zone is $\boxed{}$, or $\boxed{}$ %.

Lesson Check • Do you UNDERSTAND?

Reasoning In the figure at the right, $\dfrac{SQ}{QT} = \dfrac{1}{2}$. What is the probability that a point on $\overline{ST}$ chosen at random will lie on $\overline{QT}$? Explain.

25. If $SQ = x$, then $QT = \boxed{}$ and $ST = \boxed{}$.

26. What is $P(\text{point on } \overline{QT})$? Explain.

_____

Math Success

Check off the vocabulary words that you understand.

☐ length ☐ area ☐ geometric probability

Rate how well you can *use geometric probability*.

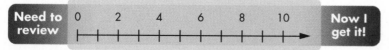

Lesson 10-8

Vocabulary

● Review

Complete each statement with the correct word from the list.

edge   edges   vertex   vertices

1. A(n) _?_ is a segment that is formed by the intersections of two faces.

_____

2. A(n) _?_ is a point where two or more *edges* intersect.

_____

3. A cube has eight _?_.

_____

4. A cube has twelve _?_.

_____

● Vocabulary Builder

> **polyhedron** (noun) **pahl ih HEE drun** (plural: polyhedra)
>
> **Related Words:** face, edge, vertex
>
> **Definition:** A *polyhedron* is a space figure, or three-dimensional figure, whose surfaces are polygons.
>
> **Origin:** The word *polyhedron* combines the Greek prefix *poli-*, meaning "many," and *hedron*, meaning "base."
>
> **Examples:** prism, pyramid
>
> **Non-Examples:** circle, cylinder, sphere

polyhedra

Pyramid   Prism

● Use Your Vocabulary

5. Cross out the figure below that is NOT a *polyhedron*.

         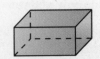

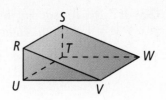

Problem 1 Identifying Vertices, Edges, and Faces

Got It? How many vertices, edges, and faces are in the polyhedron at the right? List them.

6. Identify each description as a *vertex*, an *edge*, or a *face*.

a point where three or more edges intersect	polygon	a segment where two or more faces intersect
_____	_____	_____

7. List the vertices.

8. List the edges. Remember to list the dashed hidden edges.

9. List the faces. Remember to list the hidden faces.

10. The polyhedron has _____ vertices, _____ edges, and _____ faces.

Key Concept   Euler's Formula

The sum of the number of faces (*F*) and vertices (*V*) of a polyhedron is two more than the number of its edges (*E*).

$$F + V = E + 2$$

Problem 2 Using Euler's Formula

Got It? Use Euler's Formula to find the number of faces for a polyhedron with 30 edges and 20 vertices.

11. Use the justifications at the right to find the number of faces.

$F + V = E + 2$	Use Euler's Formula.
$F + \boxed{} = \boxed{} + 2$	Substitute with given information.
$F + \boxed{} = \boxed{}$	Simplify.
$F = \boxed{} - \boxed{}$	Subtraction Property of Equality
$F = \boxed{}$	Simplify.

12. A polygon with 30 edges and 20 vertices has _____ faces.

Lesson 11-1

Problem 3 Verifying Euler's Formula in Two Dimensions

Got It? Use the solid at the right. How can you verify Euler's Formula
$F + V = E + 2$ for the solid?

13. Count the number of vertices.

⬚ on the bottom + ⬚ on the top = ⬚ vertices

14. Count the number of faces.

⬚ bases + ⬚ lateral faces = ⬚ faces

15. Count the number of edges.

⬚ solid edges + ⬚ dashed hidden edges = ⬚ edges

16. Now verify Euler's Formula for the values you found.

$$F + V = E + 2$$ Write Euler's Formula.

⬚ + ⬚ = ⬚ + 2   Substitute.

⬚ = ⬚   Simplify.

 Problem 4 Describing a Cross Section

Got It? For the solid at the right, what is the cross section formed by
a horizontal plane?

Underline the correct word to complete each sentence.

17. A horizontal plane is parallel to the bottom / side of the solid.

18. A view from the side / top of the solid helps you see the shape of the cross section.

19. The cross section is a circle / trapezoid .

Problem 5 Drawing a Cross Section

Got It? Draw the cross section formed by a horizontal plane intersecting the left
and right faces of the cube. What shape is the cross section?

20. A *horizontal* plane is parallel to which faces of the cube? Circle your answer.

front and back   left and right   top and bottom

21. Circle the diagram that shows the intersection of the horizontal plane and the left
and right faces of the cube.

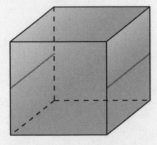   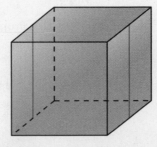

22. Use the cube to draw and shade the cross section.

23. The cross section is a __?__

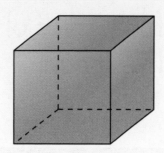

Lesson Check • Do you UNDERSTAND?

Vocabulary Suppose you build a polyhedron from two octagons and eight squares. Without using Euler's Formula, how many edges does the solid have? Explain.

24. Complete the problem-solving model below.

Know	Need	Plan
The octagons and squares are __?__. An edge is a segment formed by the intersection of two __?__.	To find the number of __?__ without using Euler's Formula	Count the number of edges formed by the squares and the top octagon. Count the number of edges formed by the squares and the bottom octagon. Count the number of edges formed by the squares.

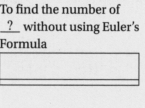

25. The intersections of the squares and the top octagon form ____ edges.

26. The intersections of the squares and the bottom octagon form ____ edges.

27. The intersection of the eight squares form ____ edges.

28. The solid has ____ + ____ + ____ = ____ edges.

Math Success

Check off the vocabulary words that you understand.

☐ polyhedron ☐ face ☐ edge ☐ vertex ☐ cross section

Rate how well you can *recognize polyhedra and their parts.*

Lesson 11-1

Vocabulary

● Review

Write T for *true* or F for *false*.

_____ **1.** A *lateral face* is a polygon surface of a solid.

_____ **2.** *Lateral faces* are surfaces of a polyhedron.

_____ **3.** A *lateral face* may be a circle.

_____ **4.** A base is a *lateral face*.

● Vocabulary Builder

| oblique | (adjective) | **oh** BLEEK |

Definition: An **oblique** object is slanting, not straight.

Main Idea: **Oblique** means indirect and not straight to the point.

Other Word Forms: obliquely (adverb)

Math Usage: An **oblique** polyhedron has no vertical edge so an **oblique** prism is not a right prism.

● Use Your Vocabulary

5. Circle the *oblique* prism.

6. Circle the *oblique* cylinder.

7. Complete with *oblique* or *obliquely*.

A right prism is not an __?__ prism.

_____

Your classmate answered the question __?__ .

_____

Problem 1 **Using a Net to Find Surface Area of a Prism**

Got It? What is the surface area of the triangular prism? Use a net.

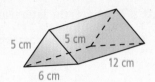

8. Label the missing dimensions in the net below.

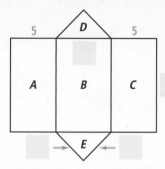

9. The altitude a of each triangle forms a right triangle with legs of lengths a cm and ☐ cm.

10. Use the Pythagorean Theorem to find a.

$$☐^2 + a^2 = 5^2$$

$$a^2 = 25 - ☐$$

$$a^2 = ☐$$

$$a = ☐$$

11. Find the surface area of the prism.

S.A. = L.A. + area of base

= areas of two lateral rectangles + areas of two lateral triangles + area of base

= (Area A + Area C) + (Area D + Area E) + Area B

= $5 \cdot ☐ + 5 \cdot ☐ + \frac{1}{2}(☐ \cdot ☐) + \frac{1}{2}(☐ \cdot ☐) + ☐ \cdot ☐$

= ☐ + ☐ + ☐ + ☐ + ☐

= ☐

12. The surface area of the triangular prism is ☐ cm².

take note

Theorem 11-1   Lateral and Surface Areas of a Prism

The lateral area of a right prism is the product of the perimeter of the base and the height of the prism.

L.A. = ph

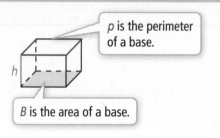

p is the perimeter of a base.

B is the area of a base.

The surface area of a right prism is the sum of the lateral area and the areas of the two bases.

S.A. = L.A. + 2*B*

13. Write the formula for S.A. using *p* and *h*.

S.A. = ☐ + 2*B*

Lesson 11-2

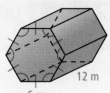

Problem 2 Using Formulas to Find Surface Area of a Prism

Got It? What is the lateral area of the prism at the right?

14. Complete the flow chart below.

L.A. = ph

→ p = perimeter of base
= ☐ · ☐ = ☐

→ h = height of prism
= ☐

→ L.A. = ☐ · ☐
= ☐

15. The lateral area of the prism is ☐ m².

take note

Theorem 11-2 Lateral and Surface Areas of a Cylinder

16. Use the diagram at the right to complete the formulas below.

The lateral area of a right cylinder is the product of the circumference of the base and the height of the cylinder.

L.A. = $2\pi r \cdot h$, or L.A. = $\pi \cdot$ ☐ $\cdot h$

The surface area of a right cylinder is the sum of the lateral area and the areas of the two bases.

S.A. = L.A. + 2B
= ☐ + $2\pi r^2$

> *B* is the area of a base.

Problem 3 Finding Surface Area of a Cylinder

Got It? A cylinder has a height of 9 cm and a radius of 10 cm. What is the surface area of the cylinder in terms of π?

17. Use the information in the problem to complete the reasoning model below.

Think	Write
I can use the formula for the surface area of a cylinder.	S.A. = L.A. + 2B
Then I can substitute the formulas for lateral area and area of a circle.	= ☐ + 2 · ☐
Next I substitute 10 for the radius and 9 for the height.	= $2\pi \cdot$ ☐ $\cdot$ ☐ $+ 2\pi \cdot$ ☐^{2}
Now I simplify.	= ☐ · π + ☐ · π = ☐ · π

18. The surface area of the cylinder is ☐ π cm².

Problem 4 Finding Lateral Area of a Cylinder

Got It? A stencil roller has a height of 1.5 in. and a diameter of 2.5 in. What area does the roller cover in one turn? Round your answer to the nearest tenth.

19. Underline the correct words to complete the sentence. The distance that is covered

in one turn is the circumference / diameter of the circular base of the cylinder / prism .

20. Find the area the roller covers in one turn.

21. The roller covers about ⬜ in.^{2} in one turn.

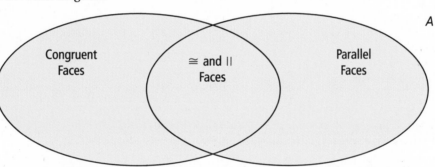

Lesson Check • Do you UNDERSTAND?

Vocabulary Name the lateral faces and the bases of the prism at the right.

22. Write the name of each of the ⬜ faces of the prism in the correct region of the Venn diagram.

Congruent Faces

≅ and ‖ Faces

Parallel Faces

23. Name the bases of the prism.

24. Name the lateral faces of the prism.

 ## Math Success

Check off the vocabulary words that you understand.

☐ right prism   ☐ oblique prism   ☐ right cylinder   ☐ oblique cylinder

Rate how well you can *find the surface area of a prism and a cylinder.*

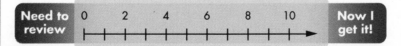

Need to review   0   2   4   6   8   10   Now I get it!

Lesson 11-2

11-3 Surface Areas of Pyramids and Cones

Vocabulary

● **Review**

Label each diagram *cone* or *pyramid*.

1.

2.

3.

4.

_____   _____   _____   _____

● **Vocabulary Builder**

slant height, ℓ

| slant height | (noun) | **slant hyt** |

Related Words: regular pyramid, lateral face

Definition: The **slant height** ℓ of a regular pyramid is the length of the altitude of a lateral face of the pyramid. The **slant height** ℓ of a cone is the distance from the vertex of a cone to a point on the circumference of the base.

Math Usage: The **slant height** of a regular pyramid divides the lateral face into two congruent right triangles.

● **Use Your Vocabulary**

5. Circle the figure that shows a three-dimensional figure with *slant height* 5 m.

5 m

5 m

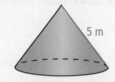
5 m

6. Is the *slant height* the same as the *height* of a pyramid or cone?   Yes / No

7. The *slant height* of the cone at the right is ____ in.

2 in. ← 3 in.

Theorem 11-3   Lateral and Surface Areas of a Pyramid

The lateral area (L.A.) of a regular pyramid is half the product of the perimeter p of the base and the slant height ℓ of the pyramid.

The surface area (S.A.) of a regular pyramid is the sum of the lateral area and the area B of the base.

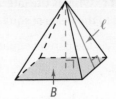

8. In a square pyramid with base side length s, $p =$ ☐ .

9. If the base of a regular pyramid has a perimeter of $6q$ and its side length is 6, the pyramid has ☐ sides.

Draw a line from each description in Column A to the corresponding formula in Column B.

Column A	Column B
10. lateral area (L.A.) of a pyramid	$\frac{1}{2}p\ell$
11. surface area (S.A.) of a pyramid	$\frac{1}{2}p\ell + B$

  Problem 1 Finding the Surface Area of a Pyramid

Got It? A square pyramid has base edges of 5 m and a slant height of 3 m. What is the surface area of the pyramid?

12. Complete the problem-solving model below.

Know	Need	Plan
The base is a square with side length ☐ m. Slant height ℓ is ☐ m.	Lateral area Surface area	Find the perimeter ☐ of the base. Find the area ☐ of the base. Use p and ℓ to find ☐ Use L.A. and B to find ☐

13. Find p.

$p = 4(s)$

$\quad = 4(\ ☐\ )$

$\quad = ☐$

14. Find B.

$B = s^2$

$\quad = ☐^2$

$\quad = ☐$

15. L.A. $= \frac{1}{2}p\ell$

$\quad = \frac{1}{2}(\ ☐\ )(\ ☐\ )$

$\quad = ☐$

16. S.A. $=$ L.A. $+ B$

$\quad = ☐ + ☐$

$\quad = ☐$

17. The surface area of the pyramid is ☐ m².

Lesson 11-3

Problem 2 Finding the Lateral Area of a Pyramid

Got It? What is the lateral area of the hexagonal pyramid at the right? Round to the nearest square foot.

18. Circle the correct equation for the perimeter of the hexagonal base.

$$42 \cdot 36 = 1512 \qquad 6 \cdot 18 = 108 \qquad \tfrac{1}{2}(36)(18\sqrt{3}) \approx 561 \qquad 6 \cdot 36 = 216$$

19. The slant height ℓ of the pyramid is the hypotenuse of a right triangle. Label the legs of the right triangle at the right.

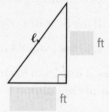

20. Use the Pythagorean Theorem to find the slant height ℓ of the pyramid.

$$\ell = \sqrt{\boxed{}^2 + \boxed{}^2}$$

$$= \sqrt{\boxed{} + \boxed{}}$$

$$= \sqrt{\boxed{}}$$

21. Use the formula L.A. $= \tfrac{1}{2}p\ell$ to find the lateral area of the pyramid.

$$\text{L.A.} = \tfrac{1}{2}(\boxed{})(\boxed{}) \approx \boxed{}$$

22. The lateral area of the hexagonal pyramid is about $\boxed{}$ ft².

> **take note**

Theorem 11-4 Lateral and Surface Areas of a Cone

The lateral area of a right cone is half the product of the circumference of the base and the slant height of the cone.

$$\text{L.A.} = \tfrac{1}{2} \cdot 2\pi r \cdot \ell, \text{ or L.A.} = \pi r \ell$$

The surface area of a cone is the sum of the lateral area and the area of the base.

23. S.A. = L.A. + $\boxed{}$

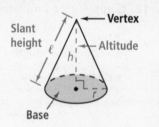

Problem 3 Finding the Surface Area of a Cone

Got It? The radius of the base of a cone is 16 m. Its slant height is 28 m. What is the surface area in terms of π?

24. Use the justifications at the right to find the surface area.

S.A. = L.A. + B	Use the formula for surface area.
$= \boxed{} + \boxed{}$	Substitute the formulas for L.A. and B.
$= \pi(\boxed{})(\boxed{}) + \pi(\boxed{})^2$	Substitute for r and for ℓ.
$= \pi(\boxed{}) + \pi(\boxed{})$	Simplify.
$= \pi(\boxed{})$	Add.

25. The surface area of the cone in terms of π is $\boxed{}$ m².

Chapter 11

292

Problem 4 Finding the Lateral Area of a Cone

Got It? What is the lateral area of a traffic cone with radius 10 in. and height 28 in.? Round to the nearest whole number.

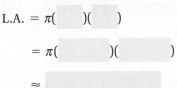

26. Let ℓ be the slant height of the cone. Label the missing dimensions on the cone at the right.

27. Use the Pythagorean Theorem to find ℓ.

$$\ell = \sqrt{\boxed{}^2 + \boxed{}^2}$$

$$= \sqrt{\boxed{} + \boxed{}}$$

$$= \sqrt{\boxed{}}$$

28. Use the formula for lateral area of a cone.

$$\text{L.A.} = \pi(\boxed{})(\boxed{})$$

$$= \pi(\boxed{})(\boxed{})$$

$$\approx \boxed{}$$

29. To the nearest square inch, the lateral area of the traffic cone is $\boxed{}$ in.^{2}.

 Lesson Check • **Do you UNDERSTAND?**

Compare and Contrast How are the formulas for the surface area of a prism and the surface area of a pyramid alike? How are they different?

30. Use the descriptions in the list at the right. Write the letter for each description under the correct polyhedron.

Prism	Pyramid

31. How are the formulas alike? How are they different?

_____

_____

_____

_____

A. Base is a polygon.

B. Faces are rectangles.

C. Faces are triangles.

D. S.A. = L.A. + B

E. S.A. = L.A. + 2B

F. Uses height

G. Uses perimeter

H. Uses slant height

Math Success

Check off the vocabulary words that you understand.

☐ pyramid   ☐ slant height   ☐ lateral area   ☐ surface area   ☐ cone

Rate how well you can *find the surface area of pyramids and cones.*

| Need to review | 0 2 4 6 8 10 | Now I get it! |

Lesson 11-3

Volumes of Prisms and Cylinders

Vocabulary

● **Review**

Label each diagram *cylinder* or *prism*.

1.

_____

2.

_____

3.

_____

4.

_____

● **Vocabulary Builder**

composite (adjective, noun) **kum PAHZ it**

Related Words: compound, combination, component

Definition: **Composite** means put together with distinct parts.

Main Idea: A **composite** is a whole made up of different parts.

● **Use Your Vocabulary**

Complete each statement with the correct phrase from the list below. Use each phrase only once.

| *composite* function | *composite* map | *composite* number | *composite* sketch |

5. A _?_ combines different descriptions of features.

_____

6. A _?_ has factors other than one and the number.

_____

7. A _?_ shows the locations of shopping malls, houses, and roads in one illustration.

_____

8. A _?_ shows how to apply at least one function to another function.

_____

Theorem 11-5 Cavalieri's Principle

take note

If two space figures have the same height and the same cross-sectional area at every level, then they have the same volume.

9. The three prisms below have the same height and the same volume. The first is a square prism. Label the missing dimensions.

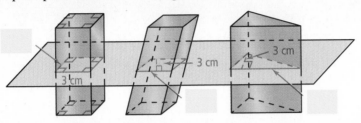

10. Circle the solid(s) that may have the same cross-sectional area at every level.

cone	cylinder	prism	pyramid

Theorem 11-6 Volume of a Prism

take note

The volume of a prism is the product of the area of the base and the height of the prism.

$V = Bh$

11. A prism with a base area of 15 m² and a height 4 m has a volume of ▢ m³.

12. A prism with a volume of 81 ft³ and a height of 3 ft has a base area of ▢ ft².

Problem 1 Finding the Volume of a Rectangular Prism

Got It? What is the volume of the rectangular prism at the right?

13. Circle the measurements of a base of the prism.

3 ft × 4 ft	3 ft × 5 ft	4 ft × 5 ft

14. Underline the correct word to complete the sentence.

The base is a rectangle / square .

15. Find *B*.

$B = $ ▢ · ▢

$= $ ▢ · ▢

$= $ ▢

16. Find *V*.

$V = $ ▢ · ▢

$= $ ▢ · ▢

$= $ ▢

17. Underline the correct word to complete the sentence.

The units for this volume are cubic / square feet .

18. The volume of the prism is ▢ .

Lesson 11-4

Finding the Volume of a Triangular Prism

Got It? What is the volume of the triangular prism at the right?

19. The base is a right triangle with legs of length ▢ m and ▢ m.

20. The height of the prism is ▢ m.

21. Complete the formula for volume of a prism. $V = $ ▢ $\cdot$ ▢

22. Find the area of the base.

$A = \dfrac{1}{2} \cdot$ ▢ $\cdot$ ▢

$\quad = \dfrac{1}{2} \cdot$ ▢

$\quad = $ ▢

23. Find the volume of the prism.

$V = $ ▢ $\cdot$ ▢

$\quad = $ ▢

24. The volume of the triangular prism is ▢ m^3.

---

take note

Theorem 11-7 Volume of a Cylinder

The volume of a cylinder is the product of the area of the base and the height of the cylinder.

$\quad V = Bh$, or $V = \pi r^2 h$

25. Shade a base of the cylinder at the right.

26. Describe the shape of the base.

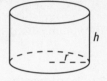

_____

Finding the Volume of a Cylinder

Got It? What is the volume of the cylinder at the right in terms of π?

27. Compete the reasoning model below.

Think	Write
First I need to find the radius.	$r = \dfrac{\text{▢}}{2} = $ ▢
I can use the formula $V = \pi r^2 h$ and substitute for r and h.	$V = \pi \cdot$ ▢$^2 \cdot$ ▢
Now I simplify.	$V = \pi \cdot$ ▢

28. The volume of the cylinder is ▢ m^3.

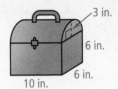

✓ Problem 4 Finding Volume of a Composite Figure

Got It? What is the approximate volume of the lunch box shown at the right? Round to the nearest cubic inch.

29. The top and bottom of the lunch box are sketched below. Label the dimensions.

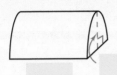   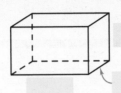

30. Find the volume of the top.

$$V = \frac{1}{2}\pi r^2 h$$

$$= \frac{1}{2}\pi(\quad^2)(\quad)$$

$$= \boxed{}$$

31. Find the volume of the bottom.

$$V = Bh$$

$$= (\quad \cdot \quad)(\quad)$$

$$= \boxed{}$$

32. Find the sum of the volumes.

$$V = \boxed{}\,\pi + \boxed{}$$

$$\approx \boxed{}$$

 33. The approximate volume of the lunch box is $\boxed{}$ in.³.

✓ Lesson Check • Do you UNDERSTAND?

Reasoning How is the volume of a rectangular prism with base 2 m by 3 m and height 4 m related to the volume of a rectangular prism with base 3 m by 4 m and height 2 m? Explain.

34. Cross out the formula that does NOT give the volume of a rectangular prism.

$$V = Bh \qquad\qquad V = \pi r^2 h \qquad\qquad V = \ell wh$$

35. The Commutative / Identity Property of Multiplication states that the product of factors is the same when listed in a different order.

36. Now answer the question.

_____

✓ Math Success

Check off the vocabulary words that you understand.

☐ volume   ☐ composite space figure

Rate how well you can *find the volume of prisms and cylinders*.

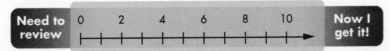

Lesson 11-4

11-5 Volumes of Pyramids and Cones

Vocabulary

● Review

1. Write *L*, *W*, or *H* to label the *length, width*, and *height* of the rectangular prism at the right.

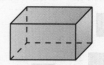

2. Explain how the *length, width*, and *height* of a cube are related.

_____

Circle the correct statement in each exercise.

3. The *width* of a cylinder is the radius of a base of the cylinder.

   The *height* of a cylinder is the *length* of an altitude of the cylinder.

4. The *height* of a pyramid is the length of a segment perpendicular to the base.

   The slant *height* of a pyramid is the length of a segment perpendicular to the base.

● Vocabulary Builder

volume (noun) VAHL **yoom**

Related Word: capacity

Main Idea: **Volume** measures quantity of space or amount, such as loudness of sound or a collection of books.

Definition: **Volume** is the amount of space that a three-dimensional figure occupies, measured in cubic units.

Example: The **volume** of a bottle of juice is 2 liters.

● Use Your Vocabulary

Write T for *true* or F for *false*.

_____ 5. A synonym for *volume* is capacity.

_____ 6. *Volume* is measured in square units.

_____ 7. You can find the *volume* of a circle.

Theorem 11-8 Volume of a Pyramid

The volume of a pyramid is one third the product of the area of the base and the height of the pyramid.

8. Complete the formula for the volume of a pyramid.

$$V = \boxed{} \cdot Bh$$

Theorem 11-9 Volume of a Cone

The volume of a cone is one third the product of the area of the base and the height of the cone.

$$V = \frac{1}{3} Bh$$

9. Circle an equivalent formula for the volume of a cone.

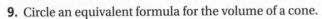

$$V = \frac{1}{3} \pi r^2 h \qquad\qquad V = \frac{1}{3} \cdot 2\pi r \cdot h$$

Write the formula for the volume of each figure below.

10.

$$V = \frac{1}{3} \cdot \boxed{} \cdot \boxed{}$$

11.

$$V = \boxed{}$$

Problem 1 Finding Volume of a Pyramid

Got It? A sports arena shaped like a pyramid has a base area of about 300,000 ft² and a height of 321 ft. What is the approximate volume of the arena?

12. Complete the problem-solving model below.

Know	Need	Plan
$B \approx \boxed{}$ $h = \boxed{}$	Volume of the pyramid	Substitute the given values into the formula $\boxed{}$.

13. Solve for V.

14. The approximate volume of the arena is ft³.

✓ **Problem 2** **Finding the Volume of a Pyramid**

Got It? What is the volume of a square pyramid with base edges 24 m and slant height 13 m?

15. Label the pyramid at the right.

16. Find the height of the pyramid.

$$13^2 = h^2 + \boxed{}^2$$

$$169 = h^2 + \boxed{}$$

$$h^2 = \boxed{}$$

$$h = \boxed{}$$

17. Find the area of the base.

$$B = \boxed{} \cdot \boxed{}$$

$$= \boxed{}$$

18. Find the volume of the pyramid.

$$V = \boxed{} \cdot Bh$$

$$= \boxed{} \cdot \boxed{} \cdot \boxed{}$$

$$= \boxed{}$$

19. The volume of the pyramid is $\boxed{}$ m^3.

✓ **Problem 3** **Finding the Volume of a Cone**

Got It? A small child's teepee is 6 ft high with a base diameter of 7 ft. What is the volume of the child's teepee to the nearest cubic foot?

20. Label the cone at the right with the dimensions of the teepee.

21. The radius of the teepee is $\boxed{}$ ft.

22. Use the justifications to find the volume of the teepee.

$V = \boxed{}$	Use the formula with π for the volume of a cone.
$V = \boxed{}$	Substitute for r and h.
$= \boxed{}$	Square the radius.
$= \boxed{}$	Simplify in terms of π.
$\approx \boxed{}$	Use a calculator.

23. The volume of the child's teepee to the nearest cubic foot is $\boxed{}$ ft^3.

✓ **Problem 4** **Finding the Volume of an Oblique Cone**

Got It? What is the volume of the oblique cone at the right in terms of π and rounded to the nearest cubic meter?

12 m

6 m

24. The radius of the base is $\boxed{}$ m and the height is $\boxed{}$ m.

25. Cross out the formula that is NOT a formula for the volume of a cone.

$$V = \frac{1}{3}Bh \qquad\qquad V = Bh \qquad\qquad V = \frac{1}{3}\pi r^2 h$$

26. Find the volume of the cone.

27. The volume of the cone in terms of π is [ ] m^3.

Rounded to the nearest cubic meter, the volume of the cone is [ ] m^3.

Lesson Check • Do you UNDERSTAND?

Error Analysis A square pyramid has base edges 13 ft and height 10 ft. A cone has diameter 13 ft and height 10 ft. Your friend claims the figures have the same volume because the volume formulas for a pyramid and a cone are the same: $V = \frac{1}{3}Bh$. What is her error?

28. Is $V = \frac{1}{3}Bh$ the volume formula for both a pyramid and a cone?   Yes / No

Underline the correct word to complete each sentence.

29. The base of a square pyramid is a circle / polygon .

30. The base of a cone is a circle / polygon .

31. Circle the base used in the formula for the volume of a cone. Underline the base used in the formula for the volume of a square pyramid.

$B = \pi r^2$ $\qquad\qquad$ $B = \frac{1}{2}bh$ $\qquad\qquad$ $B = s^2$

32. Now explain your friend's error.

_____

_____

Math Success

Check off the vocabulary words that you understand.

☐ pyramid $\qquad$ ☐ cone $\qquad$ ☐ oblique $\qquad$ ☐ volume

Rate how well you can *find the volumes of pyramids and cones*.

Need to review 0 2 4 6 8 10 Now I get it!

Lesson 11-5

11-6 Surface Areas and Volumes of Spheres

Vocabulary

● Review

Underline the correct word to complete each sentence.

1. The *diameter / radius* of the circle at the right is 5 cm.

2. The circumference of a circle is the product of its *diameter / radius* and π.

3. The *diameter / radius* of a circle is a segment containing the center with endpoints on the circle.

● Vocabulary Builder

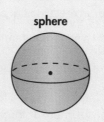

sphere

sphere (noun) **sfeer**

Related Words: spherical (adjective), hemisphere (noun)

Main Idea: A **sphere** is formed by the revolution of a circle about its diameter.

Definition: A **sphere** is the set of all points in space equidistant from a given point called the *center*.

Example: A basketball is a **sphere**.

Non-Example: A football is not a **sphere**.

● Use Your Vocabulary

4. Complete each statement with *sphere* or *spherical*.

ADJECTIVE   Each __?__ candy looks like a rock.

NOUN   A baseball is in the shape of a __?__.

Write T for *true* or F for *false*.

_____ 5. Celestial bodies such as the sun or Earth are often represented as *spheres*.

_____ 6. A *sphere* is a two-dimensional figure.

Theorem 11-10 Surface Area of a Sphere

The surface area of a sphere is four times the product of π and the square of the radius of the sphere.

7. Complete: S.A. = ☐ · ☐ · ☐^{2}

Problem 1 **Finding the Surface Area of a Sphere**

Got It? What is the surface area of a sphere with a diameter of 14 in.? Give your answer in terms of π and rounded to the nearest square inch.

8. The radius of the sphere is ☐ in.

9. Find the surface area.

$$\text{S.A.} = 4\pi(\ \ )^2 \qquad \text{Use the formula for surface area of a sphere.}$$

$$= 4\pi(\ \ )^2 \qquad \text{Substitute for } r.$$

$$= \pi(\ \ ) \qquad \text{Simplify.}$$

$$\approx \boxed{} \qquad \text{Use a calculator.}$$

10. The surface area in terms of π is ☐ π in.^{2}, or about ☐ in.^{2}.

Problem 2 **Finding Surface Area**

Got It? What is the surface area of a melon with circumference 18 in.? Round your answer to the nearest ten square inches.

11. Complete the problem-solving model below.

Know	Need	Plan
The circumference is ☐ in.	The radius r of the sphere The surface area of the sphere	Solve the formula for circumference for ☐. Substitute ☐ into the formula for surface area of a sphere.

12. Find r in terms of π.

$C = 2\pi r$

13. Use your value for r to find the surface area.

S.A. $= 4\pi r^2$

14. To the nearest ten square inches, the surface area of the melon is ☐ in.^{2}.

Lesson 11-6

Theorem 11-11   Volume of a Sphere

15. Complete the model below.

Relate | The volume of a sphere | is | four thirds the product of π and the cube of the radius of the sphere.

Write | V | $=$ |

Draw a line from each measure in Column A to its corresponding formula in Column B.

Column A

Column B

16. surface area of a sphere $\frac{4}{3}\pi r^3$

17. volume of a sphere $4\pi r^2$

Problem 3   Finding the Volume of a Sphere

Got It? A sphere has a diameter of 60 in. What is its volume to the nearest cubic inch?

18. Complete the missing information in the diagram.

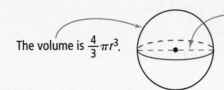

The volume is $\frac{4}{3}\pi r^3$.

The diameter is 60 in., so the radius is   in.

19. Complete to find the volume.

$$V = \frac{4}{3}\pi(\qquad)^3$$

$$= \frac{4}{3}\pi(\qquad)$$

$$= \pi(\qquad)$$

$$\approx \qquad$$

20. The volume is about _____ in.³.

Problem 4   Using Volume to Find Surface Area

Got It? The volume of a sphere is 4200 ft³. What is its surface area to the nearest tenth?

21. Circle the correct formula for the volume of a sphere.

$$V = \frac{4}{3}\pi r^2 \qquad\qquad V = \frac{4}{3}\pi r^3$$

22. Complete the reasoning model below.

Think	Write
I need to solve the volume formula for the radius.	$V = \frac{4}{3}\pi r^3$
I can substitute the given volume into the formula.	$\boxed{} = \frac{4}{3}\pi r^3$
Now, I can solve for r^3.	
If I take the cube root of both sides, I can solve for r. I need to use a calculator to simplify.	$\sqrt[3]{\boxed{}} = r$ $\boxed{} \approx r$
Then, I can substitute r into the formula for surface area of a sphere.	$S.A. = 4\pi\,\boxed{}^2$
Finally, I can simplify.	$S.A. \approx \boxed{}$

23. To the nearest tenth of a foot, the surface area is $\boxed{}$ ft^2.

Lesson Check • Do you UNDERSTAND?

Vocabulary What is the ratio of the area of a great circle to the surface area of the sphere?

24. A great circle is a circle whose center is the center of the __?__. $\underline{}$

25. $A = \boxed{}$ **26.** S.A. $= \boxed{}$ **27.** The ratio is $\underline{}$, or $\underline{}$.

Math Success

Check off the vocabulary words that you understand.

☐ sphere (radius, diameter, circumference) ☐ great circle ☐ hemisphere

Rate how well you can *find surface area and volume of a sphere*.

Need to review 0 2 4 6 8 10 Now I get it!

Lesson 11-6

Vocabulary

● Review

Complete each statement with the appropriate word from the list. Use each word only once.

similar   similarities   similarity   similarly

1. There are several _?_ house styles in the neighborhood. _____

2. The sequel may end _?_ to the original movie. _____

3. There is not one _?_ between his first and second drawings. _____

4. You could find several _?_ between the two video games. _____

● Vocabulary Builder

scale factor (noun) **skayl FAK tur**

Main Idea: The **scale factor** for similar polygons is the ratio of the lengths of their corresponding sides.

Definition: The **scale factor** for two similar solids is the ratio of their corresponding linear dimensions.

Example: The **scale factor** of a map may be 1 inch : 5 miles.

● Use Your Vocabulary

Write T for *true* or F for *false*.

_____ **5.** You can find the *scale factor* for any two figures.

_____ **6.** You can find the *scale factor* for similar figures.

_____ **7.** You can write a *scale factor* as a ratio $(a : b)$ or as a fraction $\left(\frac{a}{b}\right)$.

_____ **8.** A *scale factor* is always written as the ratio $a : b$.

Problem 1 | **Identifying Similar Solids**

Got It? Are the two cylinders similar? If so, what is the scale factor of the first figure to the second figure?

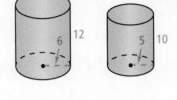

Underline the correct word to complete each sentence.

9. You can check whether prisms are similar by comparing the ratios of
   two / three dimensions.

10. You can check whether cylinders are similar by comparing the ratios
    of two / three dimensions.

11. Always compare the ratios of corresponding / similar dimensions.

12. The ratio of the height of the larger cylinder to the height of the smaller cylinder

    is ——. Simplified, this ratio is ——.

13. The ratio of the radius of the larger cylinder to the radius of the smaller cylinder

    is ——.

14. Underline the correct words to complete the sentence. The ratios you found in
    Exercises 12 and 13 are/are not equal, so the cylinders are/are not similar.

15. The scale factor is ☐.

---

take note

Theorem 11-12 Areas and Volumes of Similar Solids

If the scale factor of two similar solids is $a : b$, then

- the ratio of their corresponding areas is $a^2 : b^2$
- the ratio of their volumes is $a^3 : b^3$

16. Complete the model below.

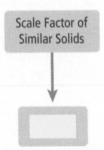   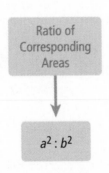   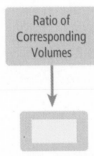

17. If the scale factor of two similar solids is $1 : 2$, then the ratio of their corresponding
    areas is ☐^{2} : ☐^{2}, or ☐ : ☐.

18. If the scale factor of two similar solids is $1 : 2$, then the ratio of their corresponding
    volumes is ☐^{3} : ☐^{3}, or ☐ : ☐.

Lesson 11-7

✓ Problem 2 Finding the Scale Factor

Got It? What is the scale factor of two similar prisms with surface areas 144 m^2 and 324 m^2?

19. Complete the reasoning model below.

Think	Write
I can write the ratio of the lesser surface area to the greater surface area.	$\dfrac{a^2}{b^2} = \dfrac{\boxed{}}{\boxed{}}$
I can take the square roots of the surface areas and write the scale factor as $a : b$.	$\sqrt{\dfrac{a^2}{b^2}} = \dfrac{a}{b} = \dfrac{\boxed{}}{\boxed{}}$

20. The scale factor is $\boxed{} : \boxed{}$, which can be simplified to $\boxed{} : \boxed{}$.

✓ Problem 3 Using a Scale Factor

Got It? The volumes of two similar solids are 128 m^3 and 250 m^3. The surface area of the larger solid is 250 m^2. What is the surface area of the smaller solid?

21. Let $\dfrac{a}{b}$ represent the scale factor of the similar solids. Circle the simplified ratio of the volume of the smaller solid to the volume of the larger solid.

$$\dfrac{a^3}{b^3} = \dfrac{64}{125} \qquad\qquad \dfrac{a}{b} = \dfrac{64}{125} \qquad\qquad \dfrac{a^3}{b^3} = \dfrac{125}{64}$$

22. Find the scale factor $a : b$.

$$\dfrac{a}{b} = \dfrac{\sqrt[3]{\boxed{}}}{\sqrt[3]{\boxed{}}} = \dfrac{\boxed{}}{\boxed{}}$$

23. Use the scale factor to find the ratio of surface areas.

$$\dfrac{a^2}{b^2} = \dfrac{\boxed{}^2}{\boxed{}^2} = \dfrac{\boxed{}}{\boxed{}}$$

24. Circle the proportion that compares the surface area of the smaller solid to the surface area of the larger solid.

$$\dfrac{a^2}{b^2} = \dfrac{x}{250} \qquad\qquad \dfrac{a}{b} = \dfrac{x}{250} \qquad\qquad \dfrac{a^2}{b^2} = \dfrac{250}{x}$$

25. Now solve for x.

26. The surface area of the smaller solid is $\boxed{}$ m^2.

Chapter 11

308

Got It? A marble paperweight shaped like a pyramid weighs 0.15 lb. How much does a similarly shaped marble paperweight weigh if each dimension is three times as large?

27. The scale factor of small paperweight to large paperweight is 1 : ☐ .

28. Let $x =$ the weight of the larger paperweight. Use the justifications at the right to find the value of x.

$$\frac{1^3}{☐^3} = \frac{0.15}{x}$$ The weights are proportional to their volumes.

$$\frac{1}{☐} = \frac{0.15}{x}$$ Simplify.

$$x = ☐$$ Use the Cross Products Property.

29. The paperweight that is three times as large weighs ☐ lb.

Lesson Check • Do you UNDERSTAND?

Error Analysis Two cubes have surface areas 49 cm² and 64 cm². Your classmate tried to find the scale factor of the larger cube to the smaller cube. Explain and correct your classmate's error.

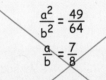

The scale factor of the larger cube to the smaller cube is 7 : 8.

Underline the correct word(s) to complete each sentence.

30. The larger cube has the greater / lesser surface area.

31. The scale factor of larger cube to smaller cube is greater / less than the scale factor of smaller cube to larger cube.

32. Your classmate found the scale factor of the smaller / larger cube to the smaller / larger cube.

33. Find the correct scale factor.

Begin with the proportion $\frac{a^2}{b^2} = $ ——. Then, $\frac{a}{b} = $ ——.

Math Success

Check off the vocabulary words that you understand.

☐ similar solids   ☐ scale factor

Rate how well you can *find and use scale factors of similar solids.*

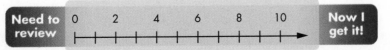

Lesson 11-7

Vocabulary

● Review

1. Cross out the word that does NOT apply to a *circle*.

arc   circumference   diameter   equilateral   radius

2. Circle the word for a segment with one endpoint at the center of a *circle* and the other endpoint on the *circle*.

arc   circumference   diameter   perimeter   radius

● Vocabulary Builder

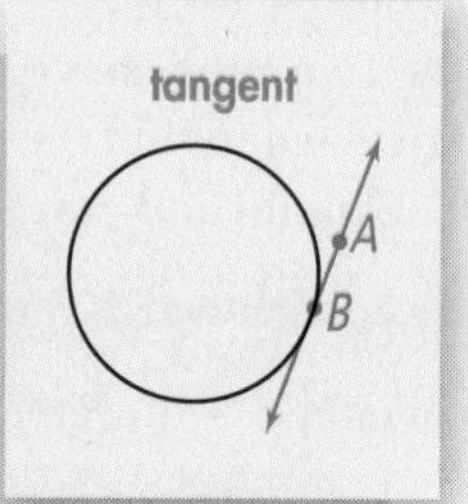

tangent (noun, adjective) TAN **junt**

Definition: A **tangent** to a circle is a line, ray, or segment in the plane of the circle that intersects the circle in exactly one point.

Other Word Form: tangency (noun)

Examples: In the diagram, $\overleftrightarrow{AB}$ is **tangent** to the circle at B. B is the *point of tangency*. $\overrightarrow{BA}$ is a **tangent** ray. $\overline{BA}$ is a **tangent** segment.

Other Usage: In a right triangle, the **tangent** is the ratio of the side opposite an acute angle to the side adjacent to the angle.

tangent

● Use Your Vocabulary

3. Complete each statement with *always*, *sometimes*, or *never*.

A diameter is __?__ a *tangent*.

A *tangent* and a circle __?__ have exactly one point in common.

A radius can __?__ be drawn to the point of tangency.

A *tangent* __?__ passes through the center of a circle.

A *tangent* is __?__ a ray.

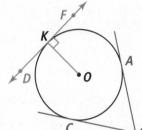

take note

Theorems 12-1, 12-2, and 12-3

Theorem 12-1 If a line is tangent to a circle, then the line is perpendicular to the radius at the point of tangency.

Theorem 12-2 If a line in the plane of a circle is perpendicular to a radius at its endpoint on the circle, then the line is tangent to the circle.

Theorem 12-3 If two tangent segments to a circle share a common endpoint outside the circle, then the two segments are congruent.

Use the diagram at the right for Exercises 4–6. Complete each statement.

4. **Theorem 12-1** If $\overleftrightarrow{DF}$ is tangent to $\odot O$ at K, then [ ] ⊥ [ ] .

5. **Theorem 12-2** If $\overleftrightarrow{DF}$ ⊥ $\overline{OK}$, then [ ] is tangent to $\odot O$.

6. **Theorem 12-3** If $\overline{BA}$ and $\overline{BC}$ are tangent to $\odot O$, then [ ] ≅ [ ] .

✓ **Problem 1** **Finding Angle Measures**

Got It? $\overline{ED}$ is tangent to $\odot O$. What is the value of x?

7. Circle the word that best describes $\overline{OD}$.

| diameter | radius | tangent |

8. What relationship does Theorem 12-1 support? Circle your answer.

| $\overline{OD} \perp \overline{ED}$ | $\overline{OD} \parallel \overline{ED}$ | $\overline{OD} \cong \overline{ED}$ |

9. Circle the most accurate description of the triangle.

| acute | isosceles | obtuse | right |

10. Circle the theorem that you will use to solve for x.

| Theorem 12-1 | Triangle Angle-Sum Theorem |

11. Complete the model below.

| **Relate** | sum of angle measures in a triangle | is | 38 | plus | measure of ∠D | plus | measure of ∠E |

| **Write** | [ ] | = | 38 | + | [ ] | + | [ ] |

12. Solve for x.

13. The value of x is [ ] .

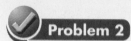

Problem 2 Finding Distance

Got It? What is the distance to the horizon that a person can see on a clear day from an airplane 2 mi above Earth? Earth's radius is about 4000 mi.

14. The diagram at the right shows the airplane at point A and the horizon at point H. Use the information in the problem to label the distances.

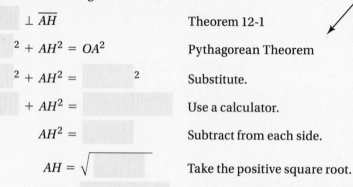

15. Use the justifications at the right to find the distance.

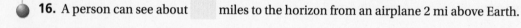

$\boxed{} \perp \overline{AH}$	Theorem 12-1
$\boxed{}^2 + AH^2 = OA^2$	Pythagorean Theorem
$\boxed{}^2 + AH^2 = \boxed{}^2$	Substitute.
$\boxed{} + AH^2 = \boxed{}$	Use a calculator.
$AH^2 = \boxed{}$	Subtract from each side.
$AH = \sqrt{\boxed{}}$	Take the positive square root.
$AH \approx \boxed{}$	Use a calculator.

 16. A person can see about ____ miles to the horizon from an airplane 2 mi above Earth.

Problem 3 Finding a Radius

Got It? What is the radius of $\odot O$?

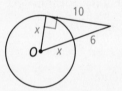

17. Write an algebraic or numerical expression for each side of the triangle.

18. Circle the longest side of the triangle. Underline the side that is opposite the right angle.

10   x $x + 6$

19. Use the Pythagorean Theorem to complete the equation.

$$\boxed{}^2 + \boxed{}^2 = \left(\boxed{} \right)^2$$

20. Solve the equation for x.

21. The radius is ____.

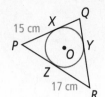

Problem 5   Circles Inscribed in Polygons

Got It? ⊙O is inscribed in △PQR, which has a perimeter of 88 cm. What is the length of $\overline{QY}$?

22. By Theorem 12-3, $\overline{PX} \cong$ [ ], $\overline{RZ} \cong$ [ ], and $\overline{QX} \cong$ [ ], so PX = [ ], RZ = [ ], and QX = [ ].

23. Perimeter p = PQ + QR + RP, so p = PX + [ ] + QY + [ ] + RZ + [ ] by the Segment Addition Postulate.

24. Use the values in the diagram and your answer to Exercise 23 to solve for QY.

Lesson Check   •   Do you UNDERSTAND?

Error Analysis A classmate insists that $\overline{DF}$ is a tangent to ⊙E. Explain how to show that your classmate is wrong.

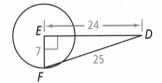

Underline the correct word or number to complete the sentence.

25. A tangent to a circle is parallel / perpendicular to a radius.

26. If $\overline{DF}$ is tangent to ⊙E at point F, then $m\angle EFD$ must be 30 / 90 / 180 .

27. A triangle can have at most [ ] right angle(s).

28. Explain why your classmate is wrong.

_____

_____

Math Success

Check off the vocabulary words that you understand.

☐ circle   ☐ tangent to a circle   ☐ point of tangency

Rate how well you can *use tangents to find missing lengths.*

Need to review 0   2   4   6   8   10   Now I get it!

Lesson 12-1

Chords and Arcs

Vocabulary

● **Review**

Circle the *converse* of each statement.

1. Statement: If I am happy, then I sing.

If I sing, then I am happy.   If I am not happy, then I do not sing.

If I do not sing, then I am not happy.

2. Statement: If parallel lines are cut by a transversal, then alternate interior angles are congruent.

| If lines cut by a transversal are not parallel, then alternate interior angles are not congruent. | If lines cut by a transversal form alternate interior angles that are not congruent, then the lines are not parallel. | If lines cut by a transversal form alternate interior angles that are congruent, then the lines are parallel. |

● **Vocabulary Builder**

chord (noun) **kawrd**

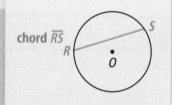

chord $\overline{RS}$

Definition: A **chord** is a segment whose endpoints are on a circle.

Related Word: arc

● **Use Your Vocabulary**

3. Complete each statement with *always*, *sometimes*, or *never*.

A *chord* is __?__ a diameter.

A diameter is __?__ a *chord*.

A radius is __?__ a *chord*.

A *chord* __?__ has a related arc.

An arc is __?__ a semicircle.

Theorems 12-4, 12-5, 12-6 and Their Converses

Theorem 12-4 Within a circle or in congruent circles, congruent central angles have congruent arcs.

4. If $\angle AOB \cong$ [____], then $\overset{\frown}{AB} \cong \overset{\frown}{CD}$.

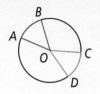

Converse Within a circle or in congruent circles, congruent arcs have congruent central angles.

5. If $\overset{\frown}{AB} \cong \overset{\frown}{CD}$, then $\angle AOB \cong$ [____].

Theorem 12-5 Within a circle or in congruent circles, congruent central angles have congruent chords.

6. If $\angle AOB \cong \angle COD$, then $\overline{AB} \cong$ [____].

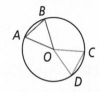

Converse Within a circle or in congruent circles, congruent chords have congruent central angles.

7. If $\overline{AB} \cong \overline{CD}$, then [____] $\cong \angle COD$.

Theorem 12-6 Within a circle or in congruent circles, congruent chords have congruent arcs.

8. If $\overline{AB} \cong$ [____], then $\overset{\frown}{AB} \cong \overset{\frown}{CD}$.

Converse Within a circle or in congruent circles, congruent arcs have congruent chords.

9. If $\overset{\frown}{AB} \cong$ [____], then $\overline{AB} \cong \overline{CD}$.

Problem 1 Using Congruent Chords

Got It? Use the diagram at the right. Suppose you are given $\odot O \cong \odot P$ and $\angle OBC \cong \angle PDF$. How can you show $\angle O \cong \angle P$? From this, what else can you conclude?

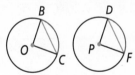

10. Complete the flow chart below to explain your conclusions.

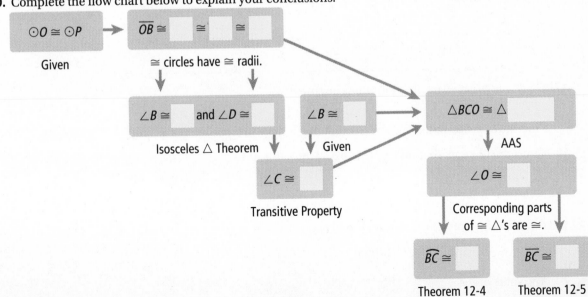

Lesson 12-2

Theorem 12-7 and Its Converse, Theorems 12-8, 12-9, 12-10

Theorem 12-7 Within a circle or in congruent circles, chords equidistant from the center or centers are congruent.

Converse Within a circle or in congruent circles, congruent chords are equidistant from the center (or centers).

11. If $OE = OF$, then $\overline{AB} \cong$ _____ .

12. If $\overline{AB} \cong$ _____ , then $OE =$ _____ .

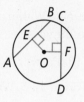

Theorem 12-8 In a circle, if a diameter is perpendicular to a chord, then it bisects the chord and its arc.

13. If $\overline{AB}$ is a diameter and $\overline{AB} \perp \overline{CD}$, then $\overline{CE} \cong$ _____ and $\overparen{CA} \cong$ _____ .

Theorem 12-9 In a circle, if a diameter bisects a chord (that is not a diameter), then it is perpendicular to the chord.

14. If $\overline{AB}$ is a diameter and $\overline{CE} \cong \overline{ED}$, then $\overline{AB} \perp$ _____ .

Theorem 12-10 In a circle, the perpendicular bisector of a chord contains the center of the circle.

15. If $\overline{AB}$ is the perpendicular bisector of chord $\overline{CD}$, then _____ contains the center of $\odot O$.

Problem 2 **Finding the Length of a Chord**

Got It? What is the value of x? Justify your answer.

16. What is the measure of each chord? Explain.

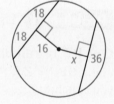

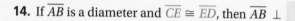

_____

_____

_____

_____

17. Circle the reason why the chords are congruent.

Chords that have equal measures are congruent.   Chords that are equidistant from the center of a circle are congruent.

18. Circle the theorem that you will use to find the value of x.

Theorem 12-5   Theorem 12-7   Converse of Theorem 12-7

Theorem 12-8   Theorem 12-10

19. Circle the distances from the center of a circle to the chords.

16   18   36 x

20. The value of x is _____ .

Problem 3 Using Diameters and Chords

Got It? The diagram shows the tracing of a quarter. What is its radius?

Underline the correct word to complete each sentence. Then do each step.

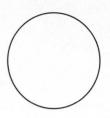

21. First draw two chords / tangents .

22. Next construct one / two perpendicular bisector(s).

23. Label the intersection *C*. It is the circle's center / chord .

24. Measure the diameter / radius .   **25.** The radius is about _____ mm.

Problem 4 Finding Measures in a Circle

Got It? Reasoning In finding *y*, how does the auxiliary $\overline{BA}$ make the problem simpler to solve?

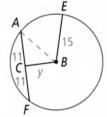

26. $\overline{BA}$ is the hypotenuse of a right __?__, so you can use the __?__ Theorem to solve for *y*.

_____   _____

Lesson Check • Do you UNDERSTAND?

Vocabulary Is a radius a chord? Is a diameter a chord? Explain your answers.

27. Circle the name(s) of figure(s) that have two endpoints on a circle. Underline the name(s) of figure(s) that have one endpoint on a circle.

| chord | diameter | radius | ray | segment |

28. Is a radius a chord? Is a diameter a chord? Explain.

_____

_____

Math Success

Check off the vocabulary words that you understand.

☐ circle   ☐ chord   ☐ radius   ☐ diameter

Rate how well you can *use chords to find measures.*

Need to review 0 2 4 6 8 10 Now I get it!

Lesson 12-2

Vocabulary

● Review

Write *noun* or *verb* to identify how *intercept* is used.

1. Defense tries to *intercept* a touchdown pass.

_____

2. The *y-intercept* of a line is the *y*-value at $x = 0$.

_____

3. Cryptographers *intercept* and decipher code messages.

_____

4. The *x-intercept* of a line is the *x*-value at $y = 0$.

_____

● Vocabulary Builder

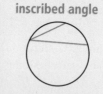

inscribed angle

inscribed (adjective) **in** SKRYBD

Related Word: circumscribed

Definition: *Inscribed* means written, marked, or engraved on.
Circumscribed means encircled, confined, or limited.

Math Usage: An **inscribed** angle is formed by two chords with a vertex on the circle.

● Use Your Vocabulary

Write *circumscribed* or *inscribed* to describe each angle.

5.

_____

6.

_____

7.

_____

8.

_____

Underline the correct word to complete each sentence.

9. $\angle ABC$ with points *A*, *B*, and *C* on a circle is a(n) circumscribed / inscribed angle.

10. An intercepted arc is between the sides of a(n) circumscribed / inscribed angle.

Theorem 12-11   Inscribed Angle Theorem

The measure of an inscribed angle is half the measure of its intercepted arc.

$m\angle B = \frac{1}{2}\, m\widehat{AC}$

11. Suppose $m\widehat{AC} = 90$.

$m\angle B = \boxed{} \cdot m\widehat{AC} = \boxed{}$

12. Suppose $m\angle B = 60$.

$m\widehat{AC} = \boxed{} \cdot m\angle B = \boxed{}$

Problem 1   Using the Inscribed Angle Theorem

Got It? In $\odot O$, what is $m\angle A$?

13. Complete the reasoning model below.

Think	Write
I know the sides of $\angle A$ are chords and the vertex is on $\odot O$.	$\angle A$ is an inscribed angle.
I can use the Inscribed Angle Theorem.	$m\angle A = \frac{1}{2}$ (measure of the blue arc) $= \frac{1}{2} (\boxed{})$ $= \boxed{}$

Corollaries to Theorem 12-11   Inscribed Angle Theorem

Corollary 1

Two inscribed angles that intercept the same arc are congruent.

Corollary 2

An angle inscribed in a semicircle is a right angle.

Corollary 3

The opposite angles of a quadrilateral inscribed in a circle are supplementary.

Use the diagram at the right. Write T for *true* or F for *false*.

_____ **14.** $\angle P$ and $\angle Q$ intercept the same arc.

_____ **15.** $\angle SRP$ and $\angle Q$ intercept the same arc.

_____ **16.** $\widehat{TSR}$ is a semicircle.

_____ **17.** $\angle PTS$ and $\angle SRQ$ are opposite angles.

_____ **18.** $\angle PTS$ and $\angle SRP$ are supplementary angles.

Lesson 12-3

Got It? In the diagram at the right, what is the measure of each numbered angle?

19. Use the justifications at the right to complete each statement.

$m\angle 4 = \frac{1}{2}($ _____ + _____)   Inscribed Angle Theorem

$m\angle 4 = \frac{1}{2}($ _____)   Add within parentheses.

$m\angle 4 =$ _____   Simplify.

20. Circle the corollary you can use to find $m\angle 2$.

| An angle inscribed in a semicircle is a right angle. | The opposite angles of a quadrilateral inscribed in a circle are supplementary. |

21. Now solve for $m\angle 2$.

22. Underline the correct word to complete the sentence.

The dashed line is a diameter / radius .

23. Circle the corollary you can use to find $m\angle 1$ and $m\angle 3$.

| An angle inscribed in a semicircle is a right angle. | The opposite angles of a quadrilateral inscribed in a circle are supplementary. |

Use your answer to Exercise 23 to find the angle measures.

24. $m\angle 1 =$ _____   25. $m\angle 3 =$ _____

26. So, $m\angle 1 =$ _____ , $m\angle 2 =$ _____ , $m\angle 3 =$ _____ , and $m\angle 4 =$ _____ .

take note

Theorem 12-12

The measure of an angle formed by a tangent and a chord is half the measure of the intercepted arc.

$m\angle C = \frac{1}{2}\, m\widehat{BDC}$

27. Suppose $m\angle C = 50$.

$m\widehat{BDC} =$ _____ · $m\angle C =$ _____

28. Suppose $m\widehat{BDC} = 80$.

$m\angle C =$ _____ · $m\widehat{BDC} =$ _____

29. In the diagram at the right, $\overrightarrow{BC}$ is tangent to $\odot O$ at B.

$m\widehat{ADB} =$ _____ $m\angle ABC =$ _____

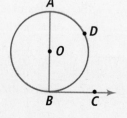

Problem 3 Finding Arc Measure

Got It? In the diagram at the right, $\overline{KJ}$ is tangent to $\odot O$. What are the values of x and y?

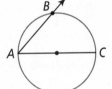

30. Circle the arc intercepted by $\angle JQL$. Underline the arc intercepted by $\angle KJL$.

$\overparen{JL}$ $\overparen{JQ}$ $\overparen{QL}$ $\overparen{QLJ}$

31. By the Inscribed Angle Theorem, $m\overparen{JL}$ = ☐ · ☐ = ☐ .

32. By Theorem 12-12, x = ☐ · $m\overparen{JL}$ = ☐ .

33. The value of x is ☐ .

34. Underline the correct words to complete the sentence.

$\overline{QL}$ is a diameter / radius , so $\angle QJL$ is a(n) acute / right / obtuse angle.

35. Use the justifications at the right to complete each statement.

$m\angle QJL + m\angle JLQ + m\angle LQJ$ = ☐   Triangle Angle-Sum Theorem

☐ $+ y +$ ☐ $=$ ☐   Substitute.

$y +$ ☐ $=$ ☐   Simplify.

$y =$ ☐   Subtract from each side.

Lesson Check • Do you UNDERSTAND?

Error Analysis A classmate says that $m\angle A = 90$. What is your classmate's error?

36. Is diameter $\overline{AC}$ a side of $\angle A$?   Yes / No

37. Is $\angle A$ inscribed in a semicircle?   Yes / No

38. What is your classmate's error? Explain.

_____

_____

_____

Math Success

Check off the vocabulary words that you understand.

☐ inscribed angle   ☐ intercepted arc

Rate how well you can *find the measure of inscribed angles.*

Need to review 0   2   4   6   8   10 Now I get it!

Vocabulary

● **Review**

1. Underline the correct word(s) to complete the sentence.

The student went off on a *tangent* when he **did / did not** stick to the subject.

2. A *tangent* to a circle intersects the circle at exactly __?__ point(s).

3. From a point outside a circle, there are __?__ *tangent(s)* to the circle.

● **Vocabulary Builder**

> **secant** (noun) SEEK **unt**
>
> **Related Word:** tangent (noun)
>
> **Definition:** A **secant** is a line that intersects a circle at two points.
>
> **Source:** The word **secant** comes from the Latin verb *secare*, which means "to cut."
>
> **Examples:** In the diagram at the right, $\overleftrightarrow{AB}$ is a **secant**, $\overrightarrow{AB}$ and $\overrightarrow{BA}$ are **secant** rays, and $\overline{AB}$ is a **secant** segment.

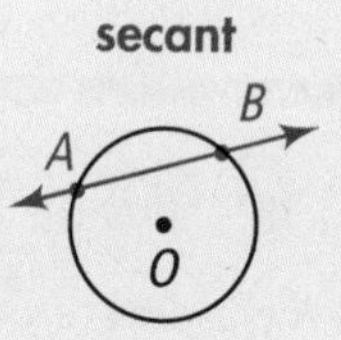

secant

● **Use Your Vocabulary**

Write *secant* or *tangent* to identify each line.

4.

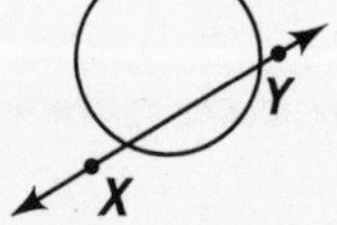

5.

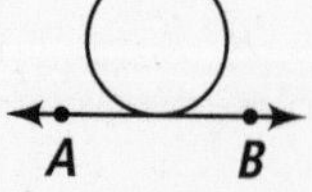

6.

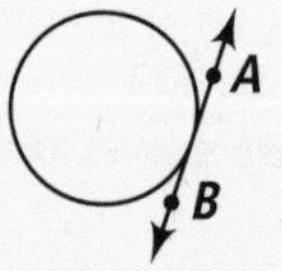

7.

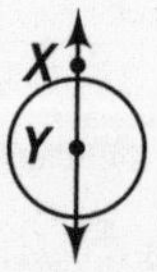

8. Is a chord a *secant*? Explain.

Theorem 12-13 The measure of an angle formed by two lines that intersect inside a circle is half the sum of the measures of the intercepted arcs.

$$m\angle 1 = \tfrac{1}{2}(x + y)$$

9. In the diagram at the right, does $m\angle 2 = \tfrac{1}{2}(x + y)$? Explain.

_____

_____

Theorem 12-14 The measure of an angle formed by two lines that intersect outside a circle is half the difference of the measures of the intercepted arcs.

$$m\angle 1 = \tfrac{1}{2}(x - y)$$

10. In the first diagam, the sides of the angle are a secant and a ___?___ .

_____

11. In the second diagram, the sides of the angle are a secant and a ___?___ .

_____

12. In the third diagram, the sides of the angle are a tangent and a ___?___ .

_____

13. Is $m\angle 1 = \tfrac{1}{2}(y - x)$ equivalent to $m\angle 1 = \tfrac{1}{2}(x - y)$?   Yes / No

Theorem 12-15 For a given point and circle, the product of the lengths of the two segments from the point to the circle is constant along any line through the point and the circle.

I.   **II.** 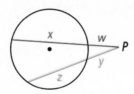   **III.**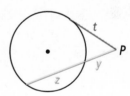

Complete each case of Theorem 12-15.

14. **Case I** $a \cdot b = c \cdot$ ▢

15. **Case II** $(w + x)\,w = ($ ▢ $+ z)$ ▢

16. **Case III** $(y + z)$ ▢ $= t^2$

Problem 1 Finding Angle Measures

Got It? What is the value of w?

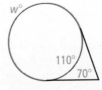

17. Use Theorem 12-14 to complete the equation.

▢ $= \tfrac{1}{2}(w -$ ▢ $)$

Lesson 12-4

18. Now solve the equation.

19. The value of w is _____ .

Got It? A departing space probe sends back a picture of Earth as it crosses Earth's equator. The angle formed by the two tangents to the equator is 20°. What arc of the equator is visible to the space probe?

20. Use 20, F, G, and the words *Earth* and *probe* to complete the diagram below.

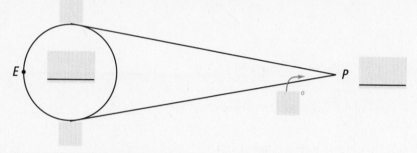

21. Complete the flow chart below.

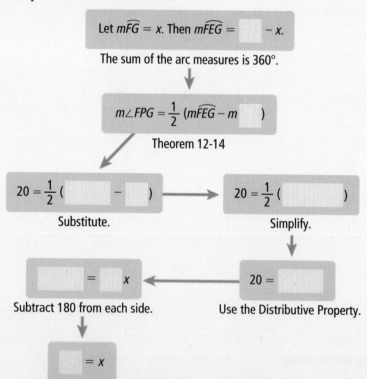

Let $m\widehat{FG} = x$. Then $m\widehat{FEG} = \boxed{} - x.$

The sum of the arc measures is 360°.

$m\angle FPG = \dfrac{1}{2}(m\widehat{FEG} - m\boxed{})$

Theorem 12-14

$20 = \dfrac{1}{2}(\boxed{} - \boxed{})$

Substitute.

$20 = \dfrac{1}{2}(\boxed{})$

Simplify.

$\boxed{} = \boxed{}\,x$

Subtract 180 from each side.

$20 = \boxed{}$

Use the Distributive Property.

$\boxed{} = x$

Divide each side by –1.

22. A $\boxed{}°$ arc of the equator is visible to the space probe.

Problem 3 Finding Segment Lengths

Got It? What is the value of the variable to the nearest tenth?

Underline the correct word to complete each sentence.

23. The segments intersect inside / outside the circle.

24. Write a justification for each statement.

$(14 + 20)14 = (16 + x)16$ _____

$476 = 256 + 16x$ _____

$220 = 16x$ _____

$13.75 = x$ _____

25. To the nearest tenth, the value of x is [____] .

Lesson Check • Do you UNDERSTAND?

In the diagram at the right, is it possible to find the measures of the
unmarked arcs? Explain.

26. You can use intercepted arcs to find the value of y.   Yes / No

27. You can use supplementary angles to find the
measures of the angles adjacent to $y°$.   Yes / No

28. You can find the sum of the unmarked arcs.   Yes / No

29. Is it possible to find the measure of each unmarked arc? Explain.

_____

_____

Math Success

Check off the vocabulary words that you understand.

☐ chord   ☐ circle   ☐ secant   ☐ tangent

Rate how well you can *find the lengths of segments associated with circles.*

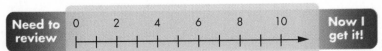

Lesson 12-4

Circles in the Coordinate Plane

Vocabulary

● **Review**

Write T for *true* or F for *false*.

_____ **1.** The *coordinate plane* extends without end and has no thickness.

_____ **2.** Only lines can be graphed in the *coordinate plane*.

_____ **3.** Any polygon can be plotted in the *coordinate plane*.

_____ **4.** (0, 5) and (5, 0) are the same point in the *coordinate plane*.

_____ **5.** The *coordinate plane* is three-dimensional.

_____ **6.** You can find the slope of a line in the *coordinate plane*.

● **Vocabulary Builder**

standard form (noun) STAN **durd fawrm**

Main Idea: The **standard form** of an equation gives information that can help you graph the equation in the coordinate plane.

Examples: The **standard form** of an equation of a circle is $(x - h)^2 + (y - k)^2 = r^2$. The **standard form** of a linear equation is $Ax + By = C$. The **standard form** of a quadratic equation is $y = ax^2 + bx + c$.

● **Use Your Vocabulary**

Draw a line from each equation in Column A to its *standard form* in Column B.

Column A

7. $y = 2x + 3$

8. $y = \frac{3}{4}x - 2$

9. $y = -x$

10. $0 = 2y - 4x + 3$

Column B

$x + y = 0$

$2x - y = -3$

$3x - 4y = 8$

$4x - 2y = 3$

Theorem 12-16 Equation of a Circle

An equation of a circle with center (h, k) and radius r is $(x - h)^2 + (y - k)^2 = r^2$.

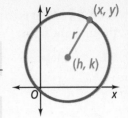

Complete each sentence with *center*, *circle*, or *radius*.

11. Each point on a __?__ is the same distance from the center.

_____

12. The equation of a circle with center $(-1, 0)$ and __?__ 6 is
$(x + 1)^2 + (y - 0)^2 = 6^2$.

_____

13. Each point on a circle is r units from the __?__ .

_____

14. The Distance Formula is $d = \sqrt{(x_2 -)^2 + (y_2 -)^2}$

15. How is d in the Distance Formula related to the radius r in the standard equation of a circle?

_____

_____

_____

16. How are the Distance Formula and the standard form of the equation of a circle alike?

_____

_____

_____

Problem 1 Writing the Equation of a Circle

Got It? What is the standard equation of the circle with center $(3, 5)$ and radius 6?

17. The x-coordinate of the center is ____ .

18. The y-coordinate of the center is ____ .

19. Is the standard equation of a circle $(x - h)^2 + (y - k)^2 = d$ Yes / No

20. Identify the values of h, k, and r.

   $h = $ ____ $k = $ ____ $r = $ ____

21. Write the standard equation of the circle with center $(3, 5)$ and radius 6.

   $(x -)^2 + (y -)^2 = ^2$

22. Simplify the equation in Exercise 21.

   $(x -)^2 + (y -)^2 = $

Problem 2 **Using the Center and a Point on a Circle**

Got It? What is the standard equation of the circle with center $(4, 3)$ that passes through the point $(-1, 1)$?

23. Complete the reasoning model below.

Know	**Need**	**Plan**
(h, k) is $(\boxed{}, \boxed{})$.	The radius $\boxed{}$	Use the Distance Formula to find $\boxed{}$.
$(-1, 1)$ is a point on the circle.	The standard equation of the circle	Then substitute for (h, k) and for $\boxed{}$.

24. Use the Distance Formula to find r.

$d = \sqrt{(x_2 - \boxed{})^2 + (y_2 - \boxed{})^2}$ Write the Distance Formula.

$r = \sqrt{(4 - \boxed{})^2 + (3 - \boxed{})^2}$ Substitute.

$r = \sqrt{(\boxed{})^2 + (\boxed{})^2}$ Simplify within parentheses.

$r = \sqrt{(\boxed{}) + (\boxed{})}$ Square each number.

$r = \sqrt{\boxed{}}$ Add.

25. Now write the standard form of the circle with center $(4, 3)$ that passes through the point $(-1, 1)$.

$(x - \boxed{})^2 + (y - \boxed{})^2 = \boxed{}^2$ Use the standard form of an equation of a circle.

$(x - \boxed{})^2 + (y - \boxed{})^2 = \boxed{}^2$ Substitute.

$(x - \boxed{})^2 + (y - \boxed{})^2 = \boxed{}$ Simplify.

 Problem 3 **Graphing a Circle Given Its Equation**

Got It? Suppose the equation $(x - 7)^2 + (y + 2)^2 = 64$ represents the position and transmission range of a cell tower. What does the center of the circle represent? What does the radius represent?

Place a ✓ in the box if the response is correct. Place an ✗ if it is incorrect.

_____ **26.** The transmission range is the same distance all around the cell tower.

_____ **27.** The center of the circle represents the position of the cell tower.

_____ **28.** The center of the circle represents the transmission range.

_____ **29.** The radius of the circle represents the position of the cell tower.

_____ **30.** The radius of the circle represents the transmission range.

Got It? What is the center and radius of the circle with equation $(x - 2)^2 + (y - 3)^2 = 100$? Graph the circle.

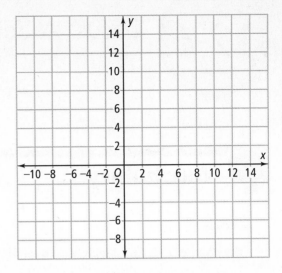

31. The center of the circle is (2,   ).

32. $r^2 = $

33. The radius of the circle is   .

34. Graph the circle on the coordinate plane at the right.

Lesson Check • Do you UNDERSTAND?

Suppose you know the center of a circle and a point on the circle. How do you determine the equation of the circle?

35. Do you know the value of h?   Yes / No

36. Do you know the value of k?   Yes / No

37. Do you know the value of r?   Yes / No

38. How can you find the missing value?

_____

_____

39. Once you know h, k, and r, how do you determine an equation of the circle?

_____

_____

Math Success

Check off the vocabulary words that you understand.

☐ circle   ☐ Distance Formula   ☐ standard form

Rate how well you can *use the standard form of a circle.*

Need to review   0   2   4   6   8   10   Now I get it!

Lesson 12-5

Vocabulary

● Review

Write *plane* or *space* to complete each sentence.

1. The set of all points in three dimensions is __?__ .

2. A __?__ is represented by a flat surface that extends without end and has no thickness.

3. An isometric drawing shows a corner view of a figure in __?__ .

4. Through any three noncollinear points there is exactly one __?__ .

● Vocabulary Builder

locus (noun) LOH kus

Other Word Form: The plural of **locus** is **loci** (LOH cy).

Related Words: location, locate

Definition: A locus is a set of points, all of which meet a stated condition.

Main Idea: The locus of points 5 in. from a point on a plane is a *circle* with radius 5 in.

● Use Your Vocabulary

Write T for *true* or F for *false.*

_____ 5. A square is the *locus* of points equidistant from a given point.

_____ 6. A sphere is the *locus* of points that are equidistant from a point in space.

_____ 7. A circle with diameter 3 cm is the *locus* of points 3 cm from a given point.

_____ 8. The *locus* of points 15 mi from a cell tower is a circle.

Problem 1 **Describing a Locus in a Plane**

Got It? **Reasoning** The sketch below shows the locus of the points in a plane 1 cm from $\overline{AB}$. How would the sketch change for the locus of points in a plane 1 cm from $\overrightarrow{AB}$?

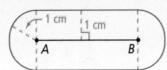

9. What is the difference between $\overleftrightarrow{AB}$ and $\overline{AB}$? Explain.

_____

_____

_____

10. Would the new sketch have a parallel line segment 1 cm above $\overleftrightarrow{AB}$? Yes / No

11. Would the new sketch have a parallel line segment 1 cm below $\overleftrightarrow{AB}$? Yes / No

12. Would the new sketch have a parallel line 1 cm above $\overleftrightarrow{AB}$? Yes / No

13. Would the new sketch have a parallel line 1 cm below $\overleftrightarrow{AB}$? Yes / No

14. Would the new sketch have semicircles at each end? Yes / No

15. Would the new sketch have anything at each end? Yes / No

16. Sketch the locus of points in a plane 1 cm from $\overleftrightarrow{AB}$.

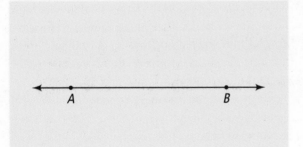

17. How would the sketch change for the locus of points in a plane 1 cm from $\overrightarrow{AB}$?

_____

_____

_____

_____

_____

Problem 2 Drawing a Locus for Two Conditions

Got It? What is a sketch of the locus of points in a plane that satisfy these conditions?

- the points equidistant from two points X and Y

- the points 2 cm from the midpoint of $\overline{XY}$

Use the diagram at the right for Exercises 18–22.

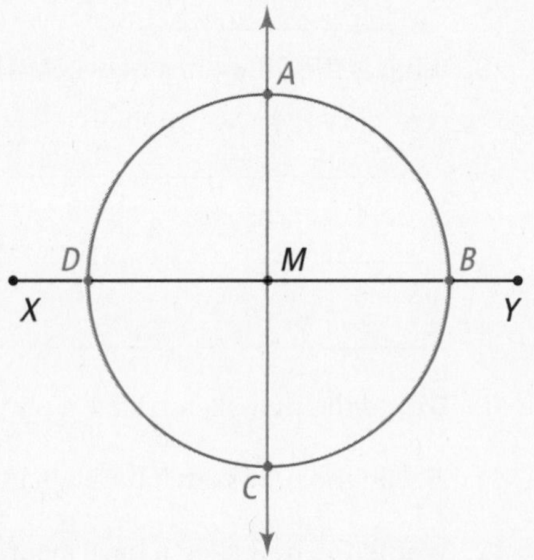

18. Circle the points in a plane that are equidistant from the endpoints of a segment.

| circle | ellipse | perpendicular bisector |

19. Circle the locus of points that are equidistant from X and Y.

| circle with center at the midpoint of $\overline{XY}$ and radius 2 cm | perpendicular bisector of $\overline{XY}$ |

20. Circle the locus of points that are a given distance from a point.

| circle | ellipse | perpendicular bisector |

21. Circle the locus of points 2 cm from the midpoint of $\overline{XY}$.

| circle with center at the midpoint of $\overline{XY}$ and radius 2 cm | perpendicular bisector of $\overline{XY}$ |

22. Points _____ and _____ are the locus of points that satisfy both conditions.

Problem 3 Describing a Locus in Space

Got It? What is the locus of points in a plane that are equidistant from two parallel lines?

Complete each statement with the appropriate word from the list below.

parallel   perpendicular   plane

23. Points that are equidistant from two __?__ lines are between the lines.

_____

24. The locus of points in a __?__ that are equidistant from two parallel lines is a line.

_____

25. The distance between parallel lines is the length of a segment __?__ to both lines.

_____

26. What is the locus of points in a plane that are equidistant from two parallel lines?

_____

_____

Got It? What is the locus of points in space that are equidistant from two parallel planes?

27. Cross out the word phrase that does NOT describe the distance between two planes.

length between two points on different planes	length of a segment perpendicular to each plane

28. Circle the word phrase that describes the locus of points in space that are equidistant from two parallel planes.

cylinder	plane halfway between the two parallel planes	plane parallel to the two parallel planes

---

Copyright © by Pearson Education, Inc. or its affiliates. All Rights Reserved.

Lesson Check • Do you UNDERSTAND?

Compare and Contrast How are the descriptions of the locus of points for each situation alike? How are they different?

- in a plane, the points equidistant from points *J* and *K*
- in space, the points equidistant from points *J* and *K*

29. Place a ✓ in the box if the description is true for the locus of points equidistant from points *J* and *K*. Place an ✗ in the box if it is not.

In a Plane	Description	In Space
	⊥ bisector of $\overline{JK}$	
	plane containing ⊥ bisector of $\overline{JK}$	
	plane ⊥ to plane containing $\overline{JK}$	

30. How are the descriptions of the loci alike?

_____

_____

_____

31. How are the descriptions of the loci different?

_____

_____

_____

Math Success

Check off the vocabulary words that you understand.

☐ locus of points   ☐ plane   ☐ space

Rate how well you can *sketch and describe a locus.*

Need to review   0   2   4   6   8   10   Now I get it!

Lesson 12-6